Your Honour

Can I Tell You My Story?

Andi Brierley

With a Foreword by Jim Hopkinson

❧ WATERSIDE PRESS

Your Honour – Can I Tell You My Story?
Andi Brierley

ISBN 978-1-909976-64-1 (Paperback)
ISBN 978-1-910979-71-6 (Epub ebook)
ISBN 978-1-910979-72-3 (Adobe ebook)

Cover design © 2019 Waterside Press by www.gibgob.com

Printed and bound in Poland by BookPress.eu

Main UK distributor Gardners Books, 1 Whittle Drive, Eastbourne, East Sussex, BN23 6QH. Tel: +44 (0)1323 521777; sales@gardners.com; www.gardners.com

North American distribution Ingram Book Company, One Ingram Blvd, La Vergne, TN 37086, USA. Tel: (+1) 615 793 5000; inquiry@ingramcontent.com

Cataloguing-In-Publication Data A catalogue record for this book can be obtained from the British Library.

Ebook *Your Honour – Can I Tell You My Story?* is available as an ebook and also to subscribers of Ebrary, Ebsco, Myilibrary and Dawsonera.

Published 2019 by
Waterside Press Ltd.
The Manor House, Lutyens Close,
Basingstoke, Hampshire, RG24 8AG.

Online catalogue WatersidePress.co.uk

Table of Contents

Publisher's Note

The views and opinions in this work are those of the author entirely and not necessarily shared. Readers should draw their own conclusions about any facts, opinions or claims it contains, concerning which the possibility of other narratives or interpretations should be borne in mind. The storyline and names of individuals together with some place names have been altered to respect privacy. Parts of the book, which seeks to portray the author's transition, are for legal reasons fiction. Details or descriptions should not be taken to bear any resemblance to actual events or individuals, past, present, living or dead.

Acknowledgements

Many people have contributed to this book, wittingly or not, including those who helped me on my journey from prisoner to law-abiding citizen. For their support and encouragement I will always be grateful.

In particular I would like to thank all those who had faith in me even if I may have taken a while to appreciate that although some things may have been due to my own efforts a great deal was due to them. Mine wasn't and isn't the only point of view I would like them to know!

Special thanks are due to: Mark Atherton, Lorraine Hopton, Phil Kent, Sarah Flanagan, Mandy Foster, Dave and Jackie Norton, Gill Garvani, Daniel Orive, Denis Lewis, Katie Wrench, Gail Faulkiner, Gary Collins, Alice Holmes, Emmal Lemdani, Steve Woodhead, Phil Robbins, Martyn Stenton, Duncan McBurney, Hollie Holdsworth, Thomas Hart, Joel Hannah, Sagir Gulzar, Jenny Bright, Rebecca Gilmour, Trevor Woodhouse, Sonia Brierley, Tina Brierley and Jim Hopkinson who kindly wrote the Foreword.

To those who shared darker days thank you from where I am now.

Finally, thanks to my wife Tami for her support. Maybe the book will help her to understand an Andi that she doesn't even recognise.

Andi Brierley

March 2019

About the author

Andi (Andrew) Brierley grew-up mainly in and around Leeds, West York-shire where he is a Children Looked After/Care Leaver Specialist within Leeds Youth Offending Service. He also spent time in the Midlands.

The author of the Foreword

Jim Hopkinson completed an MSc in Applied Social Studies at Oxford University, and became a qualified social worker. He then worked as a probation officer obtaining an MSc in Criminology and Criminal Justice at Loughborough University. Jim then moved to become a manager of a voluntary organization working with school excluded pupils. He joined Leicester Youth Offending Team at its inception in 1999 and became Head of Leeds Youth Offending Service in 2003. Since 2016 he has been Deputy Director of Children's Services in Bradford.

Foreword

'Never judge a man until you walk a mile in his shoes…'

I can still recall the day when, as Head of Leeds Youth Offending Service, I was asked to authorise the employment of Andi Brierley. It was not an easy decision to make. As a service dedicated to preventing, reducing and stopping offending we describe getting and sustaining employment as a critical protective factor. Every day youth justice staff make the case for giving young people who have offended a chance in education, training and employment. But a record like Andi's? Persistent offending. Prolific offending. Breaches of orders designed to stop offending. Several prison sentences. Could this leopard ever change its spots?

I recall taking advice from HR and others. The clear message was this is a risk—a big risk and if you take this risk Jim you are accountable for your decision. How many people would line up to say 'I told you so' if it went wrong. We often talk about a 'risk averse culture' in children's services. Children's staff are said to err on the side of caution and take risk averse decisions. But surely if I took the decision not to employ Andi I could not be accused of being risk averse with his track record?

So what swung it? Yes there was the advocacy of Wilfred who made the case for Andi to be employed—but fundamentally what swung it was the grit and determination shown by Andi himself.

Andi told me a bit about his story—but it is only on reading this book that I have fully understood just how remarkable his journey has been. A childhood surrounded by instability, numerous moves, disrupted education with adults who were it seems not consistently able to prioritise the needs of their children above their own. No wonder the escape offered by drugs became more and more central to Andi's teenage life. With drugs, offending inevitably followed and the full sanction of the criminal justice system followed close behind.

Yet this is an inspirational journey. The journey of someone who had walked through storms to reach the sunshine. Someone who has reflected deeply and developed huge insight coupled with the bravery to share his story with us. A person who packed more into his childhood years than most of us will experience in a lifetime. A person who has come to terms with his experiences and used these to become a force for change and for good.

This moving story reminds us that everyone has the capacity to change and deserves some time in the sun.

Introduction

People have various opinions about why children offend and what to do about it. I'm in a privileged position to explore this and in a unique way. My book looks at the trauma I experienced as a developing child and lets the reader decide whether it is linked to the decisions and choices I made as a young adult that led to prison.

I've served custodial sentences making-up three-and-a-half years of my young adult life, been addicted to heroin, spent time in the care system and on probation and grown-up with crime and drugs all about me. However, regardless of these experiences, I've found myself working as a professional with children that offend. How does someone overcome their past and retune the brain in this way? This is what my story is about.

I explore the impact of being in prison although as I will explain I never saw myself as a 'criminal'. It's not a story of glamour or money, rather of escaping from trauma, poverty and other negative experiences. Instead of making a case for welfare or justice for children that offend, I think it best to simply share my experiences as if by way of explanation to a judge sentencing me. You will see in the story that in my professional role I twice found myself presenting reports on children to such a judge having changed so much that they didn't recognise me (though I think one of them may have looked puzzled)! But it is also important that I tell the story in a basic and straightforward way that everyone can understand.

I invite the reader to join me on this journey as I try to unpick the nature versus nurture debate in a practical way. It is the story of my progress through care, prison and social rejection to senior youth justice worker and I hope that it contains at least some clues for those who work with young people. It begins with failures to recognise and make connections about the impact of my chaotic early life being moved from place to place, school to school, fragmented parenting and poor role models.

Encircled by the criminality of others, hard and soft drugs, violence and confusing adult examples, I ended up first in a young offender institution then in gaol. There I learned how to be, act and think like prisoners do, for my own safety and survival, something that only made matters worse when I was trying to re-adapt to the world outside after being released.

Caught in a downward spiral, hooked on drugs and partying a priority I was not strong enough to resist negative influences. My well-being deteriorated and my self-confidence was at an all time low. I try to show how, in the middle of all this, quite small things made a big difference. Random encouragement, people who took an interest in me, positive thoughts, those who gave me a chance, enlightened employers, people who let me in on their 'ordinary' lives and not least those who recognised that my past experiences could be put to good use as a youth justice volunteer and eventually, through the connections I was able to make with kids, working full-time with young people.

The story is sometimes not for the faint-hearted because it unavoidably involves offending, violence, raw descriptions of events, the rough language of the streets and prisons and a world that lies hidden to law-abiding citizens. But it also contains what I believe are messages and I hope insights for professionals and others about young people in trouble.

CHAPTER 1

Who Am I?

My name is Andi Brierley. I'm a youth justice practitioner from Leeds where I work with the city's Youth Offending Service. Most people might assume this requires a social work degree given that I work directly with children. I'm fully qualified, but I'm not a social worker, nor have I ever worked within Social Services.

I concentrate on the positive relationships I can build with children in care that have offended. A large part of this is down to the fact that I spent time in care myself and part of my young life in and out of custody. This experience allows me to open a door for children who feel the system is set against them, so they can discuss things, and because they see me as one of them not part of that system. I then offer the same advice and guidance as anyone else working in this field.

I'm married to the woman of my dreams and the father of the most amazing little girl. I don't drink alcohol or take drugs. I own my own home, have a degree in Youth Justice and work in a professional setting. I'd best describe my lifestyle and current social position as middle-class. 'How does someone go from care and custody to this?' I hear you ask. I'll try to explain.

The right way to start can only be by explaining my mother's situation and background. You'll soon get to know her, so it is only right I tell you something about her though anything I say must make allowances for her own bad time. She was born in the 1960s in Germany where her father (my grandfather) was in the military. I tell her this makes her German, but she was born in a British Army camp and is as English as anyone born in this country. Mum's slim with short dark hair but you might not notice her in a crowd. She's not an educated person and indeed never completed school due to her own chaotic childhood. She always sees the best in others and doesn't understand why some people behave in negative ways. I'd describe her as naïve and vulnerable in every sense. She was taken into care herself and lived in a children's home, ending-up there aged 15 following I believe violence and abuse at home. She was separated from her siblings and moved to Kent with her extended family. She felt lonely and wanted to be with her family, so she went back to Leeds. Her siblings' foster parents couldn't take her in as well as them, so she was placed in a children's home.

Mum tells me she was abused as a child, but I don't know the details and don't need to dwell on them to show you just how vulnerable she was. She fell pregnant with me when she was 16. When she told Charlie she was pregnant his mother wouldn't let him acknowledge me as his child. I refuse to call him my father as he hasn't earned that honour. All I know is that there was a rift between the families and mum got a house and started out on the parenthood road alone. I think Charlie was from a stable family. It would have been known that mum was in care and if he'd accepted responsibility he would have been involved in everything that follows in this story. I can understand what happened even though it left me without a father figure. His mother was looking-out for his interests not mine.

Mum then met a man called Stan. All I can remember is that he drove a red truck. She had my brother Adam with Stan (who pops-up again much later in this story) 18 months after I was born. I don't quite know what happened but I think mum left him because she found it hard to stay in a relationship with any man. She decided to take us to London. She says that she doesn't know why but that she always wanted to run away. She was on state benefits and already involved with Social Services so I can't understand why no-one asked questions about why she was going so far away with two young children. In London she met a woman from Scotland and decided to follow her north of the border. Mum was either running away from her abuse or looking for somewhere safe, or probably both. I dread to imagine some of the places I was in as a baby given mum was so young, vulnerable and in need.

After her poor start with men you'd think she would have been wary of them, or at least have taken precautions to prevent a third baby.

However, she met a man (who I don't remember enough to even know his name) and had my sister Verity. Mum was just 21 with three children under four years of age and in London with little or no support. She returned to Leeds with us kids and managed to access social housing. Mum told me that when we first came back we were placed in a hostel whilst on the waiting list. That's mum and three kids and no social care referral. Whether due to un-met need I don't know, but she always had to have a man around. So it wasn't long before she met Benny. She went on to have two more kids with him. Miles and Gail were born within 18 months of each other which meant there were now five of us and yet mum was still only 24.

She thought she'd done an excellent job finding a man to stick around. However, it wasn't long before Benny also took off. My earliest memories come from this time and are of the family living together in the Hyde Park area of Leeds. I remember mum going to town and leaving us with a babysitter. She was around 16 and lived just up the road and I can remember mum saying 'Bye' as she went.

I spent most of my time with a boy called Warren who lived not far away. Adam often followed us around and, just like most young lads, I hated having my baby brother with me. We climbed everything. This day we decided to walk across a window ledge. Warren and I shuffled across with our backs flat against the window. The ledge was quite narrow and we made sure we didn't look down as the front garden was paved with concrete slabs. After I'd made it across with Warren, I told Adam we were going to play football and he couldn't come unless he did the same. He tried but wasn't as confident as us. We could only stand and watch as he leant forward and dropped six feet from the sill. It was like slow motion. He landed flat on his face and his forehead instantly swelled-up. Mum said he looked like ET with a bee sting. We told her we'd been climbing trees and that Adam had fallen out of one of them. We were often wandering about the streets unsupervised and no-one asked any questions, not until one of us got hurt.

Mum's friend Deborah got a house across the road with her two boys and little girl and all us kids would run from house to house. Neither of them seemed to look after their health or their teeth. It wasn't a priority and so I for one never saw it as important. We would get told off when the 'bad people' (social workers, doctors and the like) visited. Danny, Deborah's boyfriend, was a tall skinny man with glasses and a moustache. His breath smelt of coffee and stale cigarettes. We liked him as he had a lot of time for us and would often play football in the street. He seemed to want to spend time with us when the other adults left us to get on with things. Since Danny was good with us kids, nobody took too much notice of how close he was with some little girls. One day the police came and arrested him. They took us one-by-one into a room and asked if he had touched us in places nobody else did. I remember thinking, 'Touched me where nobody else did? Do they mean my private bits?' They said, 'Yes, your willy or your bum, bum'. Conversations that any six-year-old should be protected from, but here I was talking about this with the police. The doctor's tests came back inconclusive. I'm pretty sure he didn't touch me whatever happened or didn't happen to others.

I believe (though I need to stress it was never proved) that Danny *was* abusing children. I remember friends of a friend of Deborah beating him up after they suspected this. Whatever really happened it caused Social Services to question the parenting skills of both mum and Deborah and led to a chain of events that meant they were back on the scene and involved with our family. This is the 'generational cycle' that professionals talk about as a child of someone in care grows-up to need similar intervention and support. If the job had been done right first time around, maybe I wouldn't have ended-up in care myself. Danny had to leave while everything was investigated, the children faced being accused of lying about the whole thing and he disappeared. But as Deborah was deemed not capable of taking care of her kids they were placed in foster care and never returned.

These days I've had the benefit of accessing my care files (as I describe more fully in a later chapter), so I now know that this wasn't the sole reason we went into care. It was only one part. This book tries to show what happens to children when they are not told the full story or not given the correct reasons why they were removed from their parents.

In 1988, Adam seems to have had a problem with lighting fires. Social Services were called in and he has always blamed himself for us being taken into care. Adam the five-year-old arsonist, just imagine! I found Social Services noted in my file that we were exposed to risks 'in unacceptably dangerous proportions'. Once we kids were found two miles away from home and brought back by the police. Benny answered the door and told the officer that we were old enough to take care of ourselves. What a caring and nurturing role model. Over the three months that Social Services tried to work with our family he often refused to allow them into the house. They recorded that Adam had what looked like burn marks and Verity had fractured her tibia on two separate occasions whilst we were 'taking care of ourselves' unsupervised. I've no idea what caused these apparent injuries and am not sure mum did either. The files show that Social Services never discovered explanations.

Benny brought a friend home one night after drinking. I'd fallen asleep on the sofa and everyone had gone upstairs to bed. They were being loud, so I asked them to stop and his friend said, 'Shut it you little idiot' and he got angry and punched me in the face. I grabbed my sore cheek and ran to my bedroom. I could hear the two of them arguing and I know Benny beat-up his friend saying he shouldn't touch any of 'his' kids. I certainly didn't see Benny as my dad. He would often hit me anyway, so I didn't understand why he wanted to shelter me from his friend. Mum felt he was protecting us.

It wasn't long before Benny got himself another girlfriend and took off with her. He would turn-up when they fell out and mum would allow him back in. When he was not there Social Services were able to get into the house to work with us and start to know our problems. In the records they noted they'd found me one morning in a chair fast asleep when I should have been at school. They asked my siblings why I wasn't there and they told them I'd been drinking vodka and couldn't wake-up. I can't remember this, but I do know that I would frequently drink alcohol when mum had parties. I would refuse to go to bed until I'd had a drink and partygoers would say things like, 'Okay then, just a sip'. I wanted to be an adult, of course, and this is what happened.

We struggled to relate to the bad people. They were always writing things down which made us distrust them still more even though they were supposed to support us. Social workers didn't like being in the

15

house. This was understandable as it wasn't the nicest of places. I felt as if I was being judged, that they were looking down their noses at the whole family. Had they been able to break down our defensive barriers then maybe they would have found out more about what was really going on. They worried about the things they knew about but there was lots they didn't get to know and we didn't trust them enough to tell them. I can't remember most of the things that happened but I do know a lot of the violence is completely missing from the files. When Benny was around, he was frequently drunk and beating-up mum or us. He used slippers and Adam would get the worst of it. He wasn't good at not getting caught. We would do things together and he would get the blame. I would sit and cry in my room when I heard Benny beating him. I knew I should've owned up, but I was scared. He slapped mum around when she wouldn't give him her benefit money for gambling. She, however, felt she had him under control because she would submit to him by cowering and he would stop. I hated him for the way he treated her and us kids. It made me feel weak because I was too young and frightened to do or say anything. I believe that if the social workers had made us feel they were there to protect us and not judge us they could have gained our trust. It wouldn't have been difficult for them, especially after what came next.

Benny disappeared completely. Mum hated being alone and the love of us children was clearly not enough to meet her needs. She'd accept any behaviour from Benny just as long as he spent time with her, even when she must have known he was seeing other women or slapping her around. She loved him without understanding what love means. What kind of man *did* she need to raise us children properly? Would she ever have been able to get a responsible man with five kids? Her answer was a man that lived up the street (whose name I can't remember and subsequently can't find out). It is clear in the files that Social Services told her he caused them concern. They told her not to leave him alone with us kids. Within two weeks he was baby-sitting on his own. If he was a risk, it's worth asking why anyone at all thought she could protect us from him.

In January 1989, a case conference was called to start care proceedings. In February, mum was taken to hospital to give birth to Gail. There was no-one else to look after us so we were taken into temporary care. Four days later mum discharged us. By the middle of the month Gail had unexplained injuries. For Social Services, to quote the files, it was 'the last straw'. They felt mum and the two youngest should be moved to a special place under supervision and the rest of us taken into care.

We went to live with a woman called Sheila in another part of the city. She was around 35 and chubby with black curly hair. She had two boys of her own called Simon and Andrew. Simon was the same age as me (seven) and Andrew was around the same age as Adam (five). They let us know that this was *their home* and we were only staying for a while. They must have known more than we did, because although we were told it was only for a short time we didn't know how long. We would talk together and say we didn't trust them. One thing I remember is that they always got information before we did. Social Services obviously told Sheila things and she told her kids. When they in turn said things about mum being put away it caused fights and then we were to blame. We were sanctioned as we were the care kids, but Sheila's kids were never in the wrong. I believed that, although just seven, I was the man in our family. I should have got information first and that would have stopped conflict. Every time we felt there was an injustice and responded in a negative way we were punished. Sheila would use words like 'aggressive' and 'disobedient', but it felt as if we were trapped and couldn't do or say anything. Whatever she said was taken as fact.

One day when out playing I decided I wanted to go back inside the house for a drink. Sheila was outside hanging-out the washing and didn't want to get me one. I was being demanding I know and saying that she should give me one but I was thirsty. So I said, 'I'll tell Social Services' and her face changed. She slapped me full around my cheek. My eyes welled-up as she said, 'Don't you ever threaten me you little shit'.

We said we would love to beat her with a stick and laughed about it. Looking back, it was important for me to feel as if someone would pro-tect me from such abuse within the care placement. I was facing abuse at home and yet here I was in care but being hit and sworn at. I couldn't tell anyone and I don't think they would have believed me anyway. Sheila said she didn't feel it would work long-term, so they were forced into action. When the social workers came for us they said the first car was for me. I knew then that they were going to split us up. I believed it was due to us being bad and Adam and I continued to believe for years that it was our fault. However, that wasn't the case. We made up a story in which we put the blame on ourselves for being separated. It feels strange to be faced years later with a fact that contradicts what you once believed to be true. I think we did it because that way we could take ownership of things beyond our control.

I signed a form stating that the most important thing in my life was a rugby club I was attending while living at Sheila's. I also said I hated my siblings annoying me. It seems silly to separate children due to the request of a seven-year-old to stay local to play sport. It suggests services are selective when they listen to kids in care. It was a mistake to do that and maybe keeping us together should have been the priority. Surely, it's normal for a seven-year-old to say that their siblings annoy them, but this shouldn't mean separating them. It compounded the trauma we faced having already been separated from mum, Miles and Gail. I can't remember much about the family I went to next as nothing stood out; they were warm and welcoming and quickly put me at ease. I can remember the woman's name was Ivy and that they got me into school.

As mum's parenting capability had revived a bit it was agreed she would be given a flat in Chapeltown and continue to be monitored. I'm not saying I believe poor families with Social Services involvement should be given nice houses in smart areas but these flats were surrounded by crime. Our social worker was called Grimley, a nice, older woman. She would collect us and take us for contact. We saw her as someone we needed to tell lies to in order to get our way and return home. I remember looking in her bag and seeing lots of paperwork then asking her if she had read it all and being told yes. I can believe this as Grimley was an academic but where she struggled was in building relationships with any of us kids. She couldn't penetrate the wall of silence we erected. Had she been able to, I would probably have told her that I *wasn't* ready to go home yet. I felt safe at Ivy's and wasn't too sure about going home.

After a few months of supervised visits I was allowed back to live with mum. This made me feel confused. I'd been at Ivy's for about a year and had started to feel settled, but this was my mum and it's normal to want to be with your parent. I wouldn't have been normal if I'd told anyone I didn't want to go home, so I told them I did. Especially as I knew mum would be upset if I didn't. These are the conflicting emotions children in care face every day. It's damaging just as much as the abuse they face. Mum's wasn't anywhere near the standard of Ivy's. But she was my mum and I was going home so I should've been happy. Deep down I wasn't. I didn't know what was going to happen and I didn't want to be with the people my mum chose to have around. Would she protect me from what happened last time? Would she be like Ivy and ask me how I felt?

As soon as I got through the door I asked, 'When are Adam and Verity coming home?' She looked straight at me with an upset face and told me that they had to wait a little bit longer. I can remember not understanding but I was getting used to this by now. All these things were happening and I didn't understand even though it was all having an impact on where I lived, who I lived with and which school I went to. By this point I was almost nine and had been to several different schools already. Documents show that I was falling behind my peers academically when I attended the local school a short bus ride away.

When we had family contact it was an emotional affair. None of us kids could understand the reasoning behind me being allowed to go home and not the others. When it was time for them to leave, Adam would kick-off and they would be forcibly bundled into the car. Looking back, I realise that this is when Adam started to have problems with authority. He just didn't respond well to knowing that three of us were at home and he was still in care. He has always been very black and white and I know he had no doubts he should have been at home with us.

We were one of the few white families in our immediate area but, as I'd lived in many areas already, this didn't bother me. People often talk about white people being racist. My experience is that children, especially, can be mean and often pick-up on difference. Although it didn't bother me, I would get abuse for being white. I believe this was because we were the poor family on the block. I would often be called 'a honky', which is a derogatory term for whites. Mum remembers one event as clearly as I do. I was sitting on a rope swing we'd made when I was approached by two black kids who later became my friends. They were asking where I was from when, all of a sudden, they grabbed a leg apiece and lifted themselves up on me as the rope dug in against my penis. 'White pussy,' they said and ran off laughing. At the time it got us down but, looking back, it was because I was the new kid and they saw difference which just happened to be colour. They didn't mean to be racist or have an issue with white people but wanted to show me they were in charge.

One day I came home and Mum told me that Adam wasn't behaving so that unlike Verity who was allowed to return the bad people said he couldn't come back yet. I burst out crying as I knew that he'd feel he was all alone and that we didn't care about him. I don't believe they had the right to exclude him in this way. Either mum was able to take care of us all or she wasn't. Let's see later whether she was or wasn't right and what these decisions meant for Adam and his life.

Mum was quite savvy when it came to the system. If she'd applied the same level of motivation to working in a proper job as she did to making sure she got every possible entitlement she could have done quite well. She would claim for the smallest thing then take all four of us kids down to Social Services to get a grant playing the poverty card. Savvy but not good with money, or the amounts we got through. I remember social workers coming to give us bus fares to get us to school. The bad people also brought us food when we ran out and yet I can remember mum spending money on things like cigarettes knowing Grimley wouldn't let us starve. It was a strange example of how to survive in the world.

We kids often played in the hallway of the flats. One day Miles was on his little bike outside by a kid called Nick's door shouting, 'Mum'. I told him she was in the bath, but he wouldn't listen and kept shouting. I became frustrated and kicked him full in the face as if his head was a football. He immediately screamed in pain. I tried to hold him and say sorry. I couldn't believe I'd just hurt my baby brother. I felt so sorry for him. Why was I capable of hurting someone I loved and cared for in an instant? It was obvious, I'd learnt this in my early years. I brushed it off after ten minutes of feeling bad. I didn't want to think about how horrible I was becoming at such a young age. Becoming violent doesn't just happen overnight. I was nine and already unable to manage my emotions. My default response to frustration or anxiety was violence. Where was all this taking me?

I'd been going to school locally but I couldn't now. It states in my care files that I told social workers I was being bullied there. I can remember that the kids knew I'd just come out of care. They used to say that I was a 'poor white boy'. It was agreed that this school wasn't the best one for me, so I was moved to another junior school. I did seem to settle there. The files also say it was felt I was slow when it came to schoolwork. The teachers said that they would have concerns if I was to move school again because I was so far behind. I was ten by now. These changes of school had far from finished as we will see.

I'd started hanging around with the young lads on the estate and we were spending time together outside the flats. One day we talked about which family had most money. Many of the lads thought my family had the lowest 'go figure', partly because of the clothes my younger siblings wore. I argued that Miles and Gail were always in nice clothes. Leslie, a small black kid that always made me aware I was white, wouldn't let this drop and said we were tramps. Although I knew they were right and we probably were the poorest family around, I was adamant they were wrong. Leslie said, 'Show us what they wear then'. I took them to my house and knocked on the door. When mum answered, she was about to give them a bath and they followed her to the door in their birthday suits. They stood there with no idea that they had a group of kids mocking them. If you can imagine young lads in this situation you will know what came next. Shouting, laughing and belittling mum, not that she was interested. My reaction was to shout at her to go inside the house and shut the door. I went upstairs thinking that I'd blown it and that I was never going to be accepted. Why was mum who she was I thought. I wished I'd never had my family.

When we had family contact Adam would ask mum why she didn't want him to come home and she would say it wasn't up to her and that he must stay out of trouble until he was allowed home. I know now from the files that, due to Adam's unpredictable behaviour, Social Services thought he would be too much for her to handle. It makes me wonder why they didn't at least try as not being with his family surely contributed towards his behaviour. After all, they were coming to the house every day, and Adam claims even now that his behaviour was poor because he wanted to come home and he believes it would have been far better had they allowed him to do that. He was too young to understand. In fact, he got what he wanted at home due to kicking-off, a form of learnt behaviour.

One night we were playing football over the road. I got into a tackle with Leslie and he instantly squared-up to me and called me a honky. By now I'd become good friends with a mixed-race lad called Pete who was at the game. He would often say his mum was half white when the white card was played and this gave me a bit of confidence. I said, 'Look Leslie, I'm not taking your shit anymore'. Finding it amusing Leslie said we could sort it out later. As I was bigger than him I thought I might be able to take him on, and hey, I had Pete, one of the older lads, on my side.

The truth is it quite often has nothing to do with size. As the lads wanting to see a fight gathered, I told mum what was happening. I expected her to save me. I may have been bigger than Leslie but he was confident he would win and I was completely wetting myself. So, you can imagine how I hoped mum would say, 'Stay here son' but she instead said, 'Get out there and give him what for Andi'. Great. We got into a childish tangle and I managed to throw Leslie on the floor. I felt good and told him to keep his arse down but nope he jumped straight back to his feet. Leslie danced around me like he was a professional boxer. We then dropped to the floor together and he bit my cheek making me scream in pain. I had to walk back to the flat holding my face with his teeth marks in it. Leslie said, 'I told you white boys can't fight' which made me hate him even more. I whispered obscenities under my breath so no-one could hear. Although these were pathetic things to say, it gave me a feeling of control.

After a few months it was decided that mum was doing well. Adam *was* allowed home. This was great for us as a family and Social Services made the decision to close our case. I can't find any details or explanation for that decision. Let's see if it was a good one or if they could have done more.

CHAPTER 2

Party Time

Meeting mum's next new boyfriend opened-up my eyes to a whole new world. It was a new beginning and made me grow-up quickly. Geoff was a character to say the least. Tall and well-built with a pony tail, I remember thinking he was cool and handsome. When he was around it was always fun time. He never took life too seriously and did a good job on my mum. It was weird, as if she became a different person, with a smile on her face, singing as she cleaned the house. It was nice to see her happy for a change.

There were always parties in the house and I could get the next day off school by saying I'd not slept because of the noise. I would sneak downstairs and Geoff would let me stay. Mum let him lay the law down when it came to us kids which I also didn't mind because it often meant no rules. I got to know UB40 songs off by heart as that is all the adults played. Geoff always had his mates with him and this attracted some of my mum's women friends. My memories of the time are what you would expect from seeing a set of bad Patrick Swayze impersonators from *Dirty Dancing*. Mum and Geoff would take the lead in the living-room and grind their hips together. Although they felt they were good, it was embarrassing. One thing for sure is that we were quite often left unsupervised. The adults were too busy having fun.

Geoff certainly liked his drink and I think he was a hardened criminal. He lived quite some way from us and I remember he found it hard to drive without drinking alcohol due to getting the shakes. I remember one neighbour asking mum why she allowed us kids in the car while he had a Vodka bottle in his hand. Unthinkingly she replied, 'No my dear, he drives loads better when he's had a drink due to him shaking with withdrawals when he hasn't'.

Deborah was pregnant at this point and I remember mum asking Geoff to take her to hospital. There were others around as we waited for her to return and tell us the baby was okay. As soon as she walked through the door, she looked at my mum and collapsed on the floor. Mum picked her up and took her into the kitchen and that's when I heard Geoff say she'd lost the baby. She'd also lost two other babies when she was younger and she later lost the kids she did have to the Social Services. It was a dark time for everyone and the answer was a drinking binge.

On a more positive note, there seemed to be more money around the house. Mum hardly ever worked due to the turmoil and having five kids to look after. We were given hand me down clothes when she returned from visiting the neighbours. I hated it when they were from kids I spent time with. I tried not to wear them because I got the piss taken out of me if I went to school in them. With Geoff around, I managed to get my first pair of Nikes from the market. They were not genuine ones but I didn't care, they were my own black £10 bad boys. I felt untouchable. I was one of the lads now and it was all down to Geoff, what a guy. What a role model, all about life feeling good and stable. Having him around certainly made mum feel good as well. I remember thinking he was exactly how I wanted to be when I got older.

Geoff would come and visit early in the morning and wake me up. I would hear mum say, 'Please leave him Geoff, he's tired'. Not that Geoff took much notice. He would take me out at five or six in the morning on motorbikes (where he got them from I don't know). I loved it even though he scared the shit out of me. I guess he knew I idolised him and liked that. Most people might say he was placing me at risk, but in his own eyes he was taking care of me and I naturally felt the same.

One night I was asleep when I heard a lot of noise downstairs. I went to look and there was a group of men I'd seen from time-to-time. Geoff was being loud and excited and, as I was dazed, I slowly tried to work out what was wrong. There were black bags full of cigarettes and alcohol spread around the room and the balcony door was wide open. This was no surprise as it is how Geoff and his friends would come and go, so that nobody saw them. Grown men climbing over it so they didn't have to come through the front entrance to the building and be seen.

Verity had also woken-up and we were both standing at the back of the room wondering what it was all about. One man who was younger than the rest lay on the floor. As I looked closer, I saw he had blood down his jeans. I heard mum ask Geoff what had happened and he told her the man had caught his leg on a window on the way out of a shop. This explained the bags of cigarettes.

I don't think anyone noticed us watching from behind the sofa as mum told Geoff to get a needle and thread. She then stitched-up the man's leg while he bit on a tea towel and Geoff held him down as he struggled and screamed. It was traumatic even to watch. Once things calmed down mum sent us to bed. I don't know how she thought we would sleep after that. The men helped the injured chap down from the balcony, passing him like a parcel. I'm not sure if Geoff got arrested or if he just didn't want to spend time around the family but he stopped coming. Although I really liked him it didn't bother me that much. Mum's relationships never lasted longer than a few months. We kids were used to it.

A woman called Wyn lived in the flat directly above us and mum became friends with her as she came to the parties. Benny was still coming to see Miles and Gail from time-to-time and, somehow, he started a relationship with Wyn. Mum told her he'd been violent with other women but that she, mum, knew how to handle him. What she really meant was that she never ever challenged him, cleaned-up after him and cooked his every meal. Benny told Wyn mum was saying this out of jealousy and Wyn stopped speaking to her.

Mum now started a relationship with a man who'd been on the scene for a while called Mark. He was skinny with big eyebrows and a moustache which meant to me that he looked like he couldn't be trusted. I didn't like him from the start and as a result I made his life as difficult as I could. He was a slimy character and he wasn't cool like Geoff. He didn't bring anything I was interested in and I didn't see any point in making an effort with him. In fact, he annoyed me and I'm sure he must have put-up with my attitude simply because he wanted to be with mum.

One day there was a lot of banging and shouting from Wyn's flat while we kids were playing in the corridor. When we told mum she brushed it aside saying Wyn was an alcoholic and that there was frequently noise coming from her place. Another neighbour appeared saying that Benny was screaming at the top of his voice. Mum decided to show us it was nothing and by the time she reached Wyn's door the commotion had stopped. She opened the door and walked in. I could see blood all the way up the staircase and walls. 'Don't go in Mum,' I yelled. But she edged warily up the stairs while the neighbour rushed to telephone the police. I felt scared as mum disappeared slowly out of sight.

By the time the police and ambulance men arrived mum had been upstairs for what seemed to be a lifetime. They brought Benny down in handcuffs and Wyn on a stretcher, breathing into an oxygen mask with mum holding her hand. When mum got cleaned-up she told me that when she walked into the bathroom she saw Benny holding an unconscious Wyn who was in the bath. Benny was repeatedly saying that he was sorry. Mum said, 'These women don't know how to handle him' as if this gave her a sense of achievement because he'd never hit her like that. Benny was sent to Armley Gaol for 18 months. I remember the mask Wyn had to wear. She looked like Jason from the horror film *Friday the Thirteenth*.

Over the next few months there was a lot of arguing in the house as Mark tried to lay down the law. I never saw him as someone to trust, like or respect. I would tell him to clear off. He wasn't capable of telling me what to do and mum would just tell him to ignore me. Mark, however, was always demanding respect as he thought he had swagger. Even at a young age I could see right through him. At least Geoff had money. Even though he drank a lot and didn't work he made our lives exciting. But Mark was always asking mum for money and, even at ten-years-of-age, I knew that was wrong.

Mark bought a car and soon afterwards the gearbox went. The twist was that he was getting involved with lads on the estate and he'd bought it along with one of them. As he was driving it when the gearbox went that meant it was his responsibility to pay for the repair. This other lad was involved in all the local crime. He was therefore well-respected in the area but, believe me when I say it, no-one at all respected Mark. He was the kind of guy that would do pretty much anything to be in with the cool gang but was never really accepted and soon became their victim.

The name of the other man I can't remember, but I do recall one day he walked into our house in the middle of the day. He was a big black man with lines in his hair. He walked into the living-room and punched Mark in the face. Down Mark went and stayed there. I'm sure he was conscious but getting-up would have meant he would have to protect us. He wasn't capable of that, of keeping us children safe or guarding his woman. I'm not saying a man needs to do this to be a man, but Mark brought trouble to the house. The least he should have done is to have taken the man outside. The man just walked into the living room and took our hi-fi. It was the only thing worth any kind of money and that wasn't much. He walked out like it was his saying we could have it back when he got his money. By now we were crying and shaking.

Mum walked after him saying, 'Don't take that. It belongs to the kids'. 'Move away,' he replied, arrogantly in a way that indicated he would punch her too if she didn't do what he said. It was as if this was completely normal behaviour for him, to simply walk in and take things. This was a place where Social Services felt a vulnerable mother with five kids could live in with no support now they'd closed our case. In this kind of environment, the police didn't get involved as it made things worse, so we were stuck as a family. I remember feeling that the adults who were supposed to take care of us didn't either.

As soon as the man left, Mark miraculously recovered put his clothes together and took off. Mum asked him where he was going and he just said they would beat him up even if he paid them so he was going away for a bit. Ironic that the only way Mark felt he could protect us as a family was to create this mess and then clear off. I could never respect a man like that. He was pathetic. The next day the black man was back again but the door was locked so he couldn't get in. 'Mark's left me because of all this,' mum shouted to him as he peeped through the letterbox, she sitting directly under it with her weight against the door in case he started forcing his way in. We kids stood in the hallway crying thinking he'd do anything to get into the house. He told mum that he was going to come every day until he got the money Mark owed him.

I thought to myself, 'We can only depend on ourselves in this time of need. The police arrest family members or take children into care but can't keep us safe from people who want to cause us harm. We're at risk from criminals but they're a safer pair of hands than services'.

My friend's mother Shirley was quite friendly with mum. Shirley spoke to her boyfriend Jason. He was a big guy who looked like Candy Man and he was well-respected. Shirley sent him to see the man. He just went and told him to leave mum alone. He told him the car had nothing to do with her or us kids and Jason brought the hi-fi back and told mum that the man wouldn't return. These are street rules.

Mum kept in contact with Benny throughout his prison sentence. She hadn't been in a relationship for a while and we needed to be re-housed as our flat was dripping with condensation. Benny was released and managed to get his own house away from us. We were promised a new one, if we waited, but Benny persuaded mum to leave and go and stay with him. Another cracking decision all round!

CHAPTER 3

Shunted Back and Forth

My brothers and sisters all began primary school and I moved to middle school due to my age. Yet although my existing school stated more changes at home would be damaging, here we were about to move to the far side of the city. How on earth was I supposed to keep up with everyone in my year? Mum got herself a job for a change at the peanut factory with a friend and things settled down. Benny didn't want to take or pick-up the younger kids and he would keep me off school so I could do it. He loved playing games on the Sega Mega Drive. It was better with someone else so we'd do it together all day long which I didn't mind. After all, I was too far behind everyone else with my lessons in any event. Aged eleven I was moved again to another school where they wanted absence letters from parents. Benny once wrote me one saying I couldn't attend due to my willy being sore as I was constantly playing with myself, or so I found out later.

On the way to school one morning I met some lads who said they were off to nick a car from the golf course. Pinching cars was a favourite pastime of teenage lads on the estate. If you got away from the police you were a god. Some of us decided to go and watch. We could collect golf balls to sell later. The older lads liked the look of a Cavalier in the car park and decided that was the car they were going to take. We younger lads were just amazed and stood and watched. There were four lads and when they got into the car there was a spare seat. They stopped, pointed and shouted me over. 'Me,' I thought as ran to the car because, hey, I was a big boy now. Or so I thought, so I jumped in. I couldn't think of a reason to say no. As they flew up and down the estate I was shitting my pants. The car was going far too fast and we were swaying in and out of the traffic. The lads were screaming and laughing but not me. I felt sick. With every turn I grabbed hold of the inside of the door as tight as I could whilst pretending not to be scared. The lads were laughing at me which was clearly the reason they took me at all. I just thought that most of the kids from school had seen me get into the car. After about 20 minutes or so they drove into the woods. There they threw petrol on the seats and set the car on fire. I was just happy to be alive. My heart was beating like it was going to pop out of my chest and my knees felt weak.

Walking back to the estate a helicopter came right above us and hovered. A minute later a police car flew around the corner and they arrested the five of us. When I was booked in I put my possessions on the counter which included the letter Benny had written to my teacher. When the officer opened it and read out the contents all the lads as well as the officers began laughing at me. I remember thinking, 'I hate Benny'. The sergeant said it was the funniest thing he'd seen in ages and was going to get it photocopied and pinned-up on the notice board. It turned out they didn't have enough evidence and had to release us. We all stuck to the same story, that we were on the golf course to find lost balls.

One day me and some other lads were in a friend's garden when Benny came staggering down the street blind drunk. He could be quite funny in this mood, so we went out to give him some friendly abuse and wrestle with him. He was telling us that no matter how big or small we were we should never back down but stay and fight. Almost as if planned, a stolen car flew down the street at high speed. Our street was in a 20 mph zone and always full of kids playing. Benny shouted at the driver and it stopped with smoke rising from the wheels.

'You got an effing problem?' the driver asked Benny. 'Clear off and joyride down another road as my little boy's in this one,' he replied. With that the driver reversed out of sight then drove the car back down at a high speed and handbrake turned it right outside our house. The driver hung out of the car window and spat at us. Benny booted the back of the vehicle like he was a Ninja but he was drunk and nearly fell over. The lads got out and walked towards him when he put up his fists and said, 'Come on you bastards'. I remember thinking, 'If that was me I'd be running,' but it was as if Benny had to prove a point. The group set about him and put him on the floor. Miles ran into the house and told mum. She came out and started pushing them off which was the bravest thing I'd ever seen her do. They told her, 'Keep that dickhead in the house,' got back in the car and drove off furiously.

When Benny picked himself up and cleaned his bloodied face he claimed the last laugh, saying 'Told you lads, never run'. These messages I was getting from the adults around me seemed strange as I didn't like fighting. It made me feel scared. Yet I was being told repeatedly that to be a real man you had to fight and protect your own. I'd learned how people stole vehicles but my one experience had scared the life out of me. One thing's for sure, I felt a lot older than my years. 'Other eleven-year-olds haven't done half what I have,' I thought.

Benny had a gambling addiction and would waste lots of the money mum earned at the factory. One day she'd taken us to a friend's house in Seacroft. Earlier she'd given Benny £20 out of her wages so he could go to the bookies. He made his way to the friend's house to ask for more as he'd lost. 'The rest's for food and things,' mum told him. Without speaking he grabbed her by the hair and pulled her over the back of the chair. She was facing upwards and he took a swing and slapped her across her cheeks.

I have never felt so helpless. I was angry and upset but there was nothing I could do. I felt lots of emotions in one. Anger, fright, confusion and frustration. Mum was right. The social workers didn't care as much as they said they did. They claimed they would protect us but things were getting worse. I remember thinking, 'I wish I was back at Ivy's in care'. This made me feel even worse because I knew I should love mum and wanted to stay with her, but she never seemed to keep us safe. I just walked outside and took my temper out at a bus stop. I found a fork and damaged the shelter because it took my mind off the pain. I waited until Benny walked-out before I went back inside and asked mum what she'd done. She told me that she'd given him the money. This is what she did, control him by not challenging him. Her friend encouraged her to leave Benny and I was agreeing even though she would have to quit her job. I said, 'He'll hurt you like he did Wyn'. What we didn't know is that this so-called friend was sleeping with Benny so when mum told Benny she was leaving he just said, 'Fuck off then'. He refused to allow her to take Miles but didn't want to keep Gail. Mum was far too scared to resist, so we took off leaving Miles with him. Soon afterwards she found out that her friend wasn't around to support her because she was with Benny.

Next mum found a house in Harehills to rent privately and we moved there. Although it was a mess she insisted it would only be temporary. The street was made up of back-to-back houses, very active, and there were three or four houses occupied by young adults who often had parties. Three fellows lived over the road called Brad, Nigel and Derek. Derek was six feet four inches tall and thought he was a hard man. None of them worked so they would often be at our house and it wasn't long before Derek started a relationship with mum.

I remember I often looked after the kids as at night mum was at their party house. One day she brought Derek home late and was telling another woman who went out with Brad that Derek was unbelievable in bed saying, 'He can go for hours, like a robot'. I remember thinking, 'Gross'. They took every opportunity to make love which meant I could hear them if I was around or in bed, so I would cover my ears. If it was during the day I would collect up the kids and leave so they didn't have to wonder what was going on. Derek would slap mum's arse and say things like, 'You're getting it tonight'. Even at eleven I knew he didn't respect her and was just using the house as somewhere to stay.

Mum spent one night at a party where they smoked cannabis and drank alcohol. I was old enough to know what they were doing whereas when mum was with Geoff I hadn't been. When she came home after that party she acted weird. I asked Derek what was wrong and he told me they'd given her an ecstasy spliff and she began laughing. I remember being worried about her but after an hour she came round and was back to normal. 'Never again,' she said, 'will I allow you lot to persuade me to do that'. This was my first introduction to drugs.

One night, Brad came over and was calling Derek out. Derek answered the door and I went to the window where I saw Brad in the street with what looked like a Rambo-style knife. Derek went out and smashed a glass bottle on the wall. He told Brad that if he was big enough he should step up to him and he would slit his throat. One of Brad's mates pulled him off saying, 'He isn't joking mate, come on'.

Mum's relationship with Derek didn't last long for reasons unknown to me and he soon disappeared. She'd had money off loan men and so we moved to another part of the city. This new house was bigger, better and had a back alley to play in. I started spending time with Daniel and his brother from two doors down. He was a skinny kid and his family was just like mine, so we got along. He was the same age and smoked cigarettes. I started stealing them from mum and smoking them with him in a hut over the road aged twelve.

Due to the constant moving I'd fallen out of touch with the school system altogether and mum was finding it hard to get me to travel across the city. Education Welfare threatened her with a fine if she didn't get me back to school and I remember her dragging me to their office and saying she couldn't. She blamed me for my lack of attendance and didn't accept any responsibility for the constant moves or not giving priority to my education. This was yet another opportunity for Social Care to come back and support her, but it didn't happen. I felt I'd far too much going without school which was for immature kids, not people like me. Good kids that listen to teachers. Not kids that had been in stolen cars or smoked. No-one got out of bed in my house until twelve noon, so why should I? 'It's a waste of time,' I thought.

By now mum was 29 and had started to see another young man called Nat who was only 19 and who she met at one of Derek's house parties. As I was still around 12, he was closer to my age than he was hers! Nat shared a house with two other young people in the next street. It was a place for young adults leaving the care system as they made the transition to living independently. One morning mum asked me to go fetch Nat. When I got there he was still in bed but Simon who lived with him let me in. I woke-up Nat and he asked me if I'd ever smoked a spliff? I told him I hadn't, so he rolled one and shared it with me. It felt awful to start with but then I became relaxed. I was now being exposed to yet another great role model showing me how to make positive choices. Nat did show an interest in me. Probably as he was only eight years older, and I looked-up to him and everything he did. Mum and he got along well but he always talked to me in a sexual way. He once pulled out his willy and showed it to me saying, 'Women love this Andi. One day, you'll have a big cock like me'. It made me feel uncomfortable, but I didn't let on. He was a horny teenager which I think is what mum must have liked about him. I remember they used to disappear upstairs. One day I went up in the middle of the day and the bedroom door was open. I could make out their outline in the bed and I remember thinking mum was losing my respect. I'm sure this affected my own relationships with women later in life.

I was upset when six weeks later Nat came and told me that mum was going to spend the day with Benny. He said he thought she was going to go back to him. I ran straight upstairs and begged and pleaded with her not to go. She said I was being silly and that she was only going to talk about his children. I asked her to look me in the eyes and promise she wouldn't return to him if he asked her to. She did and said, 'I promise, I just want Miles and Gail to see more of each other'. When she came back home she said she had sorted things out and that it was going to be better for us all if we went back to live with him. I have never felt so betrayed. It seemed clear she knew when she left that her intentions were to get back with him, but I know she missed Miles. During the time mum was moving her furniture I was left with Nat. He told me he had some tablets and that he was going to commit suicide.

Looking back, he was a care leaver and probably thought he had found a family and a sense of belonging. Yet here he was about to lose that. I asked him for some tablets as well and he gave them to me. It must have been an action that he felt would maybe get my mum to change her mind and stay. It didn't get that far as we only took four tablets each. He just cried and to be honest they were far too difficult to swallow. Mum said having Nat as a partner was sometimes like having an extra child. Him giving me tablets did kind of prove her right. I liked him, but he was a bit of a wally. I just didn't want to go back to Benny's because he scared the life out of me and was so unpredictable.

Things didn't change a bit at Benny's. He just sat on his arse all day long and mum did whatever he asked. She knew she could get a slap if she didn't. I don't know why he asked us to move back. Only four weeks later he threw us out again. We moved to another house in the same area. This time he told her to take Miles with us. I don't know if he had another woman or just couldn't have us kids around after living alone. Either way, I didn't much care.

I remember that mum was at this point struggling with Adam's behaviour who would sometimes climb out of the window and run away. She had a gay friend called Arthur who lived nearby. I found him to be nice and both Adam and I used to stay at his house and watch movies and he was always fine with me. Adam, however, was younger and more vulnerable. He'd sneak out of the window at home and was often found at Arthur's. He told mum Arthur was abusing him. Nat and his friends called on Arthur and beat him up. As always in our circle the police weren't notified so the truth will never be established. Let's just say Arthur had a lot of opportunity and a hold over Adam. Another problem of course is that as a child Adam was often caught telling fibs. His behaviour was getting worse altogether, he became more difficult to parent and nobody at all could control him. He got more attention that way.

Nat had a brother called Tony and he was still in the care system as he was only 16. He would stay with us a lot because he was always running away from his care home. It was great for mum as he would look after us while she went to bingo. I remember that every Friday Tony would go to Social Services because they would give him his weekly money. He would get around £30 and buy cannabis with it. He didn't have to worry about buying food as he ate at ours. Weed became far more important than school for me now and Friday was my favourite day.

Tony became my new best friend and mum didn't question what we were doing because her standards in this regard were minimal. This became our weekly structure until I started baby-sitting for mum's friend, Georgina in Middleton. Georgina had three kids and two of them were not much younger than me. I did it with one of my distant relations, Gerald. He was 16 and I was twelve at the time, so he was the baby-sitter but enjoyed my company. Georgina saw the benefit of me being there. She knew I fancied one girl and told me if I went to school I could stay for a while at her place. Georgina's was a more stable household, so I said yes as it was the six weeks holiday anyway. 'I'll deal with school later,' I thought.

Mum's dad who we never normally saw had met a women called Mildred from Wolverhampton and moved there to live with her. When they came to visit they brought her son Len with them. Len and mum hit it off and instantly decided she was moving to Wolverhampton and starting over. I told her there wasn't anything for me in Wolverhampton, I'd discussed it with Georgina and as long as I went to school she was happy to let me remain with her in Leeds. Mum didn't argue as she knew I'd be okay with Georgina and I'd been away for a few weeks anyway. Still, amazing to think that, as a 12-year-old, I got to make massive decisions for myself. It reinforced my view that I was a man not a boy.

Although I slept on the sofa in an overcrowded house at Georgina's, I never gave my immediate family a second thought. She was quite strict compared to mum and I don't think she ever realised people she knew would take me stealing. They would do commercial burglaries for electric and petrol tools, taking things from building sites and containers. They only took me when they needed a spare pair of hands. I would then feel like a big-time gangster as they would have meetings beforehand to plan things. I felt proud as this seemed to me like a promotion.

I only went on three or four jobs. One I remember well. There was a security guard and we were watching him and following him around. When he went to the opposite end of the site Gerald called us on a walkie talkie and asked how much time there was before he came back. We unloaded a container of electrical tools into a van and took off. I remember them giving me £20, which was a complete rip-off, but Gerald got £40, so we were set for a few bags of weed and packs of cigs.

The problem came when Georgina tried to get me to go to school. As I'd never really stayed at any school for the last two years due to all the moves I didn't like the idea of playgrounds with kids. I mean, come on. In my head I was an adult. Look at the things I'd seen and done. School wasn't for me anymore. The kids there wanted to talk about things that just didn't interest me as weed and crime took over my life.

The day before I was supposed to begin at high school I wondered what I could do not to go there. A friend and I broke into the school to rob it. Whilst inside we had another lad to keep watch. He shouted that the police were outside and we grabbed a few things and climbed out of the window. Police officers were running towards the building and I saw the lookout racing across a field. We sprinted as quickly as we could to a hole in the fence. I was scared and could hardly catch my breath. The police were right behind us, within touching distance, but when we got through the fence they couldn't because they were too big and their belts got tangled-up in it.

We jumped on a bike and took off. Although the police never found out it was me, Georgina did. She told me she didn't want the police knocking on her door. She rang mum and told her that I couldn't stay any longer. A few days later mum got my grandad to drive to Leeds and pick me up. I'd grown fond of the people I spent time with and, as I was driven away, I cried. I was used to change, but this time I was leaving my home city and didn't know anything about Bilston. It was a complete contrast to living in a large city. Well let's see how well this family got on as it couldn't be worse than it was in Leeds, surely?

CHAPTER 4

Bilston

We were on the waiting list for a council house and after three months were given one in Bilston. At that time it was one of the toughest estates around and the lads there didn't take well to newcomers, especially those who spoke like farmers. I was out of my comfort zone and Len was quite strict though I found him easy to get on with. Adam, on the other hand, didn't. They clashed over just about everything. It all went too far one day when Adam lost his temper and threw a brick though the living-room window. Mildred was everything to Len and he persuaded mum to put Adam back into care as he thought he was beyond control.

To be fair to Len he came into our lives a little late to expect us to be well-behaved but he gave us treats when we did. He would take us to Haven or Butlin's holiday camps which we'd never experienced before and it wasn't really Adam's fault that the boundaries were difficult to navigate. Len had expectations of him that he simply couldn't meet due to the neglect, drugs, crime and abuse he had been exposed to throughout his childhood. The poor lad had already experienced being sent away once and he was now placed back into the care system, voluntarily due to the one man who was able to bring some structure into the lives of the rest of us. He went to a children's home in Burton-on-Trent.

Our house had a big back garden and I'd my own small bedroom. Len had a job and a car and it looked like the past was in Leeds and Wolverhampton the future. Due to the way Len was and me being in a completely new frame of mind, they got me into the local high school. It was the back end of year eight which made me 13-years-old and, although I was quite clever, they put me in the bottom stream as I'd missed so much of my education. It was frustrating as I was more intelligent generally than my peers, I'm sure. However, due to my lack of academic attainment, I was too far behind to be taught with kids above my level.

I had yet to find out where I stood with the lads there but felt I was going down a treat with the girls. They followed me from class to class. They would ask me to speak whilst we were waiting for the next class and would giggle when they heard my Yorkshire accent. I loved the attention. At the end of the first French lesson, I received a folded-up note from a girl called Deirdrie. She was an open and forward girl and had also spent time in care. The letter said she would give me a blow job after school. I would have never admitted it at the time but I was a virgin and intimidated by her. She was pretty and like me didn't comply with the rules and I fancied the pants off her.

The attention from the girls helped me with the lads. Before I knew it I was friends with a lad called Brendan. He was the hardest kid in our year. I sought out physically strong people as they made me feel safer, but the decision to become Brendan's friend backfired on me as the lads in the year above hated him. He was a big youngster and the only black lad which made him an easy target for bullies. There was me, Brendan, Frank, a chubby follower of Brendan, and Jeremy who wasn't the brightest. We all became really close.

I remember feeling good as for the first time we had stability at home and did things as a family. Without Adam, obviously, but in Len's car, so everything was nice and normal. I'll never forget that Len would play Boney M in the car and I would pretend I hated it. Deep down I would be singing along inside my head, 'There's a brown girl in the ring, nah, na, nah, na, nah'. I can admit this now but it's never cool to enjoy the same music as your parents as a teenager. My top song around that time was Will Smith's 'Summertime'. My favourite music was R&B and hip-hop and Brendan loved this kind of music too.

The four of us were more interested in getting weed and drink for the weekend than we were in schoolwork, but at least I was actually going to school. Everything stayed like this until it was time for the year elevens to leave at the end of the year. You see the hardest older lads in that year were from our own estate so they would keep an eye out for us. But the year just above us, the year tens, were mainly from another part of town. A rumour went around that the year tens were going to wait for me and Brendan. We were told they were outside the gates and going to get us now we didn't have the year elevens to stop them and watch over us. I looked out of the window and saw a crowd gathering. I started to get an awful feeling in my stomach, one I knew I was going to have to get used to. I saw a lad called Brass who although he never actually hit us was always there putting in his two pence worth. He was a Leeds United fan as well, not that he gave a shit about me. I walked to the entrance of the building where I met Daniel and Frank and we decided to walk-out and see what happened.

When we reached the gates I could see the lads who'd made it clear they didn't like us. The feeling in my stomach was getting unbearable and there was nothing at all we could do in this situation. There were loads of them and they were older. When you're young age difference really matters. Older lads seemed automatically superior. All of a sudden Graham along with some other year elevens walked round the corner and smacked a couple of the year tens in the face. They told them, 'We're leaving but we'll be back if you start giving the younger ones shit'. I felt so relieved that we didn't have to fight.

While we were on our six weeks holiday I got to meet a few lads who had been expelled from the school before I arrived there. Flax was one of these. He had an elderly mother who couldn't control him. We got on like a house on fire. He was a goofy, skinny lad with a shaved head, always up to something and not everyone trusted him. Even though he was barred from school he would still come to play football with us in the Discount Giant car park. We waited until the cars went then used two posts as a goal for headers and volleys. The security guard was forever telling us to wait until 8 pm when the store closed but we never listened, just paused until he went back inside.

It wasn't long before there was trouble at school and I found any kind of relationship with girls difficult. I believe, looking back, that mum's relationships with men made me lack respect for women, especially when anything sexual was involved. I really liked Deirdrie but didn't want to admit it. I just wanted to stay away from her. She told someone from the year above I'd hit her and he came to find me after a PE lesson. He told me that there was a gang of year elevens looking for me. I thought, 'I'll get to class and then work out what to do about it'. However, the next door I walked through took me straight into them and this guy was the first to approach me. He punched me in the face. I tried to fight back but before I knew it there were six lads all kicking me then, all of a sudden, they dispersed and walked-off. I saw Mr Jackson, our head of year, standing over me as I picked myself up. 'Get up and get to class,' was all he could say. He knew I'd been roughed-up but I wasn't exactly a star pupil, so I guess he thought I was getting what I deserved. On top of that, when I got to my history class, Mrs Aldridge told me to, 'Go and clean your face'. I can only assume that she felt I was deserving of a beating because I'd been fighting as she was usually so nice to me. I looked over at the corner of the room and Deirdrie was sitting there smirking, covering her mouth with her sleeve. I just walked-out thinking another argument with her would make things worse.

The next morning, the minute I walked through the gates, I saw that the year elevens were grouped together. Brass shouted me over as it was clear that their attention had switched to me now. He asked me what happened the day before while some bullies stood there watching. He had a big smile on his face like he was getting a buzz from it. In a quiet voice I asked, 'Why do have to hit me?' Brass took this personally as he was the one doing the talking. He came right up in my face and told me to get away or I was going to get hit again. I just turned and left. I hated feeling weak but there was nobody who could help me, and I couldn't fight them all. Not that I would have. I couldn't handle the way this made me feel. They would make me flinch when they walked past between classes. I started to take every opportunity to stay away from school.

Due to my diminishing attendance it wasn't long before the school wrote to mum and arranged a meeting. The headmaster said that they had hardly seen me and when they did I'd often been sent to his office. They were not prepared to let me interfere with the education of other pupils. I was expelled and banned from the premises. I was told that if I entered the school grounds I would be trespassing. I'm sure they knew nothing about my past and the childhood I'd had, or about my care experience, social work intervention and breakdown of earlier school placements, or maybe they would have understood. If they had asked questions without assuming why I wasn't in school things could have been dealt with in a better way. Anyway, as I didn't want to be in school, I didn't argue. After all, it's not important to keep boys in school anyway, right?!

Towards the end of that school year I had my first contact with the Criminal Justice System. I had a Men in Black soundtrack on a blank tape but with no cover. I've always liked being organized and I wanted the cover to match the rest of my collection. I tried to steal one and was caught at the entrance to HMV. I was taken to court and given a one year conditional discharge. This meant if I got into trouble within twelve months I would be sentenced for this crime as well any new one. It didn't mean anything to me so far as any decisions I made as I quickly forgot about it. I thought I'd done pretty well to get to age 15 without a conviction so having one now didn't seem all that bad. I knew crime would be something I'd be involved in sooner or later.

Len and I sat down and had a chat. He explained to me that, if I wanted things, I would need to work hard for them. We agreed that I would work with him at weekends for £20 a time. We would see if I could get into another school. It was clear Len could see something in me. After three girls, I think I was the son he never had. He was a large chubby man with cross-eyes, a self-employed painter and decorator who worked hard for a living.

Those weekends working with him seemed to go well and I enjoyed getting that £20 note in my hand each week. I also felt good about the work itself. Len would paint newly built houses. My job was to sand down and varnish the staircases. In the time it took me to do this, he painted the whole house! He used to wake me up for work and I would say, 'I don't mind the work but I hate getting-up at 6 am'. He told me, 'Andi, no-one likes getting-up for work but you have to like everyone else'. It was clear he was a good man.

CHAPTER 5

A Life of Crime

I was spending more time with Flax who was occupying most of his time burgling houses or doing anything else to pay for weed. Brendan and the rest of the boys were at school but Flax, like me, was excluded. I knew I didn't want to get involved in burgling as I was too scared. However, I did let him persuade me to help him pinch some ladders. Jack, a friend of his, and I slept at his house and we went out for the ladders in the middle of the night. Flax knew a window cleaner who would buy them for £30, the price of a bag of weed. Jack, who'd left school, was a placid lad but didn't have much to do through the day either.

When the police arrived we ran off down country lanes. We thought we'd got away but saw more policemen coming from the opposite side of a field. We ran our separate ways and I found myself on my own in a garden where there were two large boxer dogs. I got scared and jumped onto the shed roof and lay there for hours. It wasn't until the sun rose and the owners took the dogs in that I climbed down and made my way home. I was covered from head to toe in muck, tired and exhausted and all I wanted to do was get into bed. I hadn't been in the house long enough to get cleaned-up when I heard a knock at the door and a voice ask, 'Is Andi in?' 'The police are here asking for you son,' mum shouted.

At the police station I was told Jack had been caught in the fields and said he was with me and Flax. At court I was breached on my conditional discharge and given 20 hours of community service. I can remember having to travel across Wolverhampton for my first session and was with adult offenders all day. It was intimidating as I was only 16 so I knew I wouldn't go burgling again. I may have been involved in offending but they were hairy, grown men so I didn't want to be around them. I didn't care too much about the so-called consequences of my conviction. Thinking about my future or job prospects wasn't on my radar or I wouldn't have been smoking weed, getting excluded from school or spending time with criminal-types. Besides, who other than Len had given me any belief that I could get legitimate work. People like me didn't get jobs.

By now I was getting to know older lads in Bilston with too much time on their hands. As I wasn't going out burgling I could only chip in to pay for the weed using my pocket money from Len. It wasn't long before I was sneaking things out of the house and selling them to Sue, a dealer, who would happily exchange any kind of goods for drugs. Len was becoming increasingly frustrated. But any time he grounded me mum would let me out as soon as he went out of the house. It all became too much for him and, yes, before long he left. I had mixed feelings about him going as we were settled with him around. However, I knew we could do whatever we wanted with mum on her own so it didn't bother me over much. It must have been frustrating for Len as he knew what boundaries we needed. Mum, in contrast, always took the easy option and that wasn't keeping me in the house moaning at her. Len probably felt like he'd tried the best he could. The stability we'd had wasn't real, or that's how it now seemed.

Brendan and Frank's parents were strict and as a result it wasn't long before they stopped coming around my new circle. They left me to my own devices. One of my new friends was Alexis. He was 17-years-old and respected around the estate. He had uncles known for being able to fight and going in and out prison. I'll never forget the time I went to his house and waited inside whilst he got ready. It made me feel I was being accepted in this place mum had taken us to. Not just by any old people but by those who were respected there. I was surprised when Alexis told me that he'd tried heroin. I didn't know much about it but I felt uneasy towards it so I must have known taking it was risky. He said it was stronger than weed and I guess it was only a matter of time before I tried it as I idolised these guys. Four of us paid for a bag. It was good that four of us could get smashed for £10, so we were laughing. Cheaper than the weed we thought. I did a couple of lines and my eyes started to feel heavy when we heard an ice cream van in the distance. One of them asked what we each wanted and I said a Zap lolly. By the time he'd nipped out and back, I'd been sick all over the bedroom floor. He grabbed me by the scruff of the neck and dragged me to the bathroom shouting, 'You little prick, you should have done it in here' as he threw me across tiles towards the toilet.

If only this experience had put me off taking it again. The lads told me that it was real nice once you'd been sick. That after a bit you could handle it and you wouldn't throw-up any more. The thing with heroin is that it can make doing nothing all day feel great which is amazing for those with long boring days like us as it helped to pass the time. The feeling after I'd been sick was ten times better than I got when smoking weed. I remember Brendan said that I needed to stop hanging around with the lads in Bilston as they would only get me into trouble and I thought 'That's easy for you to say as you are still in school. I can't stay with mum all day'.

I forget the name of the derelict pub in the middle of the estate where we'd go when we'd scored a bag. We started becoming sneaky with each other as we would often try to avoid anyone that couldn't chip in to get gear. We didn't do freeloaders. Me and Flax were the youngest, but we were good at getting the money together to pay for it. Even if it meant taking something from home and flogging it. Sue wasn't too fussed what she got as long as she could easily turn it into cash.

Flax and I would argue about what we were going to buy. I would want gear, but he was still keen on weed. I didn't get anything from weed anymore. I think I got hooked on heroin a lot easier than him and it masked the fact I was completely bored with life. Sixteen-years-old and wanting to hide from the world.

Malcolm was 23 with a girlfriend and two baby girls. He was respected as he'd sold weed for ages which he got from McCann a Scottish guy who I believe supplied most of Wolverhampton. Malcolm was a big man with gold chains around his neck and gold rings on his fingers. He was charismatic but slimy at the same time. One day when he came to drop off some weed for me and Flax he asked if I could get him some heroin. We were suspicious but said yes when he said he would buy us a bag to share if we could score one for him. Malcolm obviously knew that we were taking some drug or other which can only have been down to the way we were presenting. I wasn't someone who prioritised my health, but once I started on heroin this got worse.

Once we got the gear, Malcolm took us to a quiet place in his car and we all sat in his little Fiesta and got high. I could run it really well by now, in fact I was the only person in the car who could, so I ran both bags for the three of us. By now, I prided myself on this skill. I could get so much out of a small amount and, no matter who we were with, I would always be asked to run it. It made me feel I was good at something.

By this time Flax and I were both getting highly addicted and my wanting to avoid burgling had to change. In the beginning we would have an urge to get some gear that was a little more urgent than that for weed. Then, before long, we would wake-up in the morning feeling like we couldn't function without a bag. I would sweat and get pains in my stomach. I wouldn't be able to take a poo, even though I needed to. Sitting on the toilet would cause intense pain in my stomach. The further I got into withdrawing, the less clean I felt and I knew that one smoke of the drug would make me feel normal again. Being young and not fully developed didn't help me deal with the withdrawals. I felt I'd no choice, so we were out burgling houses for VCRs, camcorders and widescreen TVs. We would try the door or go in through an open window. If this failed we would use screwdrivers to prize them open. We never discriminated, we just did what we thought we had to do to make sure we didn't feel poorly the following day. We became completely focused on getting money, never thinking about victims, our families or our health.

One day we climbed through a loose window and there was an elderly man lying on his back asleep on the sofa. I quietly unplugged the VCR. Flax spotted that the man was wearing a gold ring. I knew what he was thinking and told him not to touch it but he wanted the ring and I knew he was going to try and remove it. When he started taking it, the man stirred and began shouting. I darted out of the door and it seemed like a lifetime before Flax came running after me shouting, 'Got it!'. This was risky behaviour but it became our daily routine and oddly the more you did it the less serious it seemed. Not a single thought for the fact that we would inevitably get caught. The adrenaline would kick-in and we just lived in the here and now.

During another burglary we were in a house and the victim must have rung for the police from upstairs. We saw him coming downstairs and darted out of the window. It wasn't long before the police had the estate covered. While they were chasing us, I left Flax to run and darted into a garden. At the back of the house I came face-to-face with a high metal fence. I climbed over it cutting my hands to shreds on the sharp points at the top. I hid in the bushes directly behind it as a policeman arrived. They went into all the gardens with sniffer dogs because they knew we couldn't be far away. My heart was beating so fast and the adrenalin running so much that I didn't even notice my hands were cut. The dog came right up to the fence but didn't detect me. The copper left as quickly as he came. I stayed in the hedge for half-an-hour and then climbed over it and made my way home. It was only when I got home that I realised I'd got dog shit all up the back of my trackies and that must have been why the dog missed me.

Next day I went to Flax's and found out he'd been caught and bailed and that he was now on a curfew. He was by far the better burglar of the two of us and without him making money we were going struggle to maintain our habit. We needed to be creative. I started to sleep in Flax's bed whilst he went out on the graft as the police were happy looking in the room and seeing someone there. Little did they know they were looking at me not him and fortunately they never asked to see my face. Being a decoy didn't bother me. I wasn't the one out committing crimes and I hated burgling anyway. It gave me the excuse I needed not to go along with him.

My bedroom window was directly above the back door. One morning Flax woke me up by throwing stones at it. 'Eight-hundred pounds I got from a graft last night, Brierley,' he shouted. He told me to get myself ready as he was going to spend some of the money in town before we went off to get smashed. He asked if I would keep what he said were a pair of shoes in a box at my place. He then went off to sell a camcorder while I got ready. I didn't take long. I wasn't bothered about brushing my teeth or doing my hair at this point in my life. Sixteen and I already didn't care what people thought. Everyone on the estate must have known I was taking heroin so there was no point trying to hide it.

When he returned he had Jack with him. One thing about Flax was that he wasn't stingy about sharing with his friends. We were all big on hip-hop and I remember him buying DMX, Notorious BIG, Jay Z and Busta Rhymes albums. When we'd finished in town, we went to a local junkie's. Flax had bought crack cocaine as well as heroin. We hadn't tried crack before as it was more expensive. We found it went really quickly, but Flax had bought enough. It's a stimulant, so it made us feel like sprinting up the street. I couldn't believe how intense the feeling was but, although it made me feel good for a while, I preferred heroin. We spent an hour smoking crack through a pipe which lifted us to a big high. Then we spent the next hour smoking heroin to bring us back down again.

The house we were in was full of needles, ash from the cigs used to smoke the crack and tin foil. We were in a world that kids shouldn't have been anywhere near, but we were completely surrounded by it now. The heroin and crack circle embraced us and as long as we had money to spend on drugs no-one asked questions.

Whilst we sat smoking crack, a group of black and mixed-race men came running into the room screaming and shouting. They were big and we were scared stiff with no idea what was going on. They grabbed me, Flax and Jack and escorted us outside. 'You dare go in my baby's bed-room,' a small white woman said as she slapped me around my face on the way downstairs. My head was all over the place and I didn't know if I was just messed-up or if it was a dream. One moment thinking about how much my cheek was stinging made me realise this shit was really happening. When we got outside there were three high performance cars lined-up. I thought, 'These guys are going to kidnap us!'

The three of us were put in the back of the first car with two men I'd never seen before. The man in the passenger seat pulled out some wire cutters and while opening and closing them said, 'Let's take their fucking fingers off'. I was now starting to put two and two together. The money Flax came to my house with belonged to these guys. It was obvious that someone in the junkie house had grassed us up. I started playing stupid and shaking from head to toe. 'Can someone tell me what this is all about please?' I asked. The younger lad in the passenger seat back-handed me and told me to speak when asked a question and not until. 'Do you know who I am?' he asked. 'No,' I replied. He said, 'I'm Sid and this is Simon Walton and you little sods have robbed his house'. As soon as he said that all three of us started to cry because we knew how serious this was.

The Waltons were a family that everyone spoke about. None of us had ever seen them but we'd heard stories. They were well-respected and I started to think about telling them that Flax did it and it wasn't me. All three of us were saying we didn't know anything about it and I knew this was making the situation worse. I wasn't high anymore and I didn't have time to think about withdrawing. My bones were shaking, and I was just wondering where they were taking us and what they were planning to do. I took one glance at the door handle and thought about jumping out of the moving car.

They took us to a park where there was some kind of carnival going on. They walked us across a field by the scruff of the neck and to a tent where there was a group of Rastas. 'These little smackheads did my house over last night,' Sid said to the men who simply looked at us as if we had horns growing out of our heads. By this time two men were restraining the woman from getting to us as she was absolutely fuming. I worked out that she must be Sid's wife. It was their house that Flax had robbed and he'd obviously been in her kid's bedroom.

We were whispering and trying to get Flax to own up. We told them we could give them back what we had left. 'They will only let you two go,' Flax said, shaking his head. I could understand where he was coming from. But I was still very close to telling them. Simon came back to where we were and told us that he knew we didn't have a clue it was Sid's house. He said that if we gave him everything back he'd leave it at that. Jack and I then left Flax in no man's land by telling them where the stuff was. As we'd spent £400, Flax took what was left out of his pocket and handed it over. I can remember the look on his face when Simon said, 'So it *was* you then'. Although it seemed Flax was in trouble, I would be lying if I didn't say I felt relieved it wasn't me.

They put us back in the car and drove to the house where Flax sold the camcorder. It was near Jack's, so they told him to go with them. The man knew who the Waltons were, so he didn't argue and just gave it back. He told Flax he expected the money back from him. He could see he had other things to deal with right now so said, 'I'll see you later Flax'. He knew the Waltons had him and he couldn't do anything right then.

We then visited my house to get the shoes we'd left there. I went in to fetch them and when I brought them out they told me that I could go. 'If it's all the same I'd like to stay with Flax,' I said. They agreed and let me get back into the car. They took us to his house and knocked on the door. As soon as his mum answered, Sid smacked Flax and sent him flying across the garden. His mother was elderly and immediately ran over to Flax shouting, 'That's my son'. Sid said, 'Your son's robbed my house and he owes me three grand. If I don't get it within a month you won't be able to live here'. Leaving Flax lying on the ground, Sid and Simon walked-off and got into their cars.

I know the whole thing shook Flax up. However, he stopped grafting for one night and then got straight back to burgling. The incident scared us witless but after all it was only down to bad luck that he burgled a Walton household. Or at least that is what I was telling him. It was as simple as that we had a habit to feed and it was in my best interest that he kept burgling. Heroin was making me incredibly selfish. I was always thinking ahead and wondering what I'd do to get money, even if this meant stealing from mum or anyone else.

One day I came home and she told me Sid Walton had called. 'He gave me his address and you should go see him'. When I did, he answered the door with his baby in his arms, smiled and beckoned me in. He said, 'Look Andi, doing things like that shows me you're a good kid. If you keep knocking around with lads like Flax it will only end in tears'. He told me I was stupid for thinking my friends were like me, gave me a bag of weed, told me to get out and that he didn't want to see me again. It was obvious that he felt I was being led astray. I didn't agree. Flax had no control over what I did. In fact, I was the stronger of the two, so I thought and smarter. As I walked home I giggled to myself and thought, 'Stuff it, I have a smoke so happy days'.

CHAPTER 6

The Drugs Chain

After a while Malcolm must have seen he was spending too much on gear. He told me he would put money in with me if I wanted to start selling with him. I'd been scared off burgling or stealing after my experience with the Waltons. I still had an addiction to feed, so selling drugs seemed a better and safer option. Besides, he would be helping so it seemed to make perfect sense. He bought an eighth of heroin which we bagged-up into £10 wraps and got word out to local users. We did bigger wraps than anyone else and were not making much so it wasn't hard to get customers. Users go to whoever has the best deal. If you're quick to deliver you keep their custom.

Malcolm was clear that we would each buy our own bags once we'd sold the first lot and the profit would then be our own to do with as we pleased. He already had money from the weed which he continued selling throughout but I would frequently have no other income. As I had a habit, I would open the bags and take a little bit from each for myself. Due to the size of our bags this didn't have a massive impact, or so I told myself. But problems started when the eighths didn't sell quite so quickly and I had to dilute them ever more sparingly. Malcolm would only turn up now and again at the house, so I was getting away with it. I was lonely though because I wasn't sharing these experiences with anyone. Flax was locked-up and god knows where Jack was. Daniel and Frank both kept well away.

Users started to complain saying they wouldn't be coming back because the bags were getting smaller. One of the issues is that drug-dealers selling heroin are usually addicted to it. They are not reliable. I was selling but I still found myself having to score from others while I was waiting for our suppliers to get gear to us. The best way to describe it is it's like a chain. If at any given time a link is broken it has a knock-on effect and slows down the whole process. This means users can't be choosy who they buy from. I've bought from dealers when I knew it was bad heroin but it made me feel better at the time which was all that mattered.

By now a constant flow of addicts was coming to my house. I told them not to do so but if my phone was switched off they just arrived. Mum would sometimes ask what I was doing. Malcolm was always covered in gold and handing money to us kids to go to the shop for him. I told her he owned a garage and when my phone rang it was because I was going to help him fix cars. Mum always accepted what I said and I'm sure this was because it made life easier for her. I would use this and win any conflict between the two of us by shouting her down. A string of men friends had taught me how to behave with women and she'd learnt to deal with tensions by being passive. I was abusing her and she was a victim. I was also responsible for bringing drugs and crime into a house where young kids lived.

The man who used to supply us was called Bolt. He had a helper called Zipper that sold eighths and quarters to the likes of us. They bought in a bulk as this is how the drugs chain works. Zipper thought he was going to gaol and placed an eighth up his bum and said he'd lost it. Bolt guessed what had happened and beat him up within an inch of his life. Gradually, Bolt saw that Malcolm ran a tight ship and he started to view me as a replacement for his errand boy. Malcolm took me up to see Bolt who told me he thought I was a good lad. He said, 'You have an opportunity to make me some money'. He knew I was taking heroin but like everyone else he wouldn't have dreamed that Malcolm was. Malcolm was still hiding his dirty little secret from everyone and living a double life.

There were lads in Bilston that didn't like heroin. One day Malcolm rang to say his house had been smashed-up and that I was to get down there as soon as possible. By the time I arrived he had a lot of clients in his garden and they were getting tooled-up to fight for him. He'd been told that three lads had been inside his house and smashed-up his living-room while his girlfriend and kids were upstairs. They'd been shouting that he needed to stop messing with drugs. They'd worn balaclavas but he knew three particular lads were always going on about wanting to get drugs off the estate. He was fuming and wanted to go and find them there and then. McCann who was a dodgy guy was calmer and told everyone to come back at 8 pm when it was dark. I stayed with Malcolm and helped him clean up. They'd smashed the windows and his widescreen TV and he was crying as he picked-up the glass. I was starting to feel ill so was glad when he said we needed to have a bag to calm down. He was a big lad and I was thinking I would hate to be those other lads who were younger and I don't think they'd thought things through.

Malcolm had a hold over me and I would do whatever he asked. I was taking all the risks and never had any money left to fund my addiction but I was happy when he 'did me a favour' by giving me gear to stop me rattling. By 8 pm we'd cleaned-up and boarded the windows. Everybody came back and this time it seemed more organized but I got the feeling that somebody was going to get hurt. This was the first time I'd seen McCann get involved in any kind of drama. He probably felt he needed to be so that he wasn't next. He and Malcolm made sure everyone had a weapon and gave me a pick-axe handle. 'Ridiculous,' I remember thinking. 'What the hell am I going to do with this?' I was in well over my head and I knew it. Others had nunchucks, sticks and bats. I knew I shouldn't be getting involved but I couldn't turn around and say no to Malcolm.

We made our way to a flat above a shop on a main road where two of the lads lived. We hid over the road behind a fence surrounding a field and one of the lads came back while we were there. We stayed where we were as he drove up close to the front door. As soon as he went inside, Malcolm and McCann walked over the road and went down an alley at the side of the shop to see if there was a back door. As they walked back another lad, Colin, walked along hand in hand with his girlfriend towards the front door. My heart began beating faster as Malcolm and McCann ran towards them. Everyone then jumped over the fence and headed towards the couple to join in so I just followed. Colin panicked, let go of his girlfriend's hand, and tried to get inside. His hands were shaking so badly he had no chance and he dropped his keys on the floor.

Malcolm was the first to get to him with a baseball bat. Colin instantly put his hands up to protect himself. Everyone else arrived and from the constant blows it wasn't long before he hit the ground. In amongst all this madness I swung the pick-axe handle. I didn't even look. I just launched it in the same direction as the others. I went drip white when it connected with the back of Colin's head and vibrated from the blow. I stopped immediately and watched as he struggled. Someone swung a rounder's bat and that was how it ended. Colin's head fell sideways and I heard someone call out, 'He's dead'. At that everyone ran away and headed towards a house we'd arranged to meet at afterwards.

All the way back I just couldn't believe I got involved in all this. But when we ran past some lads that knew me one of them yelled 'It's Brierley'. I can remember thinking that they would think I was bad which was great. This is the way my mind was starting to work. I hadn't even officially finished school and yet here I was building my confidence by being involved in violence. It felt like a normal route to go down. Whether it was Benny saying 'Never run away' or Derek threatening people with broken bottles, this is the way things had been for a time now. I was doing things that I didn't really have the heart to do but couldn't see a way out. And as you can see I gladly accepted the reputation that came with it. When we got back to the flat girlfriends were waiting and they took the weapons and cleaned them in the kitchen. We sat down and skinned-up to recover. McCann asked, 'Who had the pick-axe handle?' I said it was me and he swore, 'Fuck me Andi it's broken'. Although I hadn't meant to use it and didn't deserve his praise I wasn't going to argue. I was that scared I could have pissed my pants. Yet here I was taking the credit for a chance blow as if I was one of the Kray twins.

I don't know how she found out but an hour later Malcolm's mother came to the house and told us Colin was in a bad way. She said he had some broken bones and a punctured lung adding, 'I hope you got the right lad'. The other two lads involved in ransacking Malcolm's house were advised to leave the estate and weren't seen again. Malcolm was happy that he got his revenge. It sent out a clear message to everybody that drugs had taken over the streets in the area. The people that were against drugs had meant to use violence to get rid of them, however drugs know violence better than most.

I felt more at ease after Bolt gave me a work phone that had belonged to Zipper and presented me with a bright orange Escort XR3i. I still wasn't old enough to drive and didn't know how to so I had to get others to motor me about. I did once attempt to reverse it out of our cul-de-sac but ran into a wall so never tried again. The phone already had a client base on it and so I didn't have to do anything in that direction. I'd now moved up the chain and away from selling £10 bags on street corners. I was dealing in eighths and tenths. From my experience, most of the street dealers were users. It was those who didn't touch the drugs that made the money exploiting users who in turn were the ones who ended-up in prison. I was an exploited dealer, picking-up two ounces a day, shifting them and getting a couple of grammes for myself. As we moved up the ladder, Malcolm' profits went up whilst I got a more intense addiction. His main money now came from heroin but he couldn't stop his weed round as this would have exposed him as a heroin dealer. But we were both getting worse addictions and he'd wake me up first thing in the morning for a smoke. His missus was noticing changes in him and asking questions.

Now Len had gone Adam who was still in a care home started spending more time at ours. He'd turn-up with things that didn't seem to belong to him and we'd have a session on the gear. I would allow him credit because I knew I'd get my money from him later when he sold something. One day I hid the gear in the back garden. After bringing it in and checking it over I was sure there was a small amount missing. The only person who knew I'd put it there was Adam. I didn't have the money to replace it and when Malcolm turned-up I had to tell him so. He straightaway asked if Adam knew where the stash was. He knew if it was someone that didn't know us they would have taken the lot. Eventually, he said he would put the money in and I would have to give it back to him when I sold my next batch. But he said I would have to beat-up Adam in front of him or he would do it himself.

No matter how much violence I'd witnessed, I couldn't find it in myself to hit someone I loved. It wouldn't have been loss of control like when

I swung the pick-axe handle. Malcolm brushed me aside and smacked Adam full in the face catching him with the gold rings he wore. Adam's faced swelled-up, his eye split open and I felt like crying, feeling so helpless, like I did when Benny used to hit mum. I wanted to protect my younger brother. The truth is he didn't deserve the cards he was being dealt. Malcolm just said that you didn't rob family and told me to get moving as we had drugs to sell. I wish I could have stuck up for Adam. Let's face it, Malcolm was in no position to lecture people about morals with all the bad stuff he was doing. In the car I told him, 'This is all a bit much for me', that I needed to stop everything and get myself clean of drugs. With that I felt a whack in the face and the gold rings again did their work. He said, 'Don't be daft. You should be happy Bolt took you on'. All the way to the drop I was holding my face and crying and he said I was a pussy. It was at times like this that I wondered if the services couldn't have helped prevent what was happening. Social Care were aware that mum was more than capable of going down that road. Where were they when I needed them? Adam was in care, so they must have had some contact with mum, but they weren't in contact with the rest of our family. Or at least I couldn't see that they were.

Malcolm would tell me I wasn't to make him look daft in front of Bolt. He saw him as his way up the ladder and I'd also become a tool in his climb to success. Going to the police was simply not an option. These people were embedded in every aspect of my life. Malcolm had become close to my family to the point that he would come and go as he pleased. Yes, the police have an obligation to keep children safe from exploitation, but I was a criminal selling drugs, so they were people I needed to avoid. There was nowhere left to turn. I had no control over anything anymore.

One day Malcolm, Adam and I were driving up to a nice estate to drop a quarter to a man that owned his own business. This guy had a big house but, like us, was being dragged down by drugs. Malcolm spotted an unmarked police car following us. I found out later that his car was on the drug squad's watch list and by chance they'd clocked us. Malcolm sped off down a side road at the last minute and they carried straight on and lost us. He had a Fiesta when I first met him but his current RS Turbo showed how much money he was making. I remember him bragging about his driving. He drove to a local school where we got out and he told us to get the drugs as far away from the car as possible. Adam and I didn't argue, but neither did he tell us he'd dropped some £10 wraps I'd given him to hold on the floor in the back of Malcolm's car.

We saw the police drive into the yard and park near to Malcolm. He was standing with a smile on his face and complied confidently when asked if they could search the vehicle. Thinking it was clean I turned to Adam and said, 'That was close, let's go'. I took with me 18 grammes of heroin bagged-up ready to go in deals of tenths and eights and hid them in some bushes. I then waited outside the school as Adam blended in with the kids gathering as the bell went. Malcolm came and told me everything was fine and that the police were just making sure his documents were in order. I went back to where I'd left the gear, picked it up and stuffed it down my pants. I couldn't have known the police would find the wraps. On the way down the main road out of the estate a load of police cars came flying towards us from every direction. We didn't even have time to blink before they had us up against the wall. 'You're under arrest for possession of and intent to supply a Class-A drug'. That was all we heard before being cuffed and placed in separate police cars.

All the way to the police station I was trying to get my hands out of the cuffs and into my jeans thinking that I could place the gear down the side of the seat so they couldn't say for certain it was mine. But it wasn't possible. By the time we got to the station I couldn't think straight any more. I didn't know what the outcome would be but I knew I was in trouble. I was young, uneducated, unaware and misguided about the impact any of this would have on me or my future. We were booked in and when the sergeant asked a load of questions I had to keep asking him to repeat them. My hands were sweating a lot and my brain wouldn't function. We were taken one by one into a room to be searched. I walked in as Malcolm was coming out and he glanced at me as if looks could kill.

'I'm about to do a search for substances,' the officer said as he asked me to remove my top. As I did he noticed the clear plastic bag sticking out of my jeans and pulled it from me. I will never forget his words: 'To say you're in a bit of trouble kid is an understatement'. He took off the rest of my clothes and made me squat and spread by bum cheeks which was degrading and borderline abuse although I understood it had to be done. We were still children but it didn't feel like it. I was put in a cell and the police told me I should get a solicitor and that they would obtain a warrant to search my mum's house. The solicitor bit was because being a young person it might come back on them at court. I was held in a cell overnight for the first time. I had to wait until late next day for the solicitor and to be interviewed. She advised me to go 'no comment' throughout if I wanted to get released.

I was told that as they'd found the drugs on me I would have to admit some knowledge but they would bail me pending further enquiries. I did as my solicitor said as I'd no idea what else to do. I was given a date to go back to the police station and released without charge. They told me that they'd found names on a list showing money I was owed from users. They had also found Methadone which must have been someone else's because I didn't use it. They'd found tin foil which would forensically match the wraps in the car. I was up shit creek without a paddle. We'd no money to catch the bus so Adam and I walked back to mum's and for some reason Malcolm was bailed at a different time. Mum asked why I was at the police station and the police were searching the house. I told her I'd been found with a friend's drugs and that they thought I was a dealer but of course I wasn't. I don't think she knew I was addicted to heroin due to lack of familiarity with it. That said, she must have had more than an inkling that I was up to no good, what with the people coming to the door day and night, the money, the car and a my expensive mobile phone, which were all a bit of a giveaway. I guess she looked the other way and accepted any excuse I gave her when she was left with no alternative but to ask questions.

A good example of this is my year nine school report. They repeatedly felt I needed to improve my attendance but the 68 days I'd had off were all signed for by her. Even when she found out I hadn't been in school she would make excuses for me. To her way of thinking she was protecting me, but it was actually preventing me from taking responsibility. With Adam still in care and returning home a lot and me missing school I don't understand why Social Care weren't involved. Now I'd been arrested for serious offences and with younger siblings in the house I can't figure out why there was still no referral to any service that might have identified us all as being at risk.

That evening Malcolm and I went to score from a rival dealer. It was at this point that we both realised just how bad our addictions really were. We had been locked-up and hadn't washed but didn't even think of getting clean until we'd had our fix. After we'd smoked the bag, Malcolm told me he was going to beat Adam to pulp. He blamed him for leaving the drugs in his car. It was perhaps fate that a week later he himself was arrested on several counts of burglary and remanded to Brinsford Young Offender Institution. Malcolm threatened to get Adam battered from prison.

Earlier along with Malcolm we had to go and see Bolt and explain why we'd lost over half an ounce of his gear. He already knew as we hadn't been in touch for days and he was surprisingly okay with the bad news. He told us that he always looked after his lads and that he already had another two ounces for us. He said that he would take the repayments for the lost gear in instalments. Declining wasn't an option. Strangely what he did made me happy. I didn't want to withdraw again the way I'd been doing overnight at the police station. I was totally dependent on heroin and couldn't rely on anyone else for it.

Malcolm told me to wait in the car while he spoke to Bolt. To this day I don't know what they discussed but it was obviously Malcolm starting to make plans to get himself out of the shit. This meant at my cost I'm sure. I felt like I was all alone and these guys were not going to help me. They were far savvier than I was at working out what to do. I don't know whether I was more dependent on heroin or they were. The answer was probably that our addictions were linked. Every decision I was making was connected to serious and violent drug-dealers that didn't care about me. There seemed little I could do to make anything better.

I took a fresh batch of gear and Malcolm and I went about our business as usual. He didn't know I'd found out he used to meet with the drug squad in secret locations. This is probably the reason he was released from the police station at a different time. I was just too young and naïve to do anything with that information. I was far too scared of him to say anything anyway. Malcolm was a police informer. Would people believe a smackhead or a well-respected drug-dealer? After one of his mysterious meetings with the police behind a pub, Malcolm said he would buy us both a bag out of the new batch. I knew the police were around because I could see the unmarked police car in the car park. You get to know the unmarked cars well when you're selling drugs.

We were in his house having a toot while his family were out and started to talk about the best way going forwards. He said that as he already had a criminal record I should keep the drugs on my person and anyway he had a family to take care of. It would also make sense so he said for me to tell the police a similar story to the one I'd told mum. I should say that I found the drugs in a guy called Cotterill's garden inside crisp packets and was keeping them for friends. This would also help take out a competitor as the police were onto Cotterill who Bolt hated for taking his business. I agreed because I liked Malcolm's daughters and girlfriend. I knew enough to understand that he would go to prison for a long time. The next day I got Malcolm to take me to the police station. I handed myself in and they quickly re-interviewed me, this time without a solicitor. It was like they were expecting me. I stated that I found the drugs in Cotterill's garden and I was going to use just a little and give the rest back to the friends who'd ask me to hide them. It was clear that the police were colluding with Malcolm. They bailed me again and of course he had his charges dropped at the next hearing along with those against Adam. Not that I think Adam would have given it a second thought. They swallowed my statement and let him go without any further inquiries.

I was straight back into the same routine. The fact I'd been caught with a boatload of drugs changed nothing. There were junkies coming to the house, the phone went all the time and I was in and out delivering. Mum never seemed to understand that she needed to lay down rules or I was going to get into more and deeper trouble. She obviously loved me but was unable to protect me. I needed protecting and services were clearly incapable of it. I know that she felt like she'd lost all control of me by now and I probably would have left home before stopping my habit. However, I really needed someone strong enough to help me. I was being exploited and groomed into a world of drugs and crime. I was back in full flow selling drugs after a few weeks. Four weeks after getting caught I was at Malcolm's with his family having dinner when I received a phone call. It was a user and I said I would have to go as it was a regular. You didn't mess around with regulars or you would've been in the shit if it had got get back to Bolt. When I got home I stashed the heroin in amongst mum's clothes in the wardrobe. I was sitting downstairs watching *Eastenders* when a dozen police officers burst into the house. 'Everyone stay where you are, we're going to conduct a search so don't move'. My heart sank.

There was no way of getting out of it this time. I was already up in court for possessing a hell of a lot of gear and here I was in my living room with a shitload more upstairs. They made sure we were all sitting on the sofa whilst they searched downstairs. When they'd finished there they took me and mum upstairs whilst a women officer looked after the kids. After looking in every bedroom I heard one copper say they couldn't find anything. 'Could it be that I'm going to scrape my way out of this?' I thought. I found out the answer straightaway as they brought an Alsatian sniffer dog into the house. They seemed so sure there was gear in the house and I wondered where this intelligence came from. Then I heard voices getting louder. Before I knew it, an officer walked into my room with the bag of gear I'd hidden earlier and said, 'Whose is this?' 'Not mine,' I responded and with that they started reading me my rights.

They took me to the police station. I sat in the cell and thought about the fact that the police seemed to know I had gear in the house. I was involved with a lot of evil people that would do whatever it took to get money and stay out of gaol. Surely Malcolm hadn't rung them to say I was on my way home to do a sale, or did he? I got to thinking that prison might be on the cards for me. I should have thought, 'It might help me,' but I didn't. I felt so low. What were my options? I would get released and return to a world where my friends were using me and making me do things I didn't want to. Or I'd go to prison, which scared the life out of me. I could tell the police everything, but I didn't know what would happen to my family and then I just thought that I needed to make sure I got out and some gear before I started withdrawing.

I denied all knowledge of the drugs. I told the police there were lots of people coming and going at home, including my brother. I wasn't trying to put him in the frame, just to cast doubt in their minds. But I'd been caught with a bag full of gear four weeks previously and I knew I was in the shit but I just didn't want to accept it. After searching the house for a second time the police found the scales I used for bagging-up, two mobile phones and £400 in cash. As an unemployed teenager with a threadbare and hand to mouth lifestyle I couldn't account for it. I didn't sleep all night because of the pain. By morning I was feeling really ill and being sick every time I thought of gear. The situation got even worse when they walked me from my cell to the courtroom. I couldn't believe it when I saw mum walk out of the cell opposite. They'd arrested her due to drugs being found in her house and her being the only adult. They found it hard to believe she knew nothing about them. She was held at a separate police station overnight as this is how they dealt with serious crimes. Her only real offences were of naïvety and maybe looking the other way. It was a strange feeling to stand in front of a magistrate's court with her next to me as my co-accused. We were charged and the court gave us bail to return a week later. My bail conditions were the more rigorous. I had to keep to a 7 pm curfew and live in a bail hostel in Sandbach. Once outside I saw two men that worked for Bolt sitting in a car. They shouted me over and told me that I needed to go see him. I told them that I had to get to Sandbach but they just said, 'Get in'. I went to say bye to my mum and she said, 'I can't believe all this Andi, what kind of a mess are you in?' I didn't answer but just jumped in the car. After all, it was a little late for a her to be asking me.

I was taken to a pub where Bolt and the rest of the dealers on the estate spent most of their time. By the time I arrived I must have looked really ill and as soon as I walked in Bolt told one of the lads to take me off for a toot and then bring me back. When I returned, I noticed Malcolm was there. We sat round a table and discussed the fact that Bolt had lost money again. They asked why I'd been given bail for a second time even though I'd been caught with so much gear. I got the impression they felt I'd said something to the police and started to feel unsafe.

I took myself off to the toilet to get my head together and think about what was going on. It was all happening so quickly and I'd no idea what was going to happen. Should I tell Bolt I thought Malcolm grassed on me? Was I even right about this? Would Malcolm beat me up there and then? I was about to walk out of the toilet when I looked-up and saw one of Bolt's toughest friends, Eddie, blocking my way. A bald-headed man he was always in fancy trainers and new clothes. I started crying and explaining that I never said anything. I said, 'I wasn't going to ask them to lock me up'. Eddie just picked me up and said, 'Stop being silly you little pussy, I need a piss'. He told me they knew I hadn't said anything and just wanted it to stay that way. They wanted me to know what would happen if it didn't. I can't even try to explain my relief. Malcolm took me home to get my stereo and CDs. All the money I'd been making and it was all I had to my name. He dropped me off at the station saying, 'See you soon mate, take care'.

With my travel warrant to Sandbach I jumped on the train and off I went. When I reached the hostel they put me in a room with a man called Tweedy. He was about 30, well-muscled and told me he'd just got out of prison after two years. I simply thought, 'I'll stay out of his way'. There was a bed on the left-hand side of the room with no bedding on it so I assumed it was mine. I said, 'Hi' and walked over to it with my head down. The first thing he asked was, 'Do you take gear?'. When I said yes he got some foil out of his drawer. My mouth started to water and he shared a bag with me. He seemed alright. I felt okay now so things didn't seem that bad. I just had to think about how I would make money here to support my addiction. I would find a way but for now I was just going to lie down and feel the heroin. Even with everything that was going on around me it didn't bother me as long as I was gouching.

When I woke-up next morning I was approached by the staff and asked how old I was. When I told them 17 they said I couldn't stay as this was an adult establishment and that the court shouldn't have sent me there. They made a few phone calls and told me that I was going to have to travel to Ellesmere Port near Liverpool. All they gave me was another travel warrant and a map as they pointed me towards the railway station.

Tweedy must have seen me as a kid that needed help as he told me to come back to the room for another quick toot before I left. Lovely lad.

I had to get the train to the local railway station and walk to the hostel using the map. I got lost as all the streets looked the same. I'd been told that my bail curfew was 7 pm so I needed to be in before then or I would get breached and sent to gaol. I started to get worried at around 6.30. I used a phone box and called my mum telling her I was lost and that I was going to get breached. As I was crying my eyes out, a man walked past and asked what was wrong. When I said I was searching for the bail hostel he told me not to worry as it wasn't far. He said he would take me there. He asked if I'd any money and pulled a load of change out of his pocket. He handed me around three pounds which, given I didn't have a penny, was a lot. I ran over the road to a shop for some sweets in the few minutes I had left. I will never forget the grace of that man. He didn't see me as a criminal but as a lost child. It was a nice touch for a kid going through a very difficult time. Although I was in trouble for supplying heroin it's ironic that given a bit of small change I showed my age by buying sweets.

When I arrived at the hostel I was inducted and shown the fire exits and they told me where to come for food. In the association room I was approached by a group of lads that all sounded like they were from Liverpool which made sense. After all it was Merseyside. I felt intimidated by them and when I told them I was from Leeds they just walked-off as if I wasn't anyone who mattered. I was shown to my room and I thought it would be best if I stayed there where I was safe. I plugged in my stereo. There was nothing apart from a bed and a wardrobe. I just lay on the bed and thought about how far away I was from everyone and the trouble I was in. At other times I just sat and cried. If things weren't bad enough, I then started to withdraw. Although I felt like I could do with a good sleep I couldn't drop off which led to a deep feeling of frustration. It felt like every second lasted an hour. I was starting to get sick, sweating and yet shivering. I wasn't tired and yet it was now three in the morning. I kept getting-up and putting a different CD on hoping this would be the one to put me to sleep. I must have got through ten or more when my wish came true until the sun started coming through the window.

I sat up and half-an-hour afterwards there was a knock on the door to tell me breakfast was being served. I wasn't hungry, but I needed to get out of that room before I started to crack-up. I didn't have the energy or enthusiasm to brush my teeth or wash my face. I was wallowing in self-pity and it was hardly a surprise.

The other lads asked lots of questions about where I was from and what I'd done. I tried to answer but after I ate one piece of sausage I threw-up in the dining area. They jumped out of their seats yelling, 'Dirty bastard'. They knew why I was sick and began calling me a smackhead. The staff heard the noise and came running. A man pushed me aside and told me to get out of the way while he cleaned-up the mess. As I was nervous I stayed by his side and he got annoyed shouting, 'Move, give me space'. I ran to my room and thought about my options. I was here with people that didn't seem to care or want to help me and there was no way of getting home. I rang Malcolm from the hostel phone and told him I'd never felt as bad as I did then and that it was down to the gear. He told me he had loads and that if I could get to Wolverhampton he would sort me out. He said he'd even bring me back up to Liverpool which surprised me. I rang mum and asked if she could get grandad to pick me up from Crewe. The thought of getting home was over whelming and all I could think about. I was completely angry with Malcolm but he was a familiar face and I was so alone.

When I arrived I could see the disappointment in their eyes and neither mum or grandad said anything. Being honest, the only thing that I could think of right then was the promise Malcolm had made to me. Soon I would have a toot in my mouth and get rid of the pain I was going through. Mum and grandad were not able to get any conversation out of me and kept having to pull over so that I could be sick. The feeling you get from heroin withdrawal is incredibly emotional. The best way to describe taking heroin while you're withdrawing psychologically is being in extreme debt and then winning the lottery. Physically you're in pain all over and struggle to walk or rest. Put the physical, emotional and psychological elements together and you'll get some idea what its like.

At Wolverhampton I thanked them and rushed to a phone box (I no longer had a mobile phone as it was with the police). I could tell by

Malcolm's voice that he didn't think for one minute I would actually come back. He told me to go Stanley Fender's house, a young lad who lived with his girlfriend. They had a baby girl, but they maintained their habit by letting dealers use their home. I made my way there and must have run into four or five people who asked what had happened. Like I was a superstar. Rumours spread quickly and they were being nosey. I didn't feel like a superstar. I still needed to clean my teeth and wash my face and by now I probably stank but cleanliness was the last thing on my mind.

When I reached Stanley's they could tell I was pretty ill. They sat me on a chair and gave me a cup of tea saying the sugar would make me feel better. I wasn't the only one waiting for Malcolm. There were another two lads he'd rung to say he was on his way. When he arrived, he sorted them out with weed and then came into the room. He didn't seem that bothered that I was poorly. He could do me a loan as all this police interest had cost him dear. I can't believe how angry I felt. The cheeky bastard persuaded me to take a drugs rap so he didn't have to spend a day away from his family. I was having to live miles away from home because I'd been making him money. He went from having a Fiesta to an RS Turbo and could only give me a loan. 'Unbelievable,' I thought. While I was smoking the gear he even had the cheek to ask me for half of the bag he'd lent me and treated me like I was just another customer. I asked what time he was planning to take me back? 'If I was you, I'd stay down here where it will be easier for you to make money. Otherwise you will just be coming back every day for gear,' he said. Even though he was right I felt like he was hanging me out to dry. I needed to fund my habit as I was on the run from now on. Talk about the system not understanding the needs of a young person, there couldn't be a better example of this. They placed a young heroin addict miles from home as if I was a hardened criminal, but I was and felt like a scared and vulnerable child.

CHAPTER 7

Grafting

Despite the lifestyle I'd been handed offending didn't come easy, even if I always seemed to gravitate towards those who were involved in it. I wasn't any good at it because I never liked taking risks and stealing went against my basic values. Hard to believe but its true. I started spending time with Colin from Bilston who'd been expelled from high school before I got there, remember? He'd been in the care system for some time. I often felt closer to those with similar experiences. Some of my friends were different though as they had stable and secure parents to set boundaries for them. I thought they weren't cool, but this was simply to justify why they'd distanced themselves from me. Colin scared me. A big guy with a shaved head he was streetwise with a reputation to match but he was not a very sophisticated burglar. He would kick doors off while the occupants were out.

Whilst we were out and about we saw a young lad around our age unlock his door and walk into a house. We guessed he was in there on his own and went to try the door. It was locked so Colin slowly pulled the handle down. Before I'd the chance to say, 'Come on, let's go' he booted the lock clean off and ran straight in. I followed him, shaking like a leaf as I stood in the hallway. The boy was still taking off his coat as we started to search the living-room. Then Colin told me to watch the lad whilst he looked upstairs. There was a very long silence when I was just staring at the lad. We didn't speak to each other. His hand was on the stair rail and his eyes full of fear. I felt sorry for him and was about to tell him so but what would he think if I did?

I felt I sigh of relief when Colin came dashing downstairs and told me to run with a handful of what looked like gold. I hated even spending time with Colin as you knew something serious could happen at any time. However, I was now on the run from the police with nowhere to live. I would take what I could get from him as he was far more able to look after himself. Even though he was crazy, he seemed loyal and told me he would stay by my side. It made me feel a strong bond with him. When no-one else cared, it seemed this guy did, offender or not.

I also started spending time with Frank. He also had a reputation and nobody trusted him. At this point I don't think anyone would have thought I was trustworthy either. I'd got myself into a situation where I was going deeper into an underground world. Malcolm had abandoned me after taking me into a drug-addicted state and that world. I was running from the police and left searching for people I felt could protect me. It might seem that they were not good for me yet they were the only people willing to spend time with me. I guess the police wanted to do that but I didn't feel it was in my best interest. They were visiting my mum's house all the time, well-aware that I was no master criminal and would return home whenever I could. I did try to slip into my home now and then for a wash. By this point it was one bath per week. My health wasn't a concern. I wasn't brushing my teeth, cleaning my clothes or doing my hair. I didn't smell good but whenever I got the chance I would climb over the back fence into her place without anyone seeing me.

One day I was sitting in the living-room when the police knocked on the door. I ran upstairs and climbed into the attic. They had a warrant and searched the property. My heart beat that hard I thought it was going to pop out of my chest. I heard them remove the entrance flap and climb up. I was under the itchy insulation material in the corner and I could see the light from their torch through it. It then slowly rose up and they must have seen my skinny backside. I looked-up and saw a police officer. It was the same one that searched me when I first got caught. He said, 'We've got you lad, come on'. I stood-up and walked across the beams.

I came to terms with the fact that I'd been caught until I saw that it was a women officer at the bottom of the stepladder. As soon as I climbed down and she got the handcuffs out I panicked, pushed her to one side and kicked away the ladder. I knew she'd fallen into the bath and would be pissed-off but I didn't have time to worry about that. I took off down the stairs and out of the back door past a van full of police officers. They seemed to just watch me, in shock, and it must have seemed like slow motion. I ran to Darley's Pond where we played football over the holidays. I could hear dogs but when I looked back I couldn't see any. I could smell freedom and managed to get to the road where I saw a lad I half knew. He jumped at the opportunity to help, probably because I was creating a name for myself by this point. He was drinking a bottle of beer, so I took his jumper and the beer and walked along calmly beside him. The adrenaline was making me feel sick but I did start to calm down as the police cars flashed by with their sirens on, heading for the pond looking for a lone male in a different coloured sweater.

I eventually got to Stanley's as it was the only place I could think of. The house was full. I can't remember the name of the smack dealer who was there but they had all heard about the chase and were pleased I'd got away though the police were still searching nearby. The dealer was in competition with Bolt and made it clear he didn't like him or Malcolm. He asked me where Malcolm was right now to prove he didn't care, which I already knew but didn't want to say in case it got back to him. The dealer gave me a bag of gear and took me into the kitchen. He said I was looking at four to six years in gaol and that if he was in my position he would grass-up Malcolm and Bolt. He pointed out that they weren't going to help me get through the gaol term. It made me think. He was good at acting like he gave a shit but maybe just wanted the competition out of the way. When he left he sorted me out with two more bags. He told everyone in the house I was a soldier and they should look after me until I got caught.

I spent the next couple of days at Stanley's where he helped me smoke the gear and told me he would buy some when he got money. Frank found out I was there and came round. He had stolen a car and this meant that we could go further afield than usual to get money. Frank said, 'We can earn some real money tonight'. The thought of getting in a stolen car made me scared but I couldn't tell anyone that. The last time

I did that I almost had heart failure. Frank told me to clear off if I didn't want to get in and the bottom line is I needed the money.

We travelled just outside of Wolverhampton and started checking-out houses. He spotted an old farmhouse with an open window. We climbed through it, opened the door and made our way into the house. Frank told me to help him with an old grandfather clock. I didn't think we ought to be taking something so heavy but he was convinced we should and knew better than I did. He said that he'd had one before and got rid of it quickly, so I helped him put it in the car. The boot wouldn't close but we weren't bothered. We got the keys to the owner's Ford Capri which were on a table by the front door. Frank just assumed that I could drive, I think, and we filled-up both cars with what we'd taken from the house.

Frank jumped in his car and asked me to take the Capri. I told him I hadn't driven before but I did as he said and started the engine. I kept stalling it and made so much noise that the lights came on inside the house. I had to jump out and make a run for it. A middle-aged man came chasing out of the front door which we'd left wide open. The fastest and fittest middle-aged man I'd seen. I didn't know the area well so I decided to go over fences and through back gardens. No matter how high the fence was this guy was over it as quickly as I was. Frank had driven off and I felt so scared because I thought the man would beat me up or, even worse, the police would get me.

It got to the stage where we were walking down a road absolutely drained of energy with about 100 metres between us. I asked the man to leave me alone saying, 'Please, I'm sorry,' struggling to speak due to exhaustion. He was also struggling to answer but told me I'd no right being in his house. He then said, 'God will have his way with you'. I knew that he had no more running left in him and that gave me the little bit of energy I needed. I took off into the next garden that came along and jumped over a fence. When he didn't follow me I felt an overwhelming sense of relief. 'Silly old bastard,' I said to myself to make me feel more like a man. Once I'd shaken him off I had to think about the long walk back, at least five miles. I found a spot in a school playground out of view of any police and took a few minutes to calm down. I knew they were going to be on the lookout. I needed to take time out as I was shattered from the chase and starting to withdraw and feeling weak. It took me until around eight next morning to get back to Stanley's. I jumped into gardens with every car that drove past. Luckily Stanley and Frank had already been out and sold the clock for what they said was £400. I didn't argue as it was Frank's grafting knowledge that got us the money.

We had a laugh about me not being able to drive the car. When I told Frank about the man saying God would have his way with me he asked me if I was walking round with my eyes closed. Frank and Stanley seemed to be in on a joke that I wasn't included in and Frank said, 'It's a priest's house'. I didn't feel too good about that. I don't know whether it was the fact that we had robbed a priest or that I was in the company of people that didn't care who they took money from. Still, I'd an addiction and was on the run looking at prison. These were the most important things right now. Although I felt bad, it wasn't going to stop the path of destruction I was set on.

Genette and Trish were sisters who lived around the corner. Genette was in my year at school and Trish older. They were both attractive and popular. Trish had always had a thing for me and Genette was with Graham. They were both taking heroin like I was but I think she didn't know Frank and I were as well. They invited us to stay over the week-end as they knew I was on the run and bedding down wherever I could. We made sure that we had some cannabis before we went because Trish would kick us out if she thought for one minute that we were on gear. We had a few drinks and a bit of a laugh and went to bed. I got into bed with Trish and was a little nervous as she was 19 and I had only just turned 17. I knew she'd been with one guy for a year and he was a lot older and more experienced than I was. When we heard Genette kicking Frank out of her bedroom we both laughed and it relaxed the mood.

Sex on heroin is pointless as you don't have control over any part of your body so, although we went through the motions, it was a long and tedious event. Eventually, Trish let me know she'd had enough as it was becoming repetitive. I was young and didn't know how to make it more creative. There was no emotion involved because my sensations had disappeared. This was a shame because I liked her, but gear was ruining everything. She fell asleep and I lay next to her thinking about just how long I'd wanted to sleep with her and yet the whole thing was spoilt when it happened. My life was a mess and I couldn't even enjoy sex at my young age. The following morning, we thanked the girls for letting us stay. I was in deep thought about what Trish was going to think of me after the night before. When we walked out of the garden Frank smiled and pulled a handful of gold from his pocket. I instantly told him to go and ask to use the toilet and put it back. I was fuming. They'd invited us in because they knew we had nowhere to stay and he'd robbed the house so it would look as if it was both of us. 'How low can we get?' I asked him.

I liked Trish and knew if I wasn't on the gear I could have had a relationship with her easily. No-one knew Frank had taken the gold and I was going to be just as much to blame when they noticed. On moral grounds I should have told him that I wouldn't go with him unless he took it back, or even gone back myself with it. The truth is I was already starting to rattle as we hadn't had any gear the night before. I could only go around ten hours max without heroin and that was usually when I slept. When he refused, I went with him to Cotterill's house and got a couple of bags for the gold and smoked them with him. Gear changes everything including your morals, values and beliefs. You try and forget about what you're doing and pretend it doesn't matter.

Later that day I was at Stanley Fender's and while Frank and I were upstairs we heard shouting. I could hear Scottie's voice saying 'Where are them two little smackhead bastards'. Before I realised what was happening, Frank climbed out of the bathroom window. Graham nearly grabbed him, but he managed to slip away. Graham and Scottie walked in to see me and I just stood up and looked straight at both of them. Graham walked over to me and began dragging me out of the room. When I started to struggle he repeatedly pricked me in the back with a dart that he'd picked-up from the floor. My back was covered in pinpricks and I asked him how he could do that to me as I thought we were friends. He said, 'If we were friends you wouldn't sleep at my girlfriend's house and steal shit'. I told him that nothing went on with Genette and that I slept with Trish. It was obvious he didn't believe this and thought someone had slept with her. Scottie then butted in with, 'Fuck that where's the gold?' Graham came towards me with the dart again and Scottie held him back. Scottie told me that I'd 24 hours to get the gold back. If I didn't he would go round to my mum's and take it out on her house. I knew he wasn't just saying that so I said, 'I will'. I'd no idea how but I had to keep my family safe.

I got Stanley's girlfriend to clean me up so I didn't need to go to the hospital. I'd a lot of dart holes in my back but I didn't have time to worry about that, got myself to Cotterill's and told him about the situation. He said that I could have the gold back if I paid him £80. That was £10 more than he bought it for, but I expected that. I'm sure he wouldn't have been so kind if he'd known I gave his name to the police as a drug-dealer. I went to the local shopping centre and pinched some designer clothes from various shops. Given I'd been burgling a few times and getting involved in violence more or less daily it was a surprise to find that I was more scared of shoplifting. It was because it was daylight and there were people around, but I didn't have much option. I took everything I got to Cotterill and he gave me the gold back. He received more value than he'd asked for but I was in a desperate situation and he knew he had the power.

On the way to Sue's, the lady weed dealer, I saw Jack. He told me he'd seen Frank a couple of hours ago and that he was laughing about me getting caught by Scottie and Graham. Frank was telling people I was dozy and should have got out of the window with him. Hearing that pissed me right off. My first thought was to confront Frank but I'd more important things to deal with. My family were far more precious than dealing with him. I got to Sue's door and hesitated before I knocked. 'Should I even knock,' I asked myself. I did and waited what for what seemed a lifetime. Trish answered and told me to go through to the living room where Sue, Scottie and Genette were.

It was completely quiet and all four of them just stared which worried me even more. To break the silence. I said, 'I don't want to drop anyone in it but I need to be clear that I didn't steal from you'. I was shitting myself as I didn't know what to expect. Scottie sat directly opposite and asked why Frank hadn't come with me. I told him that he was a little prick and that I hadn't seen him since he took off out of the bathroom window. I took the gold out in my closed hand and showed it to them. Sue came straight over to make sure that it was all there. I saw her look at Scottie and give him a nod. As soon as she did that, he jumped up out of his seat and punched me square in the face. 'Come into my house and take my things for your smack, will you?' he screamed. I immediately started crying. I wiped my face and noticed that it was covered in blood from my nose. As I was dazed, he grabbed me and picked me up out of the chair. I didn't fancy standing in front of him so he could continue hitting me so I dropped to the floor and covered my head.

I could hear Trish and Genette crying and telling him to stop. Scottie just told them to get out. 'Go get the pick-axe from the kitchen,' he said, to Sue. I was in survival mode at this point and thinking he could kill me. As I was on the floor near the kitchen door, I got between it and the sofa and clamped my feet against the door. I wriggled and kicked the door shut every time Sue tried to open it. I was still fending off Scottie who was trying to pull me back into the middle of the room. It was the most frantic moment of my life and I was going crazy screaming, 'Don't hurt me, please'. All of a sudden it all stopped and I was left shaking on the floor. Everything went silent again. Scottie calmly told me to get-up and sit in the chair. He said he wasn't going to hurt me and sat down as if nothing happened. 'Is this guy crazy or what,' I was thinking.

I was still scared when Trish and Genette came back crying their eyes out. Sue and Scottie were sitting down as if this was all a joke. I felt like a bit of amusement at a zoo as they watched me bleed on the floor, my feet still held firmly against the kitchen door which made me feel a kind of victory in this utterly helpless situation. 'You are going to stay here until that little shit comes to help you,' Scottie told me. I said Frank couldn't give a damn and that he wouldn't come for me. What did he think, that this was a movie and Frank would turn up and save the day? If I hadn't been so scared I would have laughed. Scottie rang someone and told them to get the word out that I was in a bad way. This guy was crazy, unpredictable and it made the whole situation worse. It didn't dawn on him that I was only 17 and so was Genette. We had just officially left school and become involved in such a violent world.

Scottie told me that I was to sit quietly until Frank came. The family then went on doing their daily chores as if I wasn't there. Sue and Scottie were laughing at the TV and eating. Genette and Trish just kept looking at me as if they wanted to talk but daren't. It was around five hours later before any of them spoke to me again as it was starting to get late. Scottie was getting frustrated with my constant requests to visit the toilet. One of them always came with me and stood outside the door. I was being sick and although I never said anything they must have known that I was rattling as I was getting paler by the minute. Constipation started to kick in and when it did it was extremely painful.

I just kept looking at Sue with my young puppy eyes. I was hoping she would think about the years she'd seen me growing-up and let me go. Scottie did tell me that it didn't look like Frank was a friend of mine but if he came he would let me go. I wondered if he thought he was dealing with master criminals and not kids that were shit scared of him. I started to think that he probably wasn't hard, just a little crazy. I don't know whether this made me feel better or worse. He told me after seven long hours that he was going to let me go. He said I needed to tell Frank that he was going to pay a bigger price and that I was getting off lightly because I came of my own free will and brought the gold back.

When they opened the door and I walked out of that house I began to realise my life wasn't worth a shit. It was around 2 am and I'd nowhere to go so I took myself off to a local school and sat down feeling sorry for myself. I'd just turned 17, had no real friends and was addicted, with every police officer in the area looking for me. I was facing a hefty gaol sentence when I got caught. I considered handing myself in when a camcorder caught my eye through a window. I was feeling proper sick and this was an easy opportunity to make some money. I lobbed a brick through the glass because I wasn't now bothered about being quiet. I jumped inside while the alarm was going off, grabbed the camcorder and was in and out in a flash.

I went straight to Stanley's place. He never minded grafters knocking him up if they had things to sell. He was Delboy Trotter on heroin but as he and his girlfriend were addicts they used their home to fund their habit. They had a small baby and because of that Stanley never got visibly involved in crime He probably felt that handling stolen goods was a lesser offence and made it unlikely that he'd get caught. They were both lovely people and supported those around them. However, with the baby exposed to so much drug use and crime at such an early age, Social Care should have been supporting them. If it didn't happen that child would likely have similar experiences to me.

When I arrived at their house Colin had been out grafting and they were already smoking some gear. They had heard about my run in with Scottie. As my clothes were covered in blood they sat me down and gave me a smoke straightaway. It felt so good to not just smoke but feel safe. I was living a life that, whether I liked it or not and no matter how hard I tried, was constantly placing me in violent situations that also made me feel that way. Not a probation officer or social worker to influence me but friendly and protective criminals with a bag of heroin and a warm welcome. We sat down and spoke about Frank and it seemed that nobody wanted anything to do with him now. They knew he took the gold and yet I was the one who'd taken a beating. They said they thought he was out of order. But I knew if he turned-up with gear Stanley would let him in.

Colin told me he'd been kicked-out of the care home he was living in so he had nowhere to live. He thought that we should stay together so it would be easier to make money and watch each other's backs. We tried to support one another in our own ways. The situation for each of us was unstable so things changed quickly. Stanley told us that we could get our heads down but as soon as the baby woke-up in the morning we would have to scarper. He did do his best to keep his child out of things but as always the heroin made his decisions for him.

The following day I thought it would be nice to see the family so Colin and I took a walk to my mum's house. I mean, I'd been on the run from the police, beaten, was homeless and addicted to heroin and all without my family around at my tender age. When we got there mum told me she was going back to Leeds for a week after New Year. She wanted to get away from the mess we'd caused. Adam had just been sentenced to 15 months for burglary (and of course none of it was her responsibility).

This meant I could stay at home and make it seem like nobody was there if the police came looking. It goes to show how naïve and stupid I was.

While we were having something to eat the doorbell went. Gail was the nearest to the door and, as a girl her age might, she quickly opened it. As soon as she did so in came two uniformed police officers. They asked us all to give them our names and dates of birth. I told them mine was Richard Watts speaking loudly so everyone in the room could hear. They asked if anyone had seen Andrew Brierley. Colin and I said that as friends we'd called in to tell Sonia that Andrew had sent us to tell her he was okay. We kept saying that they should leave Andrew alone in an assertive manner as he was just hoping to get through Christmas and that he was going to hand himself in after New Year.

The officers seemed relaxed about looking for me. The whole time my heart was pounding and I thought they were just playing along with our lies. They talked about me as if I wasn't there which seemed strange. I thought they were going to say, 'Yes Andrew we know who you are'. It was unreal when the two of them said, 'Just tell him to hand himself in as he's not making the situation any better'. Then they turned and left and we watched them walk down the road. It was as if they'd been told to do the visit and were about to go off duty and couldn't be bothered. It didn't matter why, everyone in the house just laughed and I did a dance I was so happy.

It was easy to make money over Christmas. Colin was booting-off doors and taking presents and none of us gave it a second thought. The best thing was that he never complained he was doing most of the grafting. He saw that I'd a big sentence looming and that I didn't need more charges on top. The reality was that he was just trying to find his place in the world. He didn't have anywhere to live, people to support him or a true identity. He had morals but they were as misplaced as mine. He took a caring role with me as it made him feel needed and important.

When Christmas was over and mum visited Leeds, I found myself squatting in the house. Colin was off grafting every day and coming back and staying there with me. He rarely returned without gear. He was happy having somewhere to stay and we felt like it was our house with no-one else there. We struggled with food because all our money went on drugs. We ate beans and sausages with pepper and that was as good as it got.

An elderly Hungarian woman lived next door. She never had visitors so we decided the easy option was to steal from her. It was something we could do together because I wouldn't need to be seen on the street, my normal excuse for not to going out stealing with Colin. The truth is we were so far gone in heroin addiction and our criminal path that robbing old people didn't bother us one bit. It might be viewed as disgusting but neither of us had been raised to believe that. We never meant the old woman harm. Most of my adult peers would have done the same so why wouldn't I in a desperate situation. We climbed over the back fence and observed her sit down in the living room to watch TV. We noticed she had a cat flap. Colin reached through it and grabbed the key on the inside of the door and we gained entry without making a noise. He went straight to the kitchen and came back with a jar healthily filled with coins. I was watching the woman through the window to make sure he knew what she was doing but I panicked when I saw her stand up. I knew if she saw him it could all go wrong and we would lose control of the situation. It was like in a *Carry On* film. Colin walked into the living room and when she walked out he silently followed her smiling at me and pulling a silly face. I was thinking he should just get out as he had lots of chances and we had some money now. Chance after chance went by and he just kept picking things up and looking at them. Eventually he did come out with a camera and some gold. A great day all round I thought.

Once we'd sold the items and set-off back to our house we bumped into Graham and Genette. Colin told me we would both take him out because he knew he'd stabbed me with the dart when Scottie was after me. Graham just said that it was the past and he had scored so we should have a session and forget about it. We all went back to the house and started smoking the gear which we knew would keep us going for a couple of days. As addicts, we weren't bothered about food or hygiene, simply making sure we had our fix. Not for a minute did any of us believe we were kids, we were grafters and streetwise and like others we knew involved in offending. That was our identity.

We were all planning on staying at mine for a few days and enjoying smoking gear. Having the house free was an absolute blessing we kept saying. Lawrence, Frank and others I knew were all injecting by now, but we were clear that none of us would do that. I enjoyed the preparation for smoking heroin, so injecting didn't attract me. Injecting means it's quicker to prepare and it hits you fast so it's ideal for the lifestyle addicts adopt. No matter how much I was rattling, I would savour the moment when the first inhalation reached my lungs.

While we were smoking we heard a car door go. We looked out and saw a police car had pulled-up outside. The old woman had obviously noticed we'd been in her house and called them. This made me nervous but I felt secure in my own house as nobody would answer the door. The police knew mum was in Leeds as she was still on bail and had to declare to them she was going there. When the police officer left he took a long look backwards. Although there were net curtains on the windows we were looking through he seemed to stare straight at us. Graham and Colin both said that we should leave as they thought he'd seen us. I think I was too hungry for the gear so I didn't listen and kept saying he couldn't have. I thought that maybe the old lady knew we were there and had told them so. As soon as the officer drove off the discussion was over. 'Let's get high,' I said.

While we were in the bedroom we heard a loud knock at the door and my face turned white. I opened the back bedroom window and noticed an officer from the drug squad climbing up a ladder. He tried to stop me shutting the window but would have lost his fingers. I think he knew that and pulled them away when I slammed it shut. I ran downstairs into the living-room and opened the front window to see the entire drug squad and uniformed officers. 'We've got you Andi. Just open the door,' came a shout. I was in a state of shock running around with my adrenaline hitting the roof. I felt like a rabbit in headlights. It was all over though I wasn't willing to accept it. They used a battering ram on the door. I gave up and shouted, 'I'll open it' but they told me to stay away from it. They must have enjoyed smashing their way in.

I went back to the living-room and sat on a speaker in the middle of the room. I waited for the door to cave in thinking about what my mum was going to think when she came back and saw it like that. While they were walking me out it was like a scene from the movie *Buster*. The whole street was out watching and I shouted to Colin to make sure he stayed at the house till mum got back. The police said that they would secure it and no-one would be allowed to stay. Little did I know that this would be the last I ever saw of the likes of Graham and Colin.

On the way to the police station I was quizzed off the record. They said they knew who I was selling with and for, things they couldn't possibly have known unless they'd been told by someone close to me. I told them, 'I know you used to get information in pub car parks'. One of them looked at me in amazement and told me that I'd be stupid if I didn't tell them on the record who I was selling for. They said they knew Bolt and that I was looking at four to five years in prison so I'd be best placed to make a statement against him. I was scared but I didn't identify as a grass and Bolt and Malcolm didn't give a damn about me any more than the police. I was caught-up in a game and losing whichever way I played it.

I was banged-up in a cell and the duty officer came to my flap. 'You deserve an Oscar young man'. He asked if I could remember his face, but I could hardly see through the tiny window. He told me that he was the officer who came to my house over Christmas and reminded me that I'd told him I was Richard Watts. I was just held overnight and taken to court next morning. I woke-up feeling like shit. I'd no chance of being released and was probably going to have to rattle. I was scared but the truth was I'd no idea what was about to happen to me which made the situation worse. Going to court in the white prison wagons was degrading, isolating and frightening. There were names scraped into the wall. 'Jimmy was 'ere 97', 'Police suck arse' and it stank of piss with adult criminals shouting that they would smash the guards' heads in. I just wanted my mum.

CHAPTER 8

A Taste of Custody

At court I met my solicitor in a cell deep underground. A different one from my police interviews who told me he'd try and get bail for me. But the fact was I'd absconded from the bail hostel and gone on-the-run so it was hardly going to be granted. I was starting to feel really bad by now and needed some gear so I just told him to do whatever was needed to get me out of there. 'Don't hold your breath,' he said. I wanted to see a familiar face or someone to tell me everything would be okay. I knew damn well it wouldn't be.

By early afternoon I was feeling weak and sick. I was hoping for bail because anything else was unthinkable right now. How could I possibly go to prison like this? Would I be able to get through my rattle? How long would that take? When my name was called out and the security men took me to the courtroom I was sweating. The walk took two minutes but it seemed like two hours. My solicitor stated that I was still young and my mother was in Leeds which was why I'd absconded. The prosecutor tore me to shreds. I felt like crying when the judge said my application would be refused and remanded me to Brinsford Young Offender Institution until my next court appearance in a week's time. 'You were given every opportunity Mr Brierley,' he told me. 'Take him down'.

I was led to another holding cell below the courts with six lads in it. Two of them had been freshly remanded but the other four had come from Brinsford and were going straight back there. I asked them what it was like. They said that they were on the YOI side which was for the over 18s. Asked how old I was, I said 17 and they started laughing. 'You'll go to the juvenile side and it's just crazy. The younger ones don't care and they're always carrying-on and fighting'.

They asked if I took smack and I lied saying 'No'. I thought, 'They don't know me, so why should I tell them my business?' I knew they would respect me less if they knew I was on heroin. 'You'll be alright then as Wolverhampton lads have it bad enough in Brinsford,' one said and the ugly little one advised, 'If you were a Wolves smackhead you'd be in double trouble'. At least I was pre-warned. I wouldn't tell anyone I was addicted to gear but wondered how I was going to hide it? I felt awful and surely this was only going to get worse. On some prison buses they have a radio and depending who the staff are turn it on. Alone in my cubicle I sat thinking about how shit life was. I was addicted, on my way to prison and didn't know how long it would be before I saw my family. Then the Spice Girls' 'Goodbye' came on. Listening and thinking about my life and how things were turning out was too much for me and I cried my eyes out. Images of mum and the girls came flooding into my head. If everyone was right and I was looking at five years when would I ever get to see them again? I wiped my face as we pulled-up so that no-one could see how inwardly lonely, anxious and scared I was.

In Brinsford it felt like I'd made a step forward and then gone back to the beginning. My mind was working overtime. I was thinking, 'Is it violent like in films?' I was given some tracksuit bottoms and told to go into a cubicle. Each had a designated officer and a half door so that he could watch an inmate getting changed in case of weapons, drugs and so on. I was then given my induction pack: a cheap toothbrush (no toothpaste), shaving brush, plastic bowl, cutlery, tea, coffee and bedding. There was also a shaving-stick, but I couldn't work out what it was for. I didn't want to ask and look silly. 'I'll work it out later,' I thought.

They marched me to the wing I was to stay on and sat me down on a chair on the landing. Three of us waited until a doctor came and asked us about our health. I was going to have to keep the fact that I was a heroin addict to myself. I told him I was fit and well and didn't need anything. This was probably the daftest thing I did at the time as I was already feeling dizzy. He could have given me prescription drugs to help with withdrawals. However, after what the lads had warned me about on the prison bus I'd decided to hide it. Besides I couldn't be sure that he would give me drugs anyway.

I was taken to the cell I would be in. I asked the screw silently escorting me if I was going to be staying in it. He told me it was an induction wing and I would be moving to the juvenile wing sometime that week. When the cell door opened I saw a kid lying on the bottom bunk, asleep facing the wall. 'Your late lunch will be served in an hour, get comfortable,' the screw said. When he slammed the door behind him it woke-up the lad who took a minute to come round. The cell was extremely cold. Nothing but a metal table, bunk beds and a few letters. I looked at the dazed lad who was staring straight through me. 'Where you from?' was the first thing he asked rubbing his eyes. A black kid with an Afro he looked like he could fight. I didn't want to have the same problems I'd had at school by saying I was from Leeds so I told him I was from Wolverhampton. 'Is this your first time?' he asked. I just nodded. 'Wolverhampton lads get a lot of shit in this prison,' he said adding that his name was Pete and that he was from Winson Green. He was on remand and had done two previous sentences. He promised to show me how to go on if we went to the juvenile wing together which made me feel more at ease.

I put my kit away and lay on the top bunk staring at the ceiling, thinking how much my stomach was turning and how weak I felt. I just thought that no matter what I would keep it to myself. After we'd been fed I started to feel really bad but tried to act normally. I couldn't sit around feeling sorry for myself. The YOI side was across the way and we could talk to them through the window. As we were bored we asked for their names and where they were from. These seemed to be the standard questions you asked any inmate along with 'What you in for?' and 'When you out?'.

What we didn't know was that the landing above housed the protection unit. When they heard us speaking to the older lads they came to their windows and started talking to us. Pete said they were muppets, paedos and nonces. He started to give them hell telling them to get their heads in which started a huge argument. They began saying things like they were going to abuse our womenfolk and other weird shit. All the lads on the landing downstairs were arguing with the entire landing of those on protection. They knew we couldn't get at them so they felt free to say the most horrible things. Some of those on protection were there as a result of bullying or getting into debt on the wings. They were easy targets and seen as weak. After a couple of hours non-stop we decided we couldn't listen to the things they were saying any more. We looked at the window and saw a flood of what looked like water flowing down. We just eyeballed each other not knowing what to do. It could have been piss so we didn't go anywhere near it. Although it was a strange situation, we were laughing like kids and jumping up and down on the beds. We put our emergency light on that alerted the officers but when one came he just told us to shut the window. To him this was a minor inconvenience but we thought it was a big deal. 'Better get used to it,' Pete said. Eventually we managed to close the window without touching the liquid and let it dry out on its own.

These daily intrusions did go some way to help me forget the fact that I was poorly. I wasn't sleeping and was sitting on the toilet and vomiting quietly so Pete didn't notice. When he woke-up he just thought I was homesick and went back to sleep. I was constipated so even trying to go to the toilet caused me pains in my stomach. Although I'd rattled before, I'd never got this far in and it was getting worse.

After a few days Pete had to return to court. He thought he had a good chance of bail. The ironic thing was two vulnerable young men in a difficult situation thanking each other for support but trying to act like hard men. I just wanted to hug him but didn't know what his response would be. I'd told him everything about me apart from my addiction. He told me not to say I was from Wolverhampton as I was going to have problems. I would be better off saying I was from Leeds as the city was known for successful crime and gangs whereas Wolverhampton wasn't. According to him, most of the lads from Wolverhampton there were smackheads. Little did he know. The morning he left the screws came and told me I was to pack my kit as I was being moved for the next stage of the induction process into the Juvenile Unit which was on C-wing. I would be on A2 while they found me a regular a cell. Underneath was A1 which was used for enhanced (or well-behaved) inmates. They cleaned the landings, served food and had kitchen and other jobs.

On A2 I was placed in a cell with Taradhish, a skinny Indian kid with a beard which was unusual for those our age. He would wave his arms when he spoke he got so excited. I'd seen him while I was on the induction wing and was pleased that he seemed alright and it was his first time in as well. I found out he was in for manslaughter because he told anyone who would listen. His version was that he had a warehouse job and after a lad at work had disrespected his mother he stabbed him with a big knife killing him. Oddly, he was a nice lad with me. However, he thought he was ten men and often got into arguments. Several times the lads he argued with would call me to the window and ask questions. As I was feeling weak, the last thing I wanted was trouble because I don't think I could have defended myself properly. I'd just go to the window and say, 'Leave me out of it'. Unfortunately this is not how prison works. They would say I sounded like one of the Wolverhampton lads so I'd obviously picked-up an accent. Ironic that while in Wolverhampton I got hassled because I was from Leeds and now because they thought I was from Wolverhampton. I hated the whole thing but couldn't persuade Taradhish to stay away from the window. His attention span was shorter than my heavily bitten finger nails.

On the first day the screws shouted, 'Lights on for gym'. When Taradhish told me that we had to press the emergency light to go I was unsure whether to believe him. So I shouted 'Boss' which is what we had to call the officers. I didn't get an answer. When I eventually pressed the button, the screw opened the door and pushed me back into my cell. 'You'll have to learn to be quicker than that little man'. Later the screws shouted my name and took me to the visits room where I saw Adam and learned he was on C2. By mistake they'd booked my visit and his for the same slot but it was against the rules to let anyone see two inmates in that way. It meant mum couldn't see him. My heart went out to him as he hadn't seen her for weeks. I knew he'd feel down and I would've swapped with him if I could. In prison there is little if any room for such things, you just have to deal with what happens. But he looked well with rounded cheeks and clear eyes and I hoped I would be as good in a few weeks' time.

As soon as mum sat down she said, 'I'm moving back to Leeds, Andi'. Georgina was going to put her up until she found somewhere permanent.

I was happy with the news as Wolverhampton had become unbearable and I didn't know what would happen if I returned there. I told her that Adam and I were finding it easy in gaol and that I'd made a lot of friends. I was lying but I didn't see the point in her being worried. We quickly ran out of things to say. Prison visits can be awkward. You say all you have to say in 15 minutes. But I still felt sad when the screws shouted 'Time'.

I went back to where Adam was still sitting. I told him they'd made a mistake and that mum said she would try and come again before she left for Leeds. As we were talking, I heard a group of lads in the opposite corner whispering. When I looked across I saw a small lad was crouched down with his trousers round his ankles. It looked like he was taking a shit with other's gathered around him. When he noticed me he shouted out, 'What you looking at? Look away now'. As he seemed to have a lot of friends I just looked away. He had obviously excreted something plugged up his bum. They all started to get excited and broke up whatever it was into pieces. I noticed that some of the group were happy but some weren't. They started to argue and, although the small lad, who I later found out was Wally, was loud and able to look after himself it became chaotic. Then a fight broke out and the screws came and grabbed the one who'd shouted, 'Your ripping me off Wally'.

Adam and I talked about how mad things were and he told me I'd not seen anything yet saying, 'Wait till you get to C-wing'. He explained that even padded-up with Flax he was still wary all the time. He said someone got hurt there every day and certain people were seen as tramps even if they had money and good clothes. It was due to many of them withdrawing and not looking well. The gang culture in the Midlands kept them away from heroin most of the time and gave status in prison. I told Adam I would say I was from Leeds. He said they would know otherwise when I spoke to him and Flax because they'd claimed to be from Wolverhampton. When they separated us it was just like I was going back to square one after starting to feel relatively safe.

Next morning a screw opened my door and shouted 'Taradhish, Brierley, pack your kit you're going to C-wing'. I had mixed feelings about this. Although Adam told me C-wing was a dangerous place to be, I was going to see him and Flax. Also Taradhish was coming too. Even though I hardly knew him and he was obviously going to get into trouble you take any relationship you can in prison so you're not on your own. I just didn't want to be his cell-mate but those on C-wing were all singles. Once there I was taken to a cell on C1 and Taradhish to one opposite which made me feel better. No sooner had the doors slammed shut than I heard him shout 'Breeli' in his badly spoken English, 'Were together brother'. I giggled to myself as he was a funny kid. Although he wasn't yet sentenced he was looking at a life term and either didn't care or didn't realise the seriousness of his situation. I liked him but I knew he was going to get into trouble.

After I'd unpacked, put my kit away and laid down on my bed I could hear everyone shouting out of their windows. There was a lot of noise on A-wing but not usually this long and loud. It seemed as if everyone on the wing was at their window and they all seemed to be arguing. After an hour it calmed down and I heard some lad shout out something. I instantly thought, 'That's my mum's address'. Without giving it a second thought I went to the window and yelled, ''Ere, what the heck are you doing, that's my mum's address?' He told me he'd swopped it for tobacco and that he was going to give her a house call when he got out. 'I'll smash your effing head in if you repeat that address,' I replied. My voice was obviously new out of the window and as soon as I'd said it I heard windows open. They were blocked in by metal cages so when someone opened one the window hit the cage and made a noise, and I heard a few. All the lads started asking the one who'd shouted who I was. He told them that he got the address when he was padded-up with Adam but he didn't know who I was. I told him 'I'm Andi Brierley, Adam's my little brother and that's my mum's address'.

A lad who sounded as if he was on my landing said that Martin, the lad with the address, was *his* brother and that I should keep my mouth shut. He asked me where I was from, so I said, Leeds. He said, 'You're not in Leeds now and you'll find out how far away you are if you don't keep your head down'. I thought it best to leave things and see if I could get this Martin guy at some point. I was equally mad with Adam. I don't know how Martin got the address but Adam should have kept it safe.

When I was first let out for dinner I looked at the lads on my landing to see which one I'd been talking to. I hoped it wasn't one of the two at the end as these guys were built like gladiators. The screws let us out landing by landing to get our food. The other C1 landing was for the basic lads so they always got their food last. When I was on my way back I saw a tall black lad leaning-up against the wall as if he was playing hide and seek. He watched another black lad walk past him and then he pulled out what looked like a sock with something in it. He repeatedly smashed the other lad around the head with it until the alarm went off. The screws got there in no time and managed to pull him off and drag him away kicking and screaming. 'Move on lads, back to your cells,' the screw said calmly. Adam was right, this was something they saw on a daily basis. I was shaking and trying not to drop my food.

Before I'd time to sit down and eat, Taradhish shouted, 'Yo, Brierley did you see that, I love it over here'. I can remember thinking, 'What an idiot'. I was trembling because although I'd been involved in violence all my life this situation was different. I couldn't get away and, if I'm totally honest, these Birmingham and Wolverhampton kids were just different. Taradhish seemed to be on another planet. He was skinny and I could see him getting hurt but it was like he didn't see that. Anyway, I had to concentrate as I'd a feeling I could get jumped at any point.

The next time I spoke to Adam I had to stop myself punching him on the nose. I was still fuming at him for letting a lad get a hold of mum's address. He told me that he was padded-up with Martin before Flax and he must have got the address from a letter. Adam didn't seem to be adapting to the environment at all. He was young and didn't know how to act to stop others kids taking advantage. It wasn't about fighting, it was about making others think you were willing to fight. Then keeping certain people close so they wouldn't want to bother you. This came naturally to me. I would use my skills to make friends but I would also not lose face. This made it easier for me to build relationships with like-minded kids. I was also starting to sleep of a night and feeling stronger and I was even brushing my teeth. Maybe this was just what I needed as I'd been weak and dirty on the outside.

Over the next couple of weeks I saw various fights, some more violent than others. Most of them were down to the fact that in Birmingham there were two gangs living close to each other. The Perry Barr Army (or Barmy for short) and the Jackson Crew had longstanding grievances with one another going back to before anyone in this prison was born or could remember. There was a lad called Cyclops upstairs on C2 and he pretty much ran the wings. Everything that went on was set-up by him. Cyclops was a member of Barmy. I hadn't seen him yet but I'd heard enough about him. In fact, meeting him wasn't something I was looking forward to. He'd been ordered to be detained indefinitely at age 14 which was unthinkable to me. The word was that he'd stamped on a rival gang member's head until he died.

A month later there was an incident on the enhanced wing. The lads that served the food had all been sacked and moved out. The regime worked on a points scheme. If an enhanced inmate got 90 points and a standard inmate 91 they would swap places. My cell was always clean and I hadn't had any fights or incidents. I often got high points, so I was one of the standard prisoners set to replace an enhanced inmate. It meant I went over to the enhanced wing where I'd been told you got a quilt, so I was excited. On standard level we were given green blankets that were horrible, along with a sheet. On enhanced although the beds were like sleeping on a Rizla, a quilt would help. After all, I was only now starting to have a full night's sleep as the drugs left my system.

Due to the fact that they had to replace the servery lads I was given a job there, one of the best in the prison that paid £7 per week. By then Adam had just moved to Hindley Prison to finish off his 15 months sentence. No-one told me until he'd gone which made me sad. Cyclops jumped at the opportunity to make some burn from the situation. He told me while I was serving him his food that Adam left owing him half-an-ounce. I didn't respond as I'd to go to my cell and think about what I was going to do. I didn't want to be taken for a muppet but he had muscles coming out of ears. He was only 16 but had been in gaol for two years in which time he'd done nothing but gym. I decided that the best thing to do would be to pay him. This was a way of making money in prison and I knew Adam could have owed him, so it was the right thing to do.

That being the only issue I had it cushy. I had a job which paid a lot in terms of gaol money and I was on the enhanced wing. It also meant I got more gym and association time. It wasn't long after I left this prison that Brinsford came under scrutiny for neglecting inmates. Even we as the most well-behaved prisoners were being told there weren't enough staff to allow association. We just got showers, phone calls and then put behind our doors (to the sound of screws playing snooker). It didn't bother us too much as sometimes we were out working. It was the basic kids that had it bad as they were confined 23 hours a day.

While serving food to inmates I always tried get on the main course. It was best to avoid being on custard or puddings. The harder lads like Cyclops always demanded more and used their reputation to get it. To make up for giving them more and avoid getting beaten-up you had to give the vulnerable kids less. However, this was a judgment call and, as I found out, it wasn't as simple as judging a book by its cover. One day I was on the curry and it should have been an easy day. All the inmates that had just come through induction and not been able to choose from the menu that day were given choice A. To select your meal for the fol-lowing day you would choose from A, B, C and D. Kitchens always sent more choice A to make up for any shortfall. These spare meals were often the least popular choice. A lad called Ronnie Dingwell was told he was getting choice A which he wasn't at all happy about. Remember I didn't really know who was who in the Birmingham youth underworld. So when he arrogantly told me to put some more on his plate I told him he wasn't getting any. 'Okay, you watch,' he said calmly and walked-off.

I eventually finished and got back to my cell with a mountain of a meal. We servery lads would get whatever was left over and never went hungry. The landing cleaner, a lad from Derby, then came to my cell and told me I'd stitched up Ronnie Dingwell. 'Who's Ronnie Dingwell,' I asked. 'He's been asking about you so, as soon as he sees you, you'll find out,' came the reply. Apparently, Ronnie had only just got out from an earlier two year sentence and was always down the block for fighting. I immediately thought, 'Why didn't I give him the extra food?' I was getting bigger than my boots because I was on the enhanced wing and becoming comfortable, but events like this reminded me I was not local and certainly not hard.

In the cell next to me was a lad called Smithy from Dudley. Smithy was on servery with me. He kept himself to himself. He was a short, muscly lad with what can only be described as a baby moustache. I used to talk to him through the hole around the pipes used by inmates to pass items such as tobacco and drugs from cell to cell. Smithy told me that he'd seen Ronnie fight and that he had a 'killer punch'. He also said that he wasn't as big as when he got out and I should be glad. I must admit I wasn't feeling lucky right now. Next day we lined up for gym and I noticed Ronnie was at the back of the queue with a large group of lads. They were chanting, 'Leeds, Leeds, Leeds' towards me which I hated, but what could I do? I decided to just ignore them and hope that I could get through the gym session without letting them piss me off so bad that I reacted. The session went ahead and I couldn't take my eyes off Ronnie. His every move made me nervous but he wasn't really taking note, so I assumed he'd had his fun. When I'd served him his food he had a jumper on so I didn't see his physique.

When it came to having a shower it was like a queue at the shopping-centre. There was no patience and the strongest lads would save the showers for their mates. This meant the less popular lads had to wait. I'd got used to the lads moving me aside by this point. I wasn't prepared for the almighty blow that hit my jaw as I was waiting with my hands over my balls. I dropped to the floor before I realised what was happening. Before I could gather my thoughts, I'd been kicked in the face by a number of bare feet. Every time I tried to pick myself up I'd get kicked back down. Dazed and confused, I looked across the floor and saw swirls of my watery blood going down the plug hole. Completely helpless, I just stayed down and hoped they'd leave me alone.

I waited until everyone was out of the shower before I picked myself up. Although I couldn't know who had kicked me, the four lads around Ronnie gave me some idea. While I was cleaning myself down alone in the shower it seemed like all the lads on the gym session were now slowly shouting 'Leeds….. Leeds….. Leeds….. Leeds'. I'd been kidnapped by the Waltons and beaten by Scottie but this was far worse. I was alone and it didn't seem like I'd anyone that cared or would help protect me. Those previous incidents were short-lived but there was no escaping this threat. I spent every day being scared, thinking something could happen at any moment.

I wondered if the attention on me might change when someone called Jeremiah came into the prison. His name was on every inmate's tongue. According to Taradhish who was always up-to-date on all Birmingham information, Jeremiah was going to fight Cyclops. He told me that a Barmy member had killed his brother and he was going to go straight for Cyclops for his affiliation to Barmy. I'd seen Jeremiah at dinner-time and he also had huge muscles, so it seemed like a heavyweight bout. He had a gold tooth and shaved head which made him look mean. This meant that everyone was talking about it as if they were WBA title fighters. That less attention was on me was all I cared about. I couldn't care less what these Brummies did to themselves.

Jeremiah was known for being unstable during previous sentences and I got first-hand evidence of this. He was in the cell directly above me and that night we heard officers running there. According to rumour, his cell-mate had asked him about his brother. As he never spoke about him, he tied-up his pad-mate and cut him with razor blades while reading the bible to him. How people knew this I don't know but he was taken down the block, so he definitely did something bad. I looked around my cell at the toilet and sink and thought to myself, 'Andi, don't you ever get yourself into a situation like this again'. If only I knew then what was to come over the next few years.

For a while Ronnie and his cronies kept giving me a slap or a punch while I was in line for the gym. I was constantly sizing-up how far I would let them push me. It was difficult as I thought I wouldn't let them hit me like they did in the shower again, but the slaps didn't bother me enough to react. Instead they were trying to degrade me, as if they were teasing me and joking. If it had been just Ronnie I would have hit him back but he was always in a gang of around five to six kids. I allowed them to get away with it as long as they didn't hurt me again. It was a judgement call whether I should react and you never knew if you're getting these right.

The bullying stopped as quickly as it started when Ronnie sent a message down for me. He told me to make sure I gave the cleaners on his wing some milk and cornflakes every morning for him. As there were always some left over this wasn't a problem. I guessed this would get him off my back and it wasn't as if the food belonged to me. The other servery lads had something going on with inmates too so they wouldn't tell. I'd only sent him food over twice before he was released without charge. I was listening to Shanks and Bigfoot — 'Sweet Like Chocolate' — and doing a dance in my cell when I found out. Happy, happy.

With Ronnie out of the I got to know the lads on the wing and felt just a bit more confident and settled. I even began selling tobacco but only to new inmates and I tried to keep this quiet. I would undercut most people and give a quarter-of-an-ounce for half-an-ounce back. The going rate was an eighth for a half. I kept to a select few which meant I didn't get into conflict. Whenever anyone came in and ask who was selling tobacco lads would often tell them 'Leeds'. I hated this but became used to it because there was nothing I could do about it.

I had no further problems until a lad called Trench from A1 bought a quarter from me. He was padded-up with a lad called Nixon who liked to start trouble. Trench was quiet with ginger hair and around my size. Nixon was a bigger, mixed-race lad. Nixon told Trench I was a mug. That he shouldn't pay me as I wouldn't do anything to him if he didn't, and that they could share what Trench had from me. When they came down to collect their meals I asked Trench where my burn was. He told me, 'Go suck your mum,' the ultimate insult which would always risk a fight. It was like a punch and you had to retaliate. These were prison rules. His pad-mate stood next to him laughing.

One of the lads I got along with was called Gizmo. He said to Trench, 'Who do you think you are you little bastard?' Gizmo can also only be described a joker. He was extremely dark-skinned. He liked me and knew how to fight so I kept him close. I told him to calm down and simply said to Trench, 'I'll catch you and when I do you're fucked'. I could tell he didn't know how to deal with the situation and so he just walked -off. I then spoke to Nixon and told him to slap him and he said, 'I might'. After all, I wouldn't then have to do it and didn't even want to.

The problem is that this was gaol and to ensure I didn't return to being a victim I might have had to confront him at some point.

Even in gaol, from time-to-time you're able to see the human side of inmates. After all they were just young lads trying to find their place in the world. Many of them had been guided in the wrong direction but most would have taken a better life if it had been on offer. Carlos was on C2 and had a stereo. He would often play his music louder than everyone else. Every now and again he played a song that would stop inmates arguing for a short while. It wasn't by 2 Pac, Biggie or even Jay Z. It was Mariah Carey's *My All*. If you don't know it take a moment and listen to it. The whole gaol would fall silent due to lads listening and thinking that some fine day they might have a woman that thought of them that way. In difficult circumstances they needed moments like this.

One day there were some prisoner moves on the landing of the kind the screws would do from time-to-time. I think it was to stop us becoming too settled. I was moved and padded-up with a tall black kid called Hyper from Winson Green. It was the only double pad on the wing so I don't know why they put us in it, but they will have had their reasons I'm sure. Hyper used to go to the window and freestyle hip-hop tracks to his mates, slamming his fingers on the window sill to create a rhythm. His hands were like shovels, so it sounded like a Wharfedale speaker.

A few days later I received a visit from my mum. I was happy to see her as it had been two months. When I walked into the holding room I instantly heard a voice say, 'Oh Leeds, look who's sat over here'. When I did I was instantly anxious as it was Trench, the kid that told me to go suck her. He was two people along from Nixon who was egging me on to beat him up. Trench must have wondered why Nixon encouraged him not to pay me and then highlight him that way. Welcome to YOI Trench. I looked-up at the camera. Two of the lads from the YOI side walked to the window so the screws couldn't see into the room. Nixon put his hand over the camera and said, 'No-one can see now'. It was a coordinated effort but this kind of thing happened every day. I really didn't want to, but I walked over and tried to punch Trench. He just blocked it with his hands so I walked-off hoping that was enough.

Nixon said, 'That was a pussy move ... The guy robbed you and told you to suck your mum and that's all he gets? You're a pussy'. I didn't want to go down the pecking order as I'd established myself by now. My heart thumping, I went back and threw blows that he couldn't block. I got lost in the moment as once I'd thrown a few punches I kind of blacked out. In the beginning I was more worried for him as I could tell he was just going to sit there. I know he had insulted my mum, and I knew he didn't truly mean it. The truth is empathy doesn't help at all in such situations. Everyone was watching and I caught him in the face with a number of blows. It was only for 30 seconds but it felt like longer. I could tell straightaway I'd hurt my hands but kept a straight face. I cut his eye and mouth and bust his nose. I told him to wipe his face in the toilets before he went on his visit. Even pumped full of adrenaline I still tried to act like I was in control of the situation. It was as strange as when I hit the lad with the pick-axe handle. I was scared but also felt empowered because I knew that others could see that I, Andi Brierley, could beat-up someone in that way. Instead of doing what I wanted and asking him if he was okay, I told him, 'Keep your mouth shut'.

A soon as he walked out of the room he went straight to the screws and told them what I'd done. They told me they were going to look at the video while I was on my visit. I couldn't really have a discussion with mum as this was on my mind. When the visit ended I was taken to the block. This is where they place inmates when they get sanctioned. I was put in front of the prison warden. It was intimidating as I was sitting down in a small room with two screws standing on either side of me. I was told to place my legs as far under the table as I could and my hands flat on top of it. It was clear they were taking every precaution to stop me assaulting the warden. I wouldn't have dared but I bet some lads in there had tried to before.

I admitted the assault straightaway. I told the warden 'I just slapped him for being cheeky to me'. He told me he would review the tape and he would see me again next day. I was then held overnight in solitary confinement. When I went back the following day, he said, 'If that was a slap, I wouldn't want to meet you down a dark alley'. He said, that this behaviour wasn't to be tolerated in his gaol and added two weeks to my sentence plus two weeks loss of canteen (shop purchases). He told me Trench had refused to go back on the wing and would be put on the protection unit. Although I didn't want to hit him initially, I knew everyone would be talking about it. I also felt bad though as he would now be with the idiots I met when I came in. Because my points had been consistently high, I managed to keep my enhanced status.

One night, Hyper and I were at the window and heard two guys arguing. Mitch was a central orderly and Dwayne a landing cleaner. Mitch was around six feet tall and Dwayne five feet two inches. They both had free run of the landings and they were usually friendly. At some point we heard Dwayne tell Mitch to 'suck his mum'. Gizmo straightaway shouted, 'Are you going to take that?' This always left you with almost no alternative. Mitch told Dwayne he would see him in the morning and then shut his window. Hyper and I spoke about the fact that Dwayne was brave to say that.

Next morning we'd served breakfast, done the cleaning and were sat in our cells talking. All of a sudden, everything went quiet. Mitch walked straight past us and into the spare room. It had more space as it only had the toilet, sink and a table in there. We got excited when Dwayne followed him in. The minute they entered the room they started swinging punches and as Mitch was easily the biggest it wasn't long before he was throwing Dwayne around. He grabbed him in a headlock with ease. Mitch had lost it and was acting like a pit-bull. We were shouting 'Stop'. He started to bite Dwayne's nose. I'd never seen him like this. It was as if he had become possessed but eventually we managed to separate them.

We eventually got everything tidied-up and went out to serve dinner. But we never got to serve Dwayne. The screws came and told us to make-up one for him and they would take it to the lad's cell. The officer in charge came straight to me. He asked to look at my knuckles and around my neck. He then went to Duster who worked on the servery and was often getting into trouble. The officer said that Dwayne had been fighting and he wouldn't tell him who with. He did say it could only be one of a small group of inmates as they were the only ones out of their cells. As Mitch was the pleasant lad he was, they sure as hell didn't think it was him. We were told that they expected someone to come forward and admit to the fight. If not, all the working inmates on the wing would be charged. Over that bang-up period Mitch told everyone that he'd come clean. Not that he had much of a choice. If he hadn't, he would have been battered by everyone working on the wing. No-one wanted to lose privileges or be moved. The thought sent shivers down my spine. We had life too good to even think about it.

By this time I'd been in Brinsford for five months on remand awaiting sentence. Although it seemed to have gone quickly, I was fed up with the trips to and from court. They meant we were put in a prison van at 6 am which always stank of urine. If that wasn't bad enough, you would drive past the everyday people going about their daily business. It was nice to see the good-looking women because we weren't getting any female attention. It was also frustrating and created this idea that if I wasn't in gaol I could get to be with any of them I liked. No thought about the fact that I'd no money, education or prospects. I just thought I was going to gym and had a little bit of a good physique now so of course any girl would want me. I was justifying my circumstances to myself or I would have felt so low. It was in a sense a way of protection.

On the 4th of May 1999 I was taken to court and decided to plead guilty on the basis that I was a saver of heroin for someone that I chose not to name. That meant accepting I'd done a limited amount of social supply as I'd admitted in interview. I didn't really know what it all meant but, as my solicitor said, that was for the best and I agreed. Waiting to go up in front of the Crown Court judge was frightening. Everyone back at Wolverhampton had told me that I was looking at around five to seven years. Those at the prison said I would get at least three and even the police told me I would get four years.

The anticipation was unbearable when the court screws collected me from the cells for sentence. They took me in handcuffs to the courtroom but took them off when the judge entered the room. I stood in front of the judge who was wearing a short greying wig like I'd seen on TV. He started off talking about the seriousness of my crime which instantly filled me with fear. He stated that heroin had taken the streets of Wolverhampton by storm. That anyone who was involved in it's supply must be punished to set an example, whatever their age. All I could think was where are Bolt or Malcolm at this point? The speech seemed to go on for around ten minutes and my T-shirt was dripping wet with sweat. I felt I was about to black out with the stress of it and I nearly had to sit back down. The room was completely silent as he took a pause. I felt like screaming at him. This man was about to create a chapter in my life and he was treating it like a dramatic performance. 'I will sentence you to 18 months on each count of possession with intent to supply. The sentences will run concurrently, go with the guards,' he said finally.

'Three years,' I thought. 'That isn't too bad. I got less than everyone thought. I've done five months already, so I will be out in two-and-a-half years'. I was handcuffed and taken downstairs and into an interview room. My solicitor came in to speak with me and to see how I was. Interviews on court cells are also like those on TV. The solicitor sits on the other side of a screen. It makes you feel you should kick-off with them just because the screen, which is meant for protection, is there. But I was happy so I didn't need to do this. He asked if I knew what concurrent meant, which of course I didn't. He explained that the sentences would run alongside each other. I still didn't know what he meant. He then explained that I would only serve 18 months in all. I paused to think. My first reaction was one of relief mixed with worry and despair. I'd to go back to the wing and let everyone know I got 18 months. I'd seen what happened to people with sentences that didn't match an expected outcome. I didn't want that to happen to me after all the work I'd put in to be accepted. I would have added a year to avoid going back with this sentence which is silly but true.

I told my solicitor that I needed all the evidence against me sent to the prison. Fortunately, I was told I was entitled to this. He let me know that he would get the paperwork to me as soon as possible. When we were walking back through the prison it felt like the whole wing was shouting, 'Leeds, how long did you get?' I shouted back that I'd got 18 months for both charges, but concurrent. All I heard was, 'Oh you're a grass'. To make it worse it was lads I thought I'd a good relationship with. It just reminded me of where I was and who I was with. I'd to remember that I was surrounded by strangers and when I left this place I would never see them again.

I told the whole wing that I'd asked my solicitor to send me my depositions. Unlike me, they were informed enough to know that these would have all my interviews and evidence in them. They seemed to give me the benefit of the doubt, for now. As soon as I got the chance, I rang mum to see what she thought of the news. She told me she had a visit booked for the next week and that Adam was due to be released in two days' time, before she came to see me. I jumped at the opportunity to ask her to bring him. 'Tell him to bring me a little something,' I said. I knew that if I was able to get the smallest amount of weed through the strict security on the wing I might build my reputation and earn respect from prisoners. I needed it now more than ever. Plus, a spliff would be nice.

I received my depositions through the post. I handed them to Simon Greatbatch who'd been a student at Oxford University. He was a bit of a con-man who was inside for conspiracy to steal classic cars. He was a tall posh kid with a curtain hairstyle but was well-respected for helping lads with their correspondence. I knew that as long as someone like him thought I didn't grass I'd be fine. He read them overnight then announced to everyone that there was no grassing in there at all.

By this time, I was in a single cell again. I was starting to feel like I was getting to grips with how you get through a prison sentence. Just make sure you know how to drop a few names that people know and respect. Put weaker people down and, if they speak back, make them feel belittled by overpowering them with confidence. Make sure people believe that you will swing the first punch if a fight breaks out. None of these things came naturally to me as I didn't like fighting. It was survival of the fittest and I was used to it from all the poor role models in my life. Although the violence was intense, I quickly adapted to it as it was all I'd experienced from a young age. It was the regime, language, knowing other criminals and lack of criminal knowledge that I was struggling with.

Other than the moment I cried for my mum on the way to Brinsford, I didn't really miss being around her. I bet other kids there who were close with their parents really struggled with separation. I believe I was well-prepped for prison in my early years and, if I hadn't been, I would have struggled. These young people were easy to identify and often ended up self-harming or in the protection unit. Most struggled at first but, like me, settled into prison when they learnt how to conduct themselves. Some would say we lack resilience, I would say we have it in abundance.

The lad next door called Smithy would always chat when banged-up. He was a lad I really respected because he had adapted well to prison life. We used to talk about making sure we never came back by getting ourselves a job when we got out. This kind of talk would make you a victim if you spoke about it freely. Most inmates wanted to talk about drugs and crime. People say that being in prison introduces you to crime but that didn't seem to be true for me. All I used to think about was sorting my life out and not coming back. It seemed that Smithy was like me and, although he was in gaol, he didn't see himself as a criminal either. I struggled at times to keep hold of my values. I didn't feel like a criminal, but I was a prisoner and that felt confusing.

One night after the food came up from the kitchen we were trying to decide who was going to serve what. The problem was that the desert was chocolate cake. Whoever served it had to make sure there was at least one full tray left for the servery lads. This wasn't easy. When the likes of Cyclops and Jeremiah came to get their deserts you would have to give them a portion and a half. This meant you would have to guess who you would get away with giving half a portion to so as to redress the balance. As I found out with Ronnie, you can't always tell. When everyone wears the same clothes they all look the same.

Duster, who was the loudest lad on the wing and a bully, told Smithy that he was serving the chocolate cake. When Smithy refused, Duster hit him round the head with the metal custard ladle. Smithy being the lad he was threw his servery jacket and hat on the floor and marched off to his cell. He would have felt embarrassed but this is what Duster did to most inmates. A screw walked past as Smithy was on his way out of the door. As Smithy didn't speak to him he knew something was wrong. He asked, 'What's wrong with him?' Duster told him that Smithy was in a sulk because he didn't want to serve the chocolate cake. 'Fuck him, I'll serve the damn thing,' the screw said, which seemed to resolve the issue.

'Start letting the landings out,' the screw shouted to kick of the process. With this the officers would let the lads out landing by landing. Those who were on the enhanced wing would often come out last as they could get the leftover food with us as an incentive. The lads that served food would stand behind the hotplate. Duster was serving the custard so he would sit on a chair at the end. When our landing was let out, I noticed that Smithy was literally the last person to arrive. I don't know whether this was what the screws did to him for quitting his job or whether he stalled his walk. I was serving the bread and fruit near the end of the line and I asked him if he was alright.

I knew he wasn't as he didn't answer me and that was not like him. Before I'd time to blink, Smithy's food was in the air as if in slow motion. He had swung his metal tray down on Duster's head. Duster tried to fight back but the screws as ever were there within seconds. It took seven of them to pull Smithy off him. Although he was pissed-off, we could see it coming. Smithy was just not the violent type. It was more and more evidence that gaol can be a dangerous place to be and it can and does change you. I must admit that the situation didn't seem fair as I never saw Smithy again. Duster was a little bashed and scarred. All he cared about was his reputation. 'Pussy took me by surprise,' he said wiping a large blob of custard from his bottom lip.

CHAPTER 9

Cyclops and Other Fine Friends

After I'd been in Brinsford for several months I was called to the reception area and told I was soon to be shipped-out to Stoke Heath Prison. It made me feel uneasy. I'd only just managed to convince the Birmingham lads I was one of them. Now I would have to start all over again. Although the gaol I was in was horrible it had become my home over the past five months and a move made me feel worried yet again. The truth is I wanted to get my arse back to Leeds and find a job.

This time I was going to Shropshire. I'd never even heard of it. When I got back to the wing I told the lads. Apparently Simon had been told he was due to be shipped-out the same day. Talk about a sigh of relief. Then out came Duster with his big mouth, 'Yo, that's me on that ride as well niggas'. I could never understand why he called everyone 'nigga'. It didn't matter whether they were white, black or Chinese. I just assumed that he liked the word but maybe he didn't even know what it meant.

Shah, the landing cleaner, came over and told Duster and Simon that he had some weed coming in that afternoon. I made sure he remembered that I'd looked after him when I got some. He looked at me in disbelief as I said, in a sarcastic voice, 'It's only right lad. I'll scratch your back if you'll scratch mine'. The next day Simon came to me and asked if Shah had got to me last night. He rubbed it in by saying that the spliff he gave him managed to get him and his padmate smashed. They'd giggled all night watching *Friends* on TV. This left me in a similar situation to when Trench had insulted my mum. I needed to keep Simon on side and make him believe I was tough. After all he was coming to Stoke Heath with me and I knew I couldn't rely on Duster. He would hang me out to dry to keep himself safe.

I worked myself up by saying to Simon that I was going to punch Shah and immediately walked-up the landing. It was as if Simon had already told the lads on the wing that there would be a fight. They sneaked up beside me and I could feel their adrenaline which pumped my own up even more. As soon as I walked around the corner, Shah was standing outside his pad talking to another lad. My stomach started to turn. 'What am I doing, this isn't me?' went through my head. I didn't go out looking for fights, especially with people I got along with. Still there was a big group of lads behind me and this was gaol. I had to deal with it.

'What the fuck did I tell ya, ya little prick?' I shouted down the landing. Why I gave him time to prepare I don't know. I should have just sneaked up on him and made it easier for myself. By the time I reached him he'd turned around and started to explain himself. I didn't give him time to begin before I smacked him in the eye. It split open and Shah fell to the floor. I couldn't believe he went down with the first punch. All I could hear was Simon shout '*Boom*, I knew Leeds would bang him'. With that Simon walked off as if he'd been entertained sufficiently. When I caught up with him I realised that he'd had a bet on with the lads about who would win. He told me that not only did he have tobacco on me but faith in me as well. I felt pride that someone like him thought I could fight.

After dinner I was banged-up and my adrenaline went down. I realised then that I'd smacked a kid over nothing but a spliff. I sat on my bed in deep thought. I told myself I had to do it and, hey, the whole wing would respect me now as a fighter. I couldn't help but feel that although I was gaining the respect of the lads I was putting myself in a vulnerable position. What if someone realised my stomach went in situations like that and called my bluff? I felt far from proud of myself and all I felt over Shah was remorse? What was happening to me? I was constantly confused about who I was and it was getting worse.

By morning I'd packed and come to terms with being shipped-out. Then a screw came to my door and told me it had all been cancelled until the following week. I didn't know whether I was glad or upset. I didn't want to go but I definitely didn't want to face round two with Shah. I managed to get through the week without speaking to him. When he saw me he ignored me but all I wanted to do was say sorry. I wasn't going to though. This environment simply didn't allow for that kind of behaviour. Society wanted us to change but in prison we got worse.

The day before we were due to go this time we were told that the Stoke Heath ship-out had been cancelled altogether. Instead we were going to Onley YOI near Rugby the next morning. Was this a joke? I'd written to my mum and told her I was going to Shropshire. Now, the day before we were due to go there they were telling me that I was going to Onley. 'Where the hell is Rugby?' I thought. The following morning I was told to re-pack and get myself down to reception. When I got to the holding area I saw that the knowledgeable Simon Greatbatch was already there pacing up and down. 'When Duster gets in here I'm gonna knock him clean out,' he said. I knew Simon could fight by the respect he got from the Birmingham lads but I thought that he would be apprehensive about hitting Duster. Firstly, Duster would fight back and secondly it could have consequences. It was clear that I didn't know much even after I'd been locked-up for six months.

When Duster walked into the holding area being as loud and annoying as usual, Simon told him to get into the toilet area. Duster guessed that Simon was going to hit him and he said, 'What's with you nigga?' Simon told him that he knew he'd robbed a friend. Definitely and he didn't want to talk about it. I thought Duster was a tough kid and wouldn't allow anyone to treat him like a muppet and surely I was about to see a fight between two hard kids. To my surprise Duster did all he could to talk Simon down. Almost as if the gods were looking-out for Duster, the screws arrived and saved him. 'Come see your new home lads'. 'I'll get you when we land,' Simon told Duster.

When we got to Onley we were told there were two wings for juvenile inmates. The rest of the gaol was for the over 18s. The two wings were J and K. The screws told us that they tried to keep the young black inmates on K-wing because there was a lot of racial tension in the prison and the two wings didn't interact. Duster was again saved by being taken to K-wing and as he walked-off backwards with a swagger he had the nerve to say, 'I'll catch up with you later, nigga'. I can remember thinking that just because someone pipes up a lot it doesn't mean he can fight. The screws took me and Simon up to the second row of cells. They looked more like those I'd seen on TV and the gaol was built in a square with the cells facing inwards and nothing in the middle apart from mesh to stop you falling. In the centre were two snooker tables, a table tennis table and television area with seats. When the screw got me to my cell he told me I'd a bit of cleaning to do. He would bring me some utensils after bang-up and then the door slammed behind me.

I noticed there was blood on the walls and floor. I knew that Simon had gone to a cell a couple of doors down so I shouted to him out of the window. 'My pad's covered in blood'. The rest of the lads filled me in as to why. They told me that the lad who'd been in my cell had been arguing with some of the black lads on K-wing. Although the wings were separate, my side of J-wing faced one side of K-wing in an L shape. The lad had been shouting racist abuse to the black kids and they were saying obscene things about his mother and sisters. The lad couldn't take the abuse and smashed his head on the sink. I noticed that it was now shiny and brand new even though all the paintwork around it was as dirty as in other cells. I looked closer and I could see that the lad had drawn Nazi symbols in blood on the wall. I don't know if I was more bothered that I'd to clean this shit myself or someone doing that kind of thing.

Once I'd had my first association I felt a lot better about being there than when I first arrived at Brinsford which was probably down to the fact that I'd at least one friend there in Simon. I also knew the way to behave to be accepted by other prisoners which helped. Gaol is a funny old place. You have to adjust your body posture, facial expression and the way you interact. If you throw in attitude and as long as people don't see that you're a nice lad really you'll do just fine. I think it's having the social skills to be accepted.

The gaol was full of lads from Leicester, Northampton, Coventry and Rugby. Most of these areas were predominantly white which explained where the racial tension arose from. There was one black kid on J-wing and, for a while, I couldn't understand why because he was very dark skinned. He seemed to talk to everyone, so I approached him and asked why he wasn't on K-wing. His name was Mitty and he told me that he was from Northampton. He said the tensions started because the screws began shipping in Brummie lads claiming to be from Barmy or Jackson Crew. He said white lads in the gaol didn't understand the whole black gangster thing and if the blacks dropped their attitude they'd be fine. Although I liked Mitty and he seemed to be a nice lad, I don't think I agreed with him. Yes, I thought he had a point in that people fear what they don't know and the way the incoming lads acted could be seen as intimidating. However, when lads are smashing their heads on sinks and drawing Nazi signs in their own blood I think the issues are a little more than attitude. Mitty seemed to identify more with being from a certain area rather than the colour of his skin. It was similar to me aligning myself with Leeds. To maintain existing friendships he distanced himself from the black kids from the Birmingham gangs. After all, they weren't his friends.

It seemed like we'd only been in Onley two minutes when we heard there had been another ship-out from Brinsford. Word went around that Jeremiah was on the ship-out and that there was trouble brewing between him and Duster. After the show that Duster had put on the morning we got shipped-out, I didn't read too much into it as I knew he wouldn't fight Jeremiah. Obviously, Jeremiah would be put onto K-wing with the rest of the black kids. As Duster was on there and with Jeremiah being a crazy kid, it wasn't long before they brought Jeremiah onto J-wing for beating-up Duster. Now, I wondered, 'Wherever is all this going'. We have the craziest black kid I have ever met with all these racist young white lads on the same wing. I thought it would only be a matter of time before they would beat-up Jeremiah.

It was as if everyone knew the first person to step-up to Jeremiah was going to be knocked-out because the wing just went on as normal. When Jeremiah left the snooker table or the showers, the lads from Northampton or Rugby would say things like, 'Don't know who that nigga thinks he is'. Jeremiah was almost acting as if he wanted someone to say something to him. He would stroll out of the shower with his towel wrapped around him knowing the screws would tell him to get dressed. He just wanted everyone to see his chest and arms as they were triple normal size. I guess you had to respect him as he was keeping all these racists quiet and he was literally on his own.

After two weeks with the wing relatively quiet it almost felt like the screws wanted to ruffle some feathers. They put the kid that smashed his head on my sink back on it. He'd been in isolation for two weeks. Most of the lads wanted him back. 'He'll sort Jeremiah out,' adding a string of expletives, I heard one lad say when he walked onto the landing. The next few days were full of tension. He didn't say anything to Jeremiah but who would blame him. I couldn't even begin to think what a punch from Jeremiah would feel like but there was an expectation that he would resolve the issue and I could feel it in the air. Jeremiah might have been a nasty piece of work but he wasn't the sharpest tool in the box. He didn't know or care about anything. He just seemed to go about his business and didn't really talk to anyone unless he was grunting at them or demanding something.

One day while we were at the gym taking a shower, Jeremiah noticed that the kid who smashed up my sink had a Nazi tattoo on his shoulder. He came over to me and Simon and said that as he knew us from Brinsford he wanted to know if we had his back. All I could think about was that I wanted to say, 'Erm, no. You're going to mess things up for us and drag us down with you'. 'Yes,' we both said without even looking at each other. I couldn't or didn't want to say no to him and, anyway, this was against prison rules. He said, 'I'm going to drop that white racist so and so. I think some of the lads will probably help him so I'm relying on you two to cover my back'. I had a little over three months left to do and here I was thinking about getting into a fight. It made it worse that it had nothing to do with me.

We lined up in pairs to go back to the wing and Jeremiah was well behind this Nazi boy. We were almost there when I said to Simon that Jeremiah must have changed his mind. I wondered whether he wanted to fight him at all. Then, all of a sudden, I saw Jeremiah step to the side of the line and smack the Nazi lad straight in the side of his face. He then ran onto the grass and shouted, 'Come on you racist bastard'. The lad wasn't one to back down and although Jeremiah scared me he didn't scare him. They went toe-to-toe.

I saw a group of screws come running over from one of the wings shouting for the gym screws who were already there to leave it be. Maybe because they knew the fight was over race as they never normally allowed inmates to fight. The Nazi kid had heart and he was screaming his head off. Jeremiah was calm. When the Nazi kid went to kick him he just moved his leg out of the way with one hand and smacked him in the eye with the other. This went on for a short time before the screws jumped in as the lad wasn't giving-up. Jeremiah had smashed his face in. It was like watching an amateur fight a world champion. A few days after the fight we heard that Jeremiah had been shipped back to Brinsford and the other lad to Glen Parva.

After an evening of playing table tennis I got banged-up behind my door to find a letter. 'It can't be mail at this time,' I thought. When I opened it I saw I was to be assessed for home detention curfew. If successful it meant I could have a tag on my ankle, be monitored in my home and be released eight weeks early which was four weeks from now. I couldn't believe it. Keep calm, I thought. 'I did go on the run when I was out and that might mean I won't be eligible'. But I still couldn't help thinking that I might be out soon and I wouldn't have to play this hard man role. It was starting to wear me down and I needed to be able to relax which I hadn't done for a while.

When I came out for breakfast I saw Simon showing a similar letter to another lad. 'I got the letter too,' I told him. Simon looked at me and said that he knew he wouldn't get home detention curfew (HDC). He skipped bail all the time and the police would oppose it. He told me that I wouldn't get it either as they knew I went on the run from the bail hostel. But I didn't think it would hurt to try. I missed my freedom and Adam had been home for months now. I knew I was going back to Leeds and I didn't want to go back to Wolverhampton so that was a good thing. I was the only sibling missing and that played on my mind. This was probably how Adam felt when he was the only child in care. Besides, if I got to have an interview, I would let them know that all the troubles I'd had were in Wolverhampton. Mum had moved back to Leeds, so I just kept my hopes to myself. I started to feel nostalgic. I didn't even know anyone there now but there would be girls.

The morning the HDC people came to interview us we made sure we had our best shirts on. Simon was up before me and seemed to be in the interview room for a lifetime. When he came out he shouted, 'Silly bastards, didn't want it anyway'. This made me feel uneasy. Despite his intelligence he didn't seem to know how to get adults onside.

'Andrew Brearley' they shouted, as they always got my name wrong. Every teacher, social worker, police officer, judge and screw seemed to do that, but I never corrected them. They held two months of my life in their hands. The strange thing was I was only eligible for HDC because I'd been given two weeks extra for fighting with Trench. It took my release date past my 18th birthday which was a basic requirement for early release under the scheme!

When they opened the door I saw my personal officer and three other people dressed to the nines. The first thing they asked about was the fight saying this was the main reason they might have to decline my application. They said, everything else was in place such as a change of city and my short offending history. I told them that I was bullied when I first went into Brinsford. I fought to prove to everyone that I could look after myself and not look foolish. They sent me out of the room while they discussed my case. I saw Simon on his way to the gym and he asked what they'd said and when I told him I was waiting for my answer he shouted, 'Good luck, I reckon you will get it'. For the first time in six-and-a-half months someone had said something supportive and didn't want anything in return. I said a prayer while I waited for what seemed like forever but was just ten minutes. When the warden beckoned me in his face was serious and I prepared myself for them to say no. They told me that they agreed that things were looking-up for me and as a result of my good behaviour in Onley I would be granted HDC. It meant I would be released in two weeks' time. I was elated but felt down when I thought about Simon.

In Onley I got on well with a lad called Bronze who happened to be one of the few trusted inmates and so worked outside of the prison. I approached him as I wanted to take a prison jumper home. I was adamant that I wasn't coming back to prison but felt I needed some memorabilia.

CHAPTER 10

Harehills

I heard Bronze had sneaked things out of gaol for others so we agreed he'd do it for me. All he asked was that I leave some weed in the same spot where he would drop the jumper, which seemed fair enough. After shaking my hand and saying goodbye he left early wearing two jumpers. 'Don't worry, I'm expecting weed and I'll make sure there's some for you,' I told him. By now mum was in a relationship with a guy called Davey. I haven't mentioned him up to this point and I've no idea how they got back together but he'd been with her before when we lived in Harehills. He agreed to come and drive me home so Adam arranged that he'd let him have some weed for me to smoke on the journey.

I went through the release process. There I stood, aged 17, no money, no prospects, no education, no useful friends, willing the gate to open as if I'd won the lottery. The moment it let me out the air felt fresher. It was sunny and there was my mum with a huge smile on her face. 'You're free,' she said, and gave me a big hug. I then spoke my first words as a fee man. 'Tell me Davey that you brought the weed'. He handed me three spliffs saying, 'Freshly rolled last night'.

I took a map Bronze had made and showed it to Davey saying, 'I need to visit this spot before we set off so I can pick-up a jumper'. He was a lump of a man. Not a bad bone in his body but dirty teeth, no hair and filthy finger nails. But, as men went, he was a good one for mum. When we got there I saw the jumper and took it thinking, 'I'm never going to see anyone in gaol ever again. Bronze will be pissed-off he's not getting any weed in exchange but who cares, take me to Leeds!'

Mum told me she'd a surprise for me. It seemed like she'd done some research when they pulled of the road by a KFC. She knew this was my favourite food. I can assure you I've never enjoyed a meal as much as that day. I know KFC may not be everyone's idea of nourishing food, but after seven months in gaol it tasted like Jamie Oliver had cooked it. By the time I arrived home I was stoned but within seconds of walking through the door reality hit. The living room which was full of people of all ages. Not the type I'd want in my house or chose to spend time with. Adam, Verity and Miles were pretty much running the house apparently. All their young friends were awaiting my entry like they knew me and acting like it was a welcome home party. It was more like a youth club.

Adam had a new girlfriend called Geraldine and had also started seeing her friend Zara, though Geraldine didn't know that. They were both in the house along with a lad called Brill who was good friends with both girls. Brill seemed like a bit of a geek but he wasn't being as loud as the rest, so my first impressions were that he was okay. There were twins my age and all of Miles' friends who were around eleven-years-old but happily swilling alcohol.

I struggled to be downstairs where all the noise and music was so took myself off upstairs to my room. It was a three-bedroom house and I was sharing a room with Adam and Miles. I sat down on the bed with my head in my hands. Although glad to be out of prison, I'd forgotten how it was to live with my family. I would just have to make it clear that this type of thing wasn't going to continue in the house. I needed to get away from it so took a walk down to Winston Tilly's on the next estate. At least I still knew someone and he was the only person around that I thought would remember me. When I arrived he was in his bedroom. I went up and we chatted about old times and how I'd ended up in gaol. Helen then came in who I'd seen once or twice while living at Georgina's. Winston asked her if she remembered me and she said she didn't. 'He's just got out of gaol, don't you fancy sorting him out?' I couldn't believe he was asking her that in front of us both and neither could Helen from the look on her face. She told him that he was out of order before walking-out and slamming the door.

That night I was the only person in the house. Everyone went to Georgina's place but I stayed in and watched TV as I was tagged. I never intended to breach my tag as I wasn't ever going back to gaol, or so I thought. I heard a knock at the door and when I answered I was surprised to see Helen. I invited her in and she told me that she'd thought about my situation and felt bad for not staying and talking to me. I thought all my Christmases had come at once, but I was nervous and asked her if she wanted to play cards. 'Cards, Andi,' I thought. 'Couldn't you have come up with something better than that?'

I didn't have any alcohol or anything else to offer her and I didn't really fancy Helen but after seven months inside that wasn't going to get in the way. We played blackjack for around ten minutes before she said, 'You must have played cards enough inside'. She asked if I wanted to take her upstairs to do what I hadn't done for a while. I was amazed at how forward she was but wasn't about to let the opportunity go by so I said, 'Of course'. After we had finished, I told her that I liked her. She told me that I didn't need to say that because she was aware I didn't really. She said, 'Look Andi, I have my own things going on'. But she said she'd enjoyed herself and this was fine by me as I didn't want anything more to develop with her anyway.

Davey worked at a Jet station where he'd been for a while. He said, they had an opportunity for me at another petrol station. A few days later he took me there and introduced me to his boss, (another) Simon, who was the manager of a number of Jet stations around Leeds. It was an informal chat but after five minutes he said he'd be happy for me to start work next day. He knew I was subject to a tag that meant I needed to be home for 7 pm and said I'd only have to work until 6 pm. He would make sure I got in 40 hours a week and when the tag came off I could work later.

I had to attend Waterloo Road probation office but my first probation officer never seemed to be there when I went. Eventually, I got a new one called Felicity. I remember we had a conversation about my ability to handle money while selling drugs. When I told her the amounts involved she felt that if I could handle that amount illegally at age 16 I could transfer these skills to a proper job. It was the first time since Len's weekend work in Wolverhampton that anyone at all had made me feel I was capable of doing something lawful for a living. It was excellent timing coinciding with Davey and Simon feeling I could do the petrol station job. It was to be a completely new beginning that included freedom, no drug-use and a job. I wasn't kidding myself though as the house was constantly crowded with people who I felt I'd little if anything in common with including my family. It made me frustrated and isolated. The lads I thought I'd get along with on the estate didn't seem to take to me at all. I think they'd formed their low opinion of us as a family well before I was released even though that didn't define me as an individual.

I got into trouble almost instantly as I liked a girl called Dot who lived around the corner. She was six months pregnant to a lad called Norman. She wasn't with him but, understandably, he didn't take well to catching me with my tongue down her throat in the street. We nearly got into a fight but whilst he was arguing with her I managed to sneak off. I'd got friendly with Norman's brother John and he spoke to Norman and sorted it out. I was glad about this as Norman was a prop forward who towered over me. I think people knowing I was fresh out of prison didn't help me to get along with anyone. The good lads were suspicious of me and the bad lads expected me to behave like them. I felt stuck as I wasn't really a criminal or a fighter and it was still difficult for me to acknowledge that I'd actually spent time in prison. I was more confused than when I was inside. Prison was all lads wanted to talk to me about. Not that I wasn't happy to do so. It was the one thing that made me feel important.

Now I was working and on the tag I eventually started meeting lads on the estate. I would invite them round to the house for drinks because I couldn't go out in the evenings except in the back garden. I knew I couldn't control who came to the house, so I just joined the party. Ben Peters, Don Williams and Drew Flax were three that never seemed to ask about my past. They just seemed to accept me for myself. Friday nights were usually quite lively and Mum would often be the first one up dancing. 'If you can't beat 'em, join 'em,' I thought.

I started to see a girl called Donna who occasionally came round to ours. Donna hadn't slept with any of the lads on the estate which I liked. Although I walked into a house full of people the day I got out of custody and hated it, I was now just as involved. Friday and Saturday nights were hectic. Donna and her friends were all partying there while I was confined on tag. I really liked her and I enjoyed spending time with her, but this suddenly changed once she allowed me to sleep with her after around three weeks. I still maintained the relationship as I didn't want her to think badly of me but it immediately changed. I questioned my ability to maintain a relationship with any woman and it was something I didn't understand. Why did I change how I felt straight after having sex?

My tag was due off in a few weeks' time so we agreed that we'd all go to a club in Leeds. Don Williams' and Drew Flax's sisters went to a place called *Uropa* all the time. The night the tag came off everyone met at mine and was ready to celebrate my freedom. This made me feel accepted as around 15 people turned up 'just for me'. It turned out to be a new but different chapter as I'd found something that I was good at, clubbing and socialising. It brought a confident side out of me that I didn't know existed. Don seemed to know everyone in the club. He was one of the best hard house dancers which meant he got lots of attention and I loved being around him when he did. 'Just what I need to bounce back,' or so I thought. We had some drinks and Don came over and told me to open my mouth. When I did he stuck something in it and told me to have a drink of water. I knew it was ecstasy as he'd told me that he tended to take pills rather than drink alcohol. I thought. 'If he does it and he gets all this attention it can't hurt me'. I was always into R&B, hip-hop and soul music so the hard house that they played in *Uropa* wasn't my cup of tea. However, after taking that pill it didn't make the slightest difference. The music, the people, the lights, the atmosphere all rolled into one and I was on top of the world. The feeling after taking that first pill was so intense.

All of a sudden the music stopped and the lights came on which took me by surprise. It felt like from taking the pill to the music stopping was just minutes. I knew it had been hours and it was time to go home, and when I asked someone the time it was 6 am. I was wet through. I'd been wearing my old school trousers and a shirt Flax had lent me. I guessed he wouldn't want it back as it had changed colour. I would have loved to have seen the dance moves I was doing! I doubt I would have been getting the attention Don did but, 'Who cares, what a night!' Some of the group had already gone home but the rest of us caught a bus. It was weird coming-out into the light of the morning. I'd never experienced anything like it, but it felt good. At least it was warm so my shirt would dry quickly, but I didn't smell good. My jaw was doing strange things and I didn't seem able to control it. I can't have looked attractive.

The following day I told Donna we were not going to work out. I said I'd too much catching-up to do and couldn't do it while I was in a relationship. It was dawning deeper on me that I was only attracted to women before sex. I wasn't aware of the reason, but I'm sure now it was due to the kind of relationships mum had. 'Sex and what else?' I thought.

I was now working until 10 pm on Thursdays and Sundays and getting more than enough hours in to finance nights out at *Uropa* at the weekend. The problem was it meant I had money to take more drink. Due to years of abuse, neglect and exposure to drugs and crime, I'd ended up a drug addict before I was legal to drink. I'd spent seven months in prison and yet not a single professional had discussed with me how my years in care had led me down that road. Nothing to help me acknowledge that the reason I got into trouble in the first place was due to being exposed to violence at such an early age and excluded from school. I didn't know that to prevent being involved in offending now I needed to stay away from substances and think hard about who I was spending my time with, about drinking, taking drugs and that I was finding it harder and harder to keep my job. One morning I rang in to let them know I wasn't coming in. I told Simon to just sack me. 'I can't do it anymore,' I told him.

I just couldn't manage both work and my chaotic social life. As I turned 18 I felt I had to make a choice. None of the kids I knocked around with were working and they were loving life. I was conscientiously attending all my probation appointments and I wasn't involved in crime due to their guidance, other than some personal drug use. But I foolishly told myself, 'It's only work. I'll have plenty of time later for that'. I couldn't work on Sundays was my initial justification. So I told Felicity, my probation officer, wrongly, that I'd been sacked for not going in. She didn't know about the drugs and parties and so far as my twisted thinking was concerned she didn't need to. I was in complete control, or so I thought.

CHAPTER 11

Work and an Evening at Elland Road

Brill and I started work in Yeadon scrapping metal boxes for the Ministry of Defence. Getting work through a recruitment agency wasn't difficult at all. I might struggle to hold down a job but I was always good at getting one and would go from agency to agency until I did. There was a lot of manufacturing work around and I could talk the talk. I would often use my prison licence as my ID because I didn't have anything else. It didn't prevent them taking me on.

Davey and mum had split-up by this point (tell me something new!) and she was no longer working but off to bingo every day and it was causing problems. She'd get her benefits on a Monday and one particular time there was no food in the cupboard so I told her she needed to get some on the way home. She arrived back around 10 pm with neither food nor money telling me she'd also borrowed some from Sam, an old friend, and that was all gone as well. I shouted and screamed at her and told her that she'd failed at being a mother. She was a mature adult but not able to overcome the childhood experiences she'd had. I was on the road to being an adult and I'd also experienced abuse, neglect and being in care. Was mum an example of where I was heading?

Mum looked at me, started crying and told me she was depressed. 'Bingo helps me forget my problems,' she said. She'd clearly not dealt with Davey leaving and it was getting on top of her. 'You're coming home to more problems,' I told her. I was trying to overcome my own barriers, but where were the positive adults helping me to counter all this shit? I didn't want to be worrying about whether my siblings were going to eat.

Georgina lived across the park. I called into Brill's on the way home after picking-up some bits from her. I told him I felt like clouting my mum and I meant it at the time. I hated even thinking like that but I couldn't sit around and watch the way things were deteriorating. I asked Brill if he fancied moving out and the two of us getting our own place. He was older than me and we were earning enough to survive on both our wages. Although I didn't know how to live alone and mum wasn't the best example to learn from I thought I could give it a try. After shaking my hand he said he would. He had just passed his driving test and had a Fiesta and we would be able to move our things in it.

We went to the council and looked into Housing Federation. Within a week we'd been offered a viewing in Beeston. This was close to the girls who clubbed at *Uropa*. We also started spending time with some of my old friends there which seemed to make sense. I'd never settled in Rothwell where mum now lived and didn't feel accepted there anyway. It was important that I found a good circle of friends given what had happened in Wolverhampton. Brill was a good kid and we had other friends who were working lads, so things were looking-up.

We had nothing when we moved in, no sofa, cooker or beds. We agreed that we'd just get ourselves in and buy things each week out of our wages. We bought a sofa, beds and living-room furniture straightaway. Brill and I often fell out as we seemed to still be at *Uropa* every week. He was more responsible than I was and pointed out that we should stay in to save money and buy things but I wasn't listening. Clubbing and spending time with the girls was my priority. So the novelty started to wear thin for him as he knew things weren't working out but I couldn't see it and I certainly wasn't listening to him.

We starting spending time with some lads nearby. Dick was 21 with a bald head and missing teeth. We called him Romper because he was always fighting and he lived in the next street. Clinton lived over the road from us. He was a local weed dealer, a mixed-race guy known for fighting and he fascinated me. He was around five feet seven inches, of slim build and yet seemed to fear nothing. He made me feel like I did when I was with Malcolm in Wolverhampton. I didn't even stop to think that I was building a similar relationship all over again.

These guys often came to spend time at the house because they lived so close. Brill being the sensible one felt uncomfortable in their company and it was only a matter of time before he wanted to leave me to my own devices. He knew that spending time with lads like these was a disaster waiting to happen. He hadn't had the experiences I had and probably didn't feel safe with them around. I didn't have the same feeling because all I knew from my earliest days was lads like these. One night after work we had a drink and Brill decided he was going to bed. He said he'd appreciate it if no-one disturbed him. I didn't want to be associated with him being a stiff and jokingly tried to persuade him to stay downstairs with the lads. This didn't go down well and he made some comment about me being stupid. I was drunk and grabbed him by the throat then pinned him against the wall. I made it clear he wasn't to talk to me like that. Especially in front of people. I felt the kind of rage that I did when I kicked Miles as a kid. It was different to hitting Trench in YOI, or using the pick-axe handle in Wolverhampton. That was because I was being pressured into violence. This was actual aggression and I could have hurt him if he'd said anything else to insult me.

Brill was close to me and acted more like a friend than anyone. He always wanted what was best for me but here I was making sure I was respected by people that couldn't give a cuss about me. The truth is I was comfortable around these types because they were 'like me'. Brill was sensible and therefore like other people. Alcohol was my new drug of choice and it was giving me a release of the anger and shame I felt due to leaving my siblings and not supporting mum more. Next day Brill left early and returned to his mother who lived around the corner. He said he'd had enough and, without any hard feelings, he wanted to go home. I just thought, 'Why would you seek your whole family for protection?' I recognised that I was out of order and allowed him to take what he wanted. I did feel a little down as I knew that I was losing a positive influence. Not enough for me to say sorry and that things would change though. I was far too proud for that.

Now I had free range to have as many people around and as many parties as I wished. I was laid off from my job but getting a few days work a week from another agency as a lorry driver's mate. I liked this as I could sleep while we were travelling so long as the driver would allow it. One benefit was that as it was only a few days a week I could still sign on and get housing benefits to pay my rent. Another was that I could have parties during the week. Brill being there had at least meant I couldn't do it all the time. He was gone now and my alcohol use was rocketing up and up. I'd little support other than weekly visits from mum.

I was no longer spending my nights at *Uropa*. We moved on to clubs such as *Casa Loco* and *Boilerhouse*. Both were renowned in my circle for violence, drugs and crime. My new social circle took ecstasy, amphetamines and cocaine through the night. It was helping me stay awake and drink what I liked without getting too drunk. We would end up at someone's house after the clubs closed and spend the night and maybe the next day drinking. Some of the people I partied with worked but most didn't. Some had bills to pay but would prioritise partying. So I didn't feel alone.

One night at *Boilerhouse* I bumped into Freddy (Big Mouth) Green who used to bully me in Chapeltown. I thought I'll make him aware that I'm not a little white boy in a black area anymore and stepped-up to him. By the time we were swinging punches, Ben, Miles and some other lads got in the way and split us up. 'I never forget a face,' he said as he walked-off pointing at me. 'I'll see you when I see you,' I replied. Not that I meant it as I only did it because of the drink. I wasn't bright enough to work this out and think about any later consequences.

One day mum popped around after bingo and I was at home with a group of Beeston lads. Leeds United were playing Galatasaray in the European Champions League. A Leeds fan had been stabbed and died at the Turkish home leg which gave the match an extra edge. Miles, Ben and I felt some allegiance to the club. Miles was more a fan and would often go to games, but Ben and I just liked to say we were. I have always supported Leeds United but I wouldn't spend money going to watch them! Mum had won at the bingo and said that she fancied a drink with us. We were planning on watching the game on TV and she was happy to drink with the lads and do the same. We didn't have any money so we were over the moon when she went and bought a crate of Carling Premier out of her Bingo winnings. I reckon this highlights my immaturity as I should have encouraged her to go home and spend the money on the family. It was almost as if feeding the kids wasn't my problem any more as I couldn't see whether it was happening. I tried my best to block out what was going on at home and concentrate on my new life.

Miles was the joker of the pack and would often place a scarf over his face and walk-out of the house saying he was off to do an armed robbery with a knife taken from the kitchen. We knew he was just acting like a clown and he wouldn't harm a fly, so we would just let him go and get on with it as he always came back 20 minutes later having changed his mind. He knew some lads that did robberies so he was just pretending he could be that kind of person. This time however, with the drink, Leeds United losing and the tension around the game, Miles persuaded us to go with him to Elland Road which was only ten minutes away. While we were walking there the fans that were leaving must have thought we'd come to get involved in trouble. They were shouting things like, 'Go get 'em lads … Show 'em what for'. This just fuelled us and we didn't need it as, when we got to the ground, hundreds of fans were hanging around to see if anything was going to happen. I remember an away fan built like a lorry shouting, 'No matter what, don't run'. By this point hundreds of Leeds fans had gathered. It was a crazy scene and we were drunk so this wasn't going to end well.

The police charged and most of us ran backwards. Every time they stopped people threw stones, bottles, sticks and anything else they could lay their hands on. One thing that sticks in my mind was the away fan stood at the front off the crowd shouting. He was a big guy but I couldn't help but think, 'What an idiot'. The fans started chanting: 'Where were you in Istanbul,' meaning the police were getting us but they didn't protect the Leeds fans in Turkey.

I came across Leeds fans setting cars on fire and smashing their windows. I was trying to stop them where I could, reminding them that these cars belonged to Leeds folk, but it didn't work. The police by this point had driven us to a metal footbridge. This helped them to get us away from the ground but, with bottles and bricks flying at them, they needed to drive us further away. They continued to charge us over the bridge which meant we ended-up in the streets of Holbeck. Things then got worse as the locals were getting their cars smashed. I watched a group of lads trash an Indian takeaway. At this point I sobered up and I just felt things had gone too far and went home. I simply thought it was an eventful night and took myself off home and to bed.

A few days later I was at the launderette. I had a quick look at the *Evening Post*. On the front page was the banner headline 'Football hooligans that shamed United'. Needless to say, I went straight to the centrespread of photos to make sure I wasn't there. It took me less than a minute to make out clear as day that Ben's was one of the faces. I rang him at work and told him but he didn't feel he had anything to worry about. That was until he got a letter through the post saying he had to hand himself in at the local police station for questioning. When he got there he was arrested and charged with affray and inciting a riot. When he went to court we felt he would get a community order as he'd never been to prison. I sat next to his mother and the feeling started to change when the judge asked to see the video. You could make out Ben throwing bricks and right next to him there I was in exactly the same bright blue jumper I was wearing in court. Slowly, I tried to edge behind his mum so the judge couldn't see me. I began to sweat. I wondered what would happen if they spotted me.

The judge asked Ben to stand and told him that although he understood his mitigation and that sending him to prison could jeopardise his tenancy and employment where he was earning £400 a week, he felt he had no choice but to make sure football fans were aware that such behaviour wasn't acceptable. He sentenced him to eight weeks' imprisonment of which he would spend just four weeks inside but lose everything. Ridiculous I thought. A longer community order or community service would have been more proportionate and less damaging. How could they not see that if they sent someone who posed little risk to the public to custody they thereby increased his risk of re-offending by dismantling his life, and just to prove a point? I suppose I can't moan too much as I could have been sitting right next to him. I had to sneak out thinking, 'Ah well mate, I guess I'll see you soon'. When he did get out I felt we'd a shared bond of gaol and we became closer. He rang me straightaway and I met him in town.

We did the same again one Tuesday night when only people with little going on in their lives would consider partying in mid-week. He asked me if I could get some girls round, so I rang Joan and asked her if she wanted to come. Lorraine and I were back in a relationship but she was baby-sitting and these were her friends anyway. Jennifer came and she brought Tara with her which I must admit I was happy about. We got some vodka in and our only aim was to have a good night. The vodka was definitely not the best idea as I can vaguely remember someone trying to take the bottle from me and refusing point blank to share it. Eighteen-years-old with a drink problem. In fact, since the age of twelve, when I first started smoking cannabis, I'd intoxicated myself with one substance or another. It could all be traced back to my early childhood experiences, the adults around me and their lifestyle.

As I continued to drink my memory became blurred but the last thing I can remember was Jennifer trying to get Tara to go home with her, then the rest of the group left to go to another party leaving me and Tara alone. There was a man who lived at the top of my street who'd made it clear that he didn't like the things that went on in the house. However, as he was about 30-years-old I just let him get on with it and never said anything back. The group walked up the street and as they were being loud this prompted him to shout at them out of his window. The exchange became aggressive. This was when they came running back to the house and he followed them. Miles came to my bedroom, woke-up Tara and I and told us that there was an eighteen stone older guy at the front door and he was going to beat them up. I can remember saying to those in the living-room, 'I can't believe they're carrying-on with the neighbours'.

By this point the guy was making his way up the street back to his house. I didn't know this so when I walked out the door and Miles placed a breadknife in my hand saying 'He's a big guy, Andi' he obviously thought he was helping me. I was drunk and everyone seemed to be pumped full of adrenaline so, being frightened, I took the knife but was intending to apologise to the neighbour. He'd nearly made it back to his house yet as soon as he realised I was there he turned back. I walked towards him and as we met he punched me before I could even open my mouth. Ben then jumped in the way putting his arms up to protect me. This is when I remembered I still had the knife. I picked myself up and placed it against the neighbour's cheek to stop him in his tracks. I don't know whether it was because I was drunk or that he moved suddenly but his face instantly filled with blood. He immediately went back towards his house. By now Ben had taken the knife off me and the others were running down the street as quickly as their legs would take them.

Ben dumped the knife down a drain and followed me into the neighbour's house. He was in his living room with a tea towel pressed against his face. I'd sobered-up pretty quickly and was telling him he shouldn't have hit me and that I hadn't mean to hurt him. His wife was screaming and everything was chaotic. She was encouraging him to beat me up and I agreed that he should. Then from nowhere Tara appeared and started shouting. 'What you doing bitch,' Ben said as he charged at her as if going to beat her, before taking her outside and trying to calm her down.

This was when I realised I was in the shit and said to the man, 'You shouldn't have hit me as I didn't do anything to you'. He replied, 'You're gonna get it you little shit'. The police pulled-up outside, instinct kicked in and I ran off down the street. We all ran to Stewart's house and woke him up. Luckily, he left his door open and slept on the sofa, so he would always get up for work. Being grumpy, he got upset and shouted, 'I've got work in the morning'. But when we told him what happened he stopped. We all sat down and no-one said anything for at least ten minutes. We were in shock that the night had ended in such disaster. After waiting a good hour, Ben and Tara walked to my street holding hands pretending to be a couple. The coast seemed to be clear so they came back for me. Miles had the door key and we knew he must have been arrested earlier. As we didn't have one, we had to climb through the window into the living-room. Ben went to Brill's old room at the top of the house and Tara and I went to my room. I couldn't remember doing anything and turned over as if we were just going back to sleep. Tara knew I couldn't remember and made it clear she wasn't happy about that saying it was early morning and she had to get some sleep.

At first light there was a loud knock on the door which woke us all up. None of us answered or even went to the window. We waited then looked out but there was no-one there, however we guessed it was the police. Tara asked me again if I could remember anything. I said 'No' which made her say she was going home. As Miles still had the keys I helped her climb out of the window. I just wanted to press rewind but in these situations the problem never goes away that easily.

Ben asked me if I could remember what I did the evening before. I looked him in the face and said, 'I cut that guy didn't I?' I couldn't remember the actual events but I was aware I'd done it. I could remember the aftermath although even that was blurry. It's a weird to do things and not remember them, but the truth is this was happening to me a lot. I wasn't just drinking, I was intoxicating myself. I was more confident, or so I thought, when I was drunk.

Later that day I decided I wasn't going back to gaol without a good night out. I threw some going out clothes into a bag and Ben and I went to Rothwell and spent the day there. Later we went to the *Observatory* which was three pounds entry and a pound a drink on Wednesdays. We partied until 3 am when I realised I'd no more money and had lost him. Knowing I'd slept with Tara and Lorraine who I was with at the time could find out, I walked three miles to Lorraine's house to tell her before someone else did. I arrived in the early hours which would be an issue in most households but, as her brothers were involved in offending, random callers at night were the norm. I made her aware that I thought I'd used a knife against someone then told her about Tara. When I said I'd slept with someone else she instantly said she knew who. This made it worse as she'd clearly picked-up on something before then meaning I must have given something away. She tried to kick me out but her brother came in as we were arguing. When I told him about my situation he said to get my head down on the sofa.

Lorraine came and told me she would forgive me but it would be hard and asked me to come to bed. Next morning she said that we could try and make a go of our relationship but that I would need to stay away from Tara. I told her I didn't want that now as my life was in bits and she would complicate things. After coming to her house in the early hours and telling her I'd cheated on her with her friend, I was now telling her I didn't want to be in a relationship with her. I was truly messed-up. Just like my family were impacting on me I was impacting on others that tried to care for me.

When I walked-out of the door there was a police car waiting in the street visiting someone over the road. I waited for the officer to come out of the house, walked over to him and told him I was wanted for assault. He took my name and radioed in. Once we arrived at the police station, the officer in charge was a woman. I felt she understood my position. She told me that although I was under arrest as I'd handed myself in there was no need to put me in a cell. I stayed in the waiting room until they were ready to interview me. They told me that Ben and Miles had been arrested. Ben had stated that he didn't know who actually cut the neighbour but Miles had told them it was me. This left me with no choice but to come clean, so I told them it was me but that I reacted after he'd punched me. They charged me with wounding with intent and bailed me with conditions. This meant I couldn't reside at the house as it was too close to the victim. I had to live at my mum's and was subject to a 9 pm curfew. I could go back to collect my stuff that's all.

When I got home I noticed the door wasn't shut and when I went in I saw everything of value had gone. Not that we had a lot but this was the last thing I needed. The police had not secured the property after they'd kicked the door off looking for me. The kids on the estate had been and taken the stereo, TV, DVD player and smashed the coffee table and TV stand. I was pretty down. I felt like I'd tried to get my life together and yet it had all managed to get out of hand once again. I was 18 and about to go back to my mother's. She had a gambling problem and the kids still ran riot. To top it all, I knew I was going back to prison. Looking back, it wasn't the decision to take the knife which was wrong. It was the earlier decision to allow Brill to leave and my house to be used for parties. I wanted to be a normal teenager but without Brill I wasn't responsible enough to live alone.

On the way home one night from visiting Stewart's I called into Ben's house to catch-up with him. I missed the bus and set off for home late and arrived there 20 minutes past curfew time. When I arrived the police were outside waiting for me. They arrested me in front of the family and said, 'If you're late, you're late'. I fully understand that police have procedures but was this necessary? The family was watching and the impact it could have had on the younger members was huge. Watching the police take friends and family when you're growing-up can make you view them as the enemy. The police are there to keep the community safe, however with this type of approach members of the community can view them as cold and horrible. I was held overnight and given bail again which was always going to happen and which seemed to show their heavy-handed approach was unnecessary.

I was being told I was looking at a custodial sentence of three to six years. Maybe I could get a job and that might help me in court. I managed to bag myself one at a cash and carry warehouse as a cashier. I needed the money and knew it would be better for me in court. It was difficult to motivate myself each day knowing that I was likely to receive a custodial sentence but I stuck it out. When I first attended the magistrates' court, my solicitor told me he had good and bad news. He said the charge was serious enough to be committed to the Crown Court but that the magistrates had lessened it to assault. He said it must've been due to the cut not needing stitches. He said, 'We seem to have got lucky and this could mean that, as you have a job, you may well not go to gaol'.

The morning of my sentencing I was worried because it was November and if they did sent me to prison I would lose my job and be there for Christmas. But my solicitor told me that there was a good chance I wouldn't go down, so fingers crossed. Mum and the kids were in court and when I walked into the dock I glanced at them and smiled. Then I looked at the lawyers and thought they looked daft in their silly wigs. Not for a minute thinking about how daft I looked behind a glass screen.

The judge came in and we stood for him as if he was royalty. He started to speak and I instantly got the wrong vibes. 'I can't believe or understand the reason this charge was lowered' he said. 'Its far more serious'. He told me that his hands were tied as the longest sentence he could give me was two years. 'Two years, is this guy for real?' I thought. He then said that as I'd pleaded guilty at the earliest possible opportunity he would deduct time for that but 'Due to everything I'm sentencing you to 20 months in a young offender institution. Take him down'.

I looked at my mum and my sisters who were crying their eyes out. I shook my head and mouthed, 'Sorry'. As the guards walked me down to the cells all I could think about was how I'd managed to get myself back to this point? I was confused about who I was and about my identity. I wasn't mature or intelligent enough to connect my early years to my current behaviour. That would come much later.

CHAPTER 12

Doncaster

I was put in the prison bus and told by the guards we'd arrive at Doncaster YOI in time for the evening meal. It was a lonely ride but it gave me time to think about how much I'd lost. Yes, I was back inside but I'd had a number of jobs and managed to experience getting my own house. Given the lack of support in the community that was quite something but no-one really cared, and here I was all alone again and on my way to another violent place. I shed a tear and tried to focus on the fact that I'd survived before and would do so again. I was just as scared as before.

When we got there I noticed it was a new prison and that the prisoners got to wear their own clothes, which seemed better. As the bus drew up inside the gates I thought, 'Whatever will work think when I don't turn-up?' I'd not mentioned it to anyone there. I'm sure they found another cashier just as certainly as I'd found a cell. I shivered down my spine as I saw the barbed wire again. A reminder that there's no quick way out. I was taken to C-wing. Doncaster is an adult prison but A, B, C and D-wings housed young offenders. C1 was the induction wing so all new inmates were taken there to begin with. I somehow managed to start talking to a lad called Nick from Beeston. I'd never met him before, but I told him I used to go out with Lorraine and he obviously knew her brothers. I dropped other names into the conversation and he took me for a friend straightaway. It helped make me feel comfortable as he was a big guy. I got the impression he wasn't intimidated by this environment even though it was his first time there too.

I was only on induction for a week before I was moved down to C3. I was happy when I noticed that Nick had already been moved there and he shouted over to me. The set-up here was that inmates ate at tables in a communal area. The wing was triangular with cells around the out-side. The pool and table tennis tables were in the centre along with the dining tables. I saw Alfie Boyd and Strutt who I knew from clubbing so I instantly felt at ease. However, this was prison so I had to make sure I wasn't too comfortable. Whether I could trust them was another question? If I'd not got along with Nick so well, I would have probably sat on Alfie's table as there was a mixture of Leeds lads there. However, I used my instincts and sat with the south Leeds lads. I did hear Alfie's table mention that Freddy (Big Mouth) Green was due to come off basic regime which was situated on D3 across the hall-way. Remember, he was the black lad that victimised me when I lived in Chapeltown and who I'd met in a club? This was the last thing I wanted as the last time he said he would catch me some other time. It was as if I'd just found out where.

The following day Greeny walked onto the wing with a big Afro and a hair pick sticking out of it, jeans around his ankles and a strut that made him look disabled. Everyone embraced him as he walked over to Alfie's table. He saw me, so I just said, 'Hi, Greeny'. He looked, cussed his teeth and said, 'I never forget a face, so I'll see you later'. I said, 'Well ya know where I am when you want it then, eh'. The lads on my table asked me what it was about. I told them he was bad with me when I was young but didn't want them to know I offered to fight him in a club. I was thinking to myself, 'You're making a bad situation worse, Andi, but you must play to the audience'. Getting the balance right is often impossible. I can remember one lad saying, 'I'd rip his black lips off if he ever said that to me'. Nick agreed. I just said, 'If he wants it he can have it'. I didn't want to come across as tough, just someone who could protect himself.

There was a lot of tension between Leeds and Sheffield lads. It's not like they didn't talk to each other but they sat apart at meal times and you could sometimes hear whispers. It was a problem when it came to things like the pool table. People would often argue over it. They would go to the shower room to have a fight and at times bite chunks out of each other. I worked it so that although I liked pool I only went on the table at certain times. Someone would come and say, 'I'm next'. If you were really next at that point you would need to back yourself. I would just watch and not put myself in that position. Not unless I knew I was on the table immediately.

One day I was sitting in my cell and as I didn't have a stereo I was playing a music channel on the radio. Suddenly my window slammed shut from the outside. It looked out on the exercise yard. I jumped out of my skin as I looked-up and saw a group of black lads standing at my window saying, 'Shut that shit up'. There was a Craig David song playing and they clearly thought that no-one should be listening to him in gaol. If they did, they were pussies because he wasn't gangster enough. It wasn't like I'd control over what music was played on air anyway but, to be honest, I loved Craig David.

All three lads were bigger than me but I said, 'What the fuck you doing?' One of them said, 'Where you from lad?' I told him I was from Harehills which shows you I'd no real identity in there. I would say whatever I felt benefitted me in the moment because I wasn't from any particular place given the number of schools and places I'd grown-up in. This time it backfired as the three were also from Harehills. One said, 'Don't you know who I am?' which highlighted me as a nobody as they were well-known, so they thought. We had an argument and again their leader said, 'I'll see you when I see you'. These things are constantly happening in custody and you're always being tested. The trick is to make others feel you will fight them if necessary; but you don't want to be known as one of the toughest lads.

There was a lad on the servery from Manchester called McColl and he was serving the bread one day. When a big lad whose name was Morton from Barnsley came to collect his he said he wanted two slices. When McColl said no, Morton took his plastic knife and stuck him with it. I didn't actually see it as I was too far back but I was close enough for it to affect me when I found out what happened. It was horrific and to think that it was over a piece of bread was ridiculous. I like to think it was something that happened between them prior to the bread incident but, apparently, it was because Morton was just crazy. They must like their bread down there in Barnsley.

Out of the blue I received a letter from Trevor, an old schoolfriend, who'd read about me in a local newspaper his parents had sent him whilst he was serving abroad in the Army. One screw was-ex military, Mr Hodge, and everyone hated him. He was always writing-up inmates for bad behaviour. He was the officer handing-out the mail that day and he asked me why I was receiving air mail? I lied telling him I'd completed my training for the Army and used some of the information Trevor had given me about his regiment to persuade him this was true. Mr Hodge was impressed by this and even went on to say, 'I could tell you were ex-military by looking at your cell'. Little did he know that this was due to the fact that I'd been in Brinsford where you had no choice but to keep your cell clean and bed pack made-up. It was a lot more relaxed at Doncaster.

For every wing there was a representative who would attend monthly meetings with other wing reps, the chief executive of the prison and officers. They held these meetings to discuss issues on the wing. The idea was that this was inclusive and might make the inmates feel part of the regime. This was the highest paid job in the prison at around £18 a week which is a lot of money for a prisoner. The current wing rep was a lad from Sheffield. Leeds lads often moaned about the fact that they never got good jobs on the wing. The wing rep was due to be shipped-out so you can imagine my surprise when Mr Hodge opened my door early one morning and said, 'Brierley, you're the new wing rep'. Although I was happy to have the job I thought this was going to give me exposure I was not sure I wanted. The Leeds lads seemed to think that they were going to benefit straightaway and started telling me I should ask for a new pool table and cupboards for the cells amongst other things.

I got a visit from Ben, Jennifer and Tara and this meant a lot to me as Doncaster was quite a distance and they'd taken the train. I was clear about my friendship with Ben and Jennifer, but I wasn't so clear how I felt about Tara. She seemed to make me feel vulnerable and insecure for some reason. I thought at the time that this was love but it was due to her not feeling the same way about me. She saw me as a friend but not as someone that she could have a relationship with. It was evident that, when it came to relationships, I was extremely confused. With men coming in and out of mum's life and, I thought, taking advantage of her this had impacted on my view of women and of myself. If someone cared for me I would push them away. The one person I thought I loved didn't feel the same way about me. I know now that this could be learnt behaviour as this is exactly how mum was. It's like we devalue someone that loves us because we don't value ourselves. But we focus on those that seemingly don't care for us. Un-met need.

The visit went well. It was nice to know that they were okay and enjoying partying. Jennifer never stopped talking. Visits were always great for the first 20 minutes. As with visits from mum, after them telling me what they wanted and asking who was on the wing the conversation stalled and became hard work. Jennifer gave me a picture of her Tara and Geraldine. Some of the lads wanted a look so I showed them and one said, 'I've slept with her with the blonde hair' meaning Tara. I took one look at him and thought 'I'd be surprised'. I said, 'Okay, let's ring her'. The whole table was intrigued and followed me to the phone. I called and Tara said that she had never heard of the guy. It goes without saying that he was torn to shreds by everyone for trying to big himself up.

Big Mouth Green approached and told me he needed a cupboard. This seemed to be him saying the problem was over, so I knew what my priority was to calm the situation down. I was in a single cell at this point but I'd become friendly with a lad called Clanger. Clanger was from East End Park and although he was only small he had been to gaol plenty of times mainly for ram-raiding. He was thus 'well-known'. Clanger didn't seem to care about anything or anybody, something I was in awe of. I always thought about the consequences of my actions when sober so people like Clanger intrigued me. When he got a job as a cleaner he asked me if I wanted us to get padded-up together as we were now both workers. He sold burn and at this point I was selling everything from pop and crisps to chocolate bars and phonecards. My rules were that you could have whatever you wanted but had to pay double back. I benefitted from building relationships within any environment. Others got their money back through force and intimidation, but I just built relationships with people which made them want to pay me back.

I was jealous of the lads from Gipton, Beeston, East End Park, Chapeltown and other local areas. They would have a group of friends on the out, but I didn't really spend time with crooks so hadn't this connection. I was a working lad and tried to talk about that life as little as I could as it would lose me prison cred. Bassline music is the one thing other than crime, drugs and clubbing stories that united the gaol population. I would often listen to Clanger's stories of him committing offences, about spending hundreds and sometimes thousands of pounds on clubbing, drugs, girls and cars. The lifestyles these young people used to say that they lived seemed glamorous to a 19-year-old who worked.

After a while Clanger started to get on my tits as he had the patience of a six-year-old. He would ask me to play cards and if I didn't want to he would get upset and start shouting at me. If I then got frustrated with him he would say things like, 'Are you taking the piss out of me? Get off the bed and we'll have it out'. It sometimes made me wonder whether he was doing it because he knew he had protection or he would actually beat me up. I wasn't by any means a tough lad, but I was convinced that I would beat him. He felt he could bully me. He would sometimes tell people that he asked me for a fight and I'd said, 'No'. When we used to talk, he would say that within his circle friends would fight when they disagreed. I found this bizarre as I liked Clanger and felt no need to do battle with him. He might have been a pain in the arse, but I assumed most people would know I'd hurt him if I had to.

Alan Dickens came onto the wing after being charged with armed robbery. This was something that needed my full concentration. Alan was a big guy and had a reputation for throwing his weight around and hadn't long finished a two-year sentence. I'd met him once and I knew he was a lad that demanded attention and respect. Alan was good friends with Graham. This meant Alan saw me as one of his own and we would often talk. It was a good thing we had these conversations as Graham told Alan that I'd written nasty letters to Lorraine and said he should beat me up. I think this put Alan in an awkward position as he knew I still had feelings for her. We had spoken about this and I told Alan I cared for Lorraine but I was messed-up so he came and told me what was being said. After that every time I was near Alan I felt uncomfortable.

I thought that he would stay loyal to his friends but as time went on I think he just allowed it to become old news. In prison I often felt that way for one reason or another. People often say you have to look over your shoulder. When you feel danger in real life you take yourself away from the problem. In prison the problem is in your back garden and you face it every day you go there.

I don't think it was due to my negotiating skills as wing rep and more that it was our turn anyway, but the wing was given new cupboards and a new cloth for the pool table. This left me in good stead with the wing and according to the lads it was because a Leeds lad was in charge. All the lads on the wing, whether from Leeds or not, were happy with me and this gave me some protection. I wasn't going to tell them I'd nothing to do with it because they thought I'd pulled strings.

One day at a gym session we came back to the shower room and when I unravelled my towel I noticed I was missing my shower gel. I made sure everyone was aware that someone had taken it. I walked down to the showers to see who had a white Radox like mine. Three months into my sentence and I was behaving like I owned the place. It just so happened that a kid called Sinbad from Chapeltown had the only white Radox. I told him it was mine and we were quickly face-to-face. Big Mouth Green stepped in and asked me to 'Leave it' and took the Radox off Sinbad and gave it back to me. 'Try that shit on me again and you'll see,' is what I told him. It was just words as I didn't want to fight but again felt I had no option but to make people aware that I would. This incident comes up again later in the story so remember the name Sinbad.

As I had it so comfortable, I put myself forward for a Duke of Edinburgh Award. This meant I would have to stay in Doncaster Prison as the course placed me on hold. Why would I want to move now I was settled? This got me into an argument with Strutt who was someone I considered a friend. His take on it was that I was scared to move gaols and, as he said it openly at the dinner table, I reacted. I think he was frustrated as he was being shipped-out and he probably didn't want to go either. We stood-up ready to fight but other lads got in the way and calmed it down. The thing is the thought of gaol is worse than the actual thing. As humans, we will always adapt to the environment we are in and gaol is no different. Once you are comfortable in prison why would you want to go through the induction process all over again? The worrying thing is young men becoming comfortable in a violent environment.

On New Year's Eve someone somehow and despite the security managed to get a fair number of ecstasy tablets into the gaol. While we were walking around the exercise yard, the lad concerned made sure some people got one. This included me as I was a good person to keep on side now I was wing rep. The whole wing was absolutely rocking throughout the night with everyone blasting out music. By midnight Clanger and I were rocking our socks off in the cell. I was drip wet and chewing my face off. I can remember saying to Clanger, 'We might be in gaol but were smashing it'. We were both jumping around the pad like rampant rabbits.

The screws started to notice that Clanger and I seemed to have things a little too good. Our cell was looking like a supermarket. Apparently there had been a complaint by someone that I was using my position to bully other lads. I was selling things on the wing, but I took offence to the screws saying I was bullying. I asked the wing officer to look me in the eye and decide whether this was my style. After all, they spent enough time with us and got to know us well. It was because of this suspicion that half-way through my Duke of Edinburgh Award course the screws came and told me, 'Pack your kit, you're moving'. They told me I was being shipped-out to Deerbolt YOI the following morning.

I wasn't happy. I told them that I couldn't be as I was on the D of E course which meant I was 'on hold'. 'If your name's on the list lad, you're going,' is what the officer said. He was the transfer screw and I didn't know him. Although I'd a lot to say about it, I didn't have a choice. I was gutted but I'd managed to save some money and I had a large collection of goods to take with me, so here's to another new start. You would have thought I'd have been used to moving by now. It still made me anxious.

CHAPTER 13

Deerbolt

When I arrived at Deerbolt which is in County Durham I noticed it was similar to Onley, but not so racist which was a good thing. I was back in prison clothes as sentenced prisons usually make everyone wear the same. It helps if everyone is seen as equal and not in fancy outfits. Just like in school when it was easy to see the kids that were poorer, not good at crime or in care as they didn't wear the best, leading to bullying.

I did three days on the induction wing banged-up for 23 hours a day. The only time I got to leave the cell was to attend sessions about the running of the gaol. It's good to slowly integrate prisoners and makes it easier for the officers to manage. It was also good to know how to apply for courses and get into the gym. It saved confusion like the time I was pushed back into my cell by the screw at Brinsford. I was then moved to F-wing and the first thing I realised was that I hardly knew anyone. Clanger and Strutt were on other wings and I didn't know when I would meet up with them. When I went out on association I found there were two Leeds lads on my wing and got to know them and one lad from Bradford. Gaol is and always will I think be tribal and this is the best way to stay safe. It's not that people from your area automatically back you, it just means you're seen to be with other lads rather than alone.

The wing was full of lads from Middlesbrough, Newcastle and Sunderland. There was also a lad called Hatton from Redcar and he was always on the pool table. He seemed to feel that he was some type of hard nut which I clocked straightaway. I have come across these types in all the gaols I was in. You can do two things with them: stay out of their way, or befriend them to a degree to bring them onside. But for now I just wanted to find my place on the wing.

Clanger managed to get a message to me saying he was putting his name down for the Community Sports Leadership Award (CSLA). I thought it was something I'd like to do and put mine down for it too. The course lasted six weeks and it was now May. I was due to be released at the end of September, so it would help make the time go. I was becoming a young man now and I knew that I didn't want to be an adult prisoner, so I focused on getting a job as soon as I got out. Over that first week I managed to build a relationship with a gym screw, Mr Bannister, who spoke to me about the fact that the CSLA could help me find work with young people in the community. I wanted to disagree with him and ask how I'd ever manage to get a job working with young people when I'd been to prison twice. He told me that as long as I'd never hurt vulnerable adults or children there was a possibility. He said, 'Keep your arse out of crime and there's always a chance as some people like to be involved in a turnaround story'. Although I hoped he was right, I also knew lots of people didn't like prisoners. But his words were helpful and inspiring.

Mr Bannister often told us all that 'offenders feel they can't get any-where and that's not true'. He said it was only a matter of opinion which could be wrong. He said, 'People will always find excuses'. I must admit that he came across as sincere, just like Felicity my probation officer had but did either of them really understand how hard I'd had it? Did they understand how my home life had impacted on me each time I wanted to improve? How I gravitated towards criminals because it was what I felt comfortable and identified with? That care and substance abuse as a child meant that I struggled to stay away from intoxicating myself, which led to offending? Or were Felicity and Mr Bannister right? Was I simply making excuses and it was all down to my own choices? What I didn't realise at the time is that I was thinking about it, which meant I was on the road to recovery from my early years of trauma. But Mr Bannister was a non-offender telling me that if he was an employer he would give me an opportunity because he liked me. I really liked Felicity and him and therefore I was willing to take on board what they said. Some offic-ers believed they were better than us so when they gave advice no-one listened. If the system really wants to implement change, it needs more people in it that build relationships like Mr Bannister did. He was hard but honest and I respected that.

My six weeks on the course seemed to fly by. I was refereeing sports, producing lesson plans and delivering them. I felt this was something I would like to do for a living. However, deep down I wondered how I could make it happen. I regularly spoke to the lad next door to me who was from Newcastle. We both used to say we were going to get jobs when we got out and the CSLA course was starting to make me think I might be able to do more than just warehouse work. Although I'd always got jobs in the past, they weren't enough to keep me out of trouble so maybe a better, more professional job might. My biggest issue was that the only way I knew to get a job was through recruitment agencies. I didn't have the self-confidence or knowledge to attend interviews for decent jobs. How would I tell them I'd lost two years of my life in prison and how would I get referees. Whenever I thought about this I'd decide a warehouse job was good enough. I'd get out, earn money, party, meet girls and catch-up on what I'd missed.

My first aim was not to get in any trouble inside. One evening on association I was waiting for my turn on the pool table and Hatton was shouting down the phone. He must have been arguing with his girlfriend or parents, as he then walked into the room red in the face. He came straight over to the pool table and said, 'I'm next'. The screws were talking at the other end of the room, but all the lads heard it and turned and looked at me. When Hatton was in this mood he turned into a bully and everyone knew it. I said, 'I've been waiting for a while, lad' in the best way I could, trying not push his buttons. I usually had the skills to bring people like him on side but for some reason this time it didn't happen. 'Listen, Leeds prick, I'm next on here okay,' was his response. I couldn't believe I was being put in this position and I got butterflies. I knew this was only going to end up one way. Like I said before these situations are difficult. Everyone was looking and remember it was prison. I was a prisoner so obviously could fight or so everyone assumed.

I repeated, 'I'm next and I don't appreciate you talking to me like I'm a dickhead'. 'You are a dickhead and I'll prove it now in the showers,'

141

Hatton said. 'Lets go then,' I replied but with my stomach going at god knows how many revs a minute. I was more concerned with my own safety than hurting him and that is why I knew I would never make a good fighter. When we got to the showers Hatton told two lads to get out. I tried to give him a last chance not to fight but before I managed to say anything he smacked me in the face. I got lost in the adrenaline at this point and punched him back. We stood toe-to-toe swinging punches for what seemed like seconds but it must have been longer. Some of the lads couldn't help but gather to watch which made the screws aware of what was going on. I seemed to be getting the better of him so he jumped at me and we landed on the floor. When the screws did arrive they dragged him off me, he'd clearly lost it and needed pinning-down

Next morning the officers came to my cell and took me to see the governor. I explained what had happened and the governor told me that, although he understood, he felt I could have avoided going to the showers. He gave me loss of canteen for two weeks. I wasn't too bothered by this but I can remember thinking he doesn't understand prison life even though he spends all his time with prisoners. Had I felt there was any other option I would have taken it. But there didn't seem to be one, other than being a victim which wouldn't have stopped the bullying. This would be recorded as me being involved in an aggressive incident. It's strange how you can find yourself in prison and yet get judged when forced to act like a prisoner. When I got back to the wing the officer told me to pack my kit as they were moving me G-wing. I still didn't know what had happened to Hatton but I wasn't bothered as Clanger and some other Leeds lads were over there. I would be far less likely to be involved in something like this with those lads around. Small as Clanger was he always had my back covered.

The CSLA course finished but the gym screws encouraged me to go straight onto another one: The British Amateur Weight Lifting Association (BAWLA) Leaders Award. This would see me to the end of my sentence. I loved sports, so why not be in the gym until my release date? I'd built-up a good relationship with the gym screws and I was going from being a smaller than average Andi to a very athletic looking one. I was becoming muscular and it was giving me a sense of confidence. I don't know how productive it was but it made me feel tough and good. The bigger I got, the more confident I became at dealing with conflict. I also knew it would help with the girls when I got out, so I started to take it more seriously as my sentence went on.

Ben, Jennifer and Stewart came to see me. Jennifer told me I should feel like I still had some friends out in the community as Deerbolt was much further for them to come than Doncaster. She told me that the party scene was as good as ever. I looked forward to getting out and a job but I really wanted to get back to that. I was known in that scene and some would say respected, although it was for who I was pretending to be. I used to watch my reflection in the TV screen in my cell and think about how fresh I would look when I got to the club. Jennifer also told me that Tara was pregnant. If I'm honest, this got me down. I'd convinced myself that I would tell her that I cared for her when I got out. Knowing she was pregnant made me realise the small chance of that had passed. But at least I knew I'd some good friends.

On G-wing I met a kid called Robbie from Birmingham. He was involved with Barmy but in a gaol a long way from home and I was the closest thing he had to a local. I knew a lot of his friends from my Brinsford sentence and they would often tell me what was going on in their city. I pretended to be interested because he was a good lad. He would borrow my CDs and had lots of his own. One track I would sit and listen to over and over again was Kelly Price and Aaron Hall singing 'Love Sets You Free'. It's about chains and being held back. I would listen to the words and think that circumstances were holding me back. The song made me remember I was a good person, that I would beat this prison situation and it will always mean a lot to me. We all have barriers but we can break through them and we should always prioritise love over hate. Not that I would talk to anyone about such thoughts in prison.

One dilemma I had before release was that I was eligible for a tag and could have been released in late-July. The problem now was that I'd experienced clubbing and the culture of partying and taking drugs. I was aware that because of this I wouldn't easily be able to comply with a curfew, so I refused to be assessed for a tag. I think I would have been approved but I saw many lads leave custody only to come back for breaching their tag and I'd no intention of following them. I also felt that if I got out on tag, 'they' would have control over me and, now I was in the prison routine, what did eight weeks matter? My thinking was that release would be spoiled by a tag. I wanted to own it.

One day I will never forget was when we were half-way through a session and someone came running into the gym. He was trying to catch his breath and when he did he told us to flick on the news. He said, 'Some gangster from Pakistan has bombed America and it's on every channel'. When the screws turned the TV on we stood staring as a second plane flew into the second of the Twin Towers live on air. The officers stopped everything and took us back to our cells. Some of the lads were kicking-off as they didn't care or thought that it was not a big enough deal to stop their activities. I was eager to get back to my cell so I could find out what was happening. Back there I just sat and watched events unfold. I refused to go out for association as I didn't want to miss anything. I couldn't comprehend that people were jumping to their deaths and that it was being shown live on TV. I'd no idea who Osama Bin Laden was but I felt disgust at what he'd done. I didn't know who the Taliban were or where Afghanistan was. Most prisoners were not bothered, but I was so interested. However due to my childhood being the way it was my need to understand such things wasn't nurtured. Prison was the only time I was clean from drink and drugs from as far back as I could remember. Drugs and alcohol had taken over my school years, but I certainly wanted to learn about this.

The BAWLA course finished and we were assessed by an Olympic referee. I felt good about the fact that I'd managed to get two nationally-recognised certificates whilst in prison. Could I really put them to good use and become more than a warehouse worker like Mr Bannister said I could? Probably not. I was a prisoner after all, but it had been better than wasting my time. Deep down I felt warehouse work was itself an achievement, which was probably right given I was in prison. I was released at the end of September 2001. I just missed being out for my 20th-birthday, but I thought 'Who cares, I'm off home'. Let's see what I made of myself after this second prison sentence. I wasn't coming back. Surely?

CHAPTER 14

Clubbing the Night Away

I was handed a travel warrant and directions to Durham Railway Station so I could catch the train to Leeds. It felt amazing to walk-out of prison and feel free. Having said this, it dawned on me that as a 20-year-old I'd no money, prospects, education or anywhere to live but mum's. That hadn't worked the first time I got out so I wasn't holding my breath and I knew I needed to lower my expectations. One thing I noticed was how nice the area was. I certainly couldn't imagine living there though. I'd become accustomed to certain places so I would stick to what I knew, and I certainly didn't know an area like this. Since birth I'd known welfare, care, scamming the system, not learning, instability and poor personal development. I'd been given criminality, social workers and care.

Back in Leeds I met-up with the family. Needless to say, it turned into a drinking bout in *Hoagy's*. Ben was also there and I ended-up going on a night out with him. I was drunk from the first pint and completely smashed by closing time. Walking down the street I noticed a guy with three pretty girls. I was fresh out of a place where being tough was eve-ryday behaviour so was finding the transition to life in the community quite difficult. I was also pumped full of muscles and wearing the biggest chip in town on my shoulder. I walked-up to the lad and put my hand out for him to shake it but he refused and ignored me. Before I knew it I'd punched him in the face. Ben jumped in front of me and shouted, 'Andi, you're not in prison now. You better sort your attitude out or I'll leave you here and now'. At the time I didn't understand why he was so stressed by it. But by now he had a responsible job and a good deal to lose. He stayed with me though because he knew this wasn't the real

Andi. The problem is snapping-out of the role you play in prison. Just because the doors open it doesn't mean you change overnight.

Mum had moved to a deprived area of the city. Although we'd always lived in fairly rough areas, I'd no plans to spend too much time there. I'd come to feel more at home in south Leeds now. I was sick of her moving from pillar to post and now I didn't have to rely on her as I was old enough to make my own living arrangements soon. It wasn't long before I got a job as usual. Stewart and a few of the other lads were working at Poundstretcher through an agency. I just asked and two weeks after getting out I was doing the same job. Remember, I never found getting work difficult. I was a hard worker and the agencies were convenient for someone like me and less choosy.

Stewart asked me if he could move in for a while and as usual mum was always happy with people staying as it meant extra cash. He was only there for a few days when Adam left. This meant there was a room for just me and Stewart. The job didn't last long as we often got laid off when the work dried up. This happened quite a lot with warehouse work and it was always temporary. So Christmas was busy and then January was when they got rid of you regardless of the fact that you were a hard worker. The full-time staff kept the jobs. When I went to see Jennifer she was a star and told me that my first priority was to get back into work and that this was the best way to stay out of prison. I knew this but it was nice to have someone motivating me. We both went to a recruitment agency and they gave me a job starting immediately in a warehouse in south Leeds.

Things seemed to be looking-up. Working in this new job introduced me to a lad called Reggie, a tall, black guy from London. He had funky dreads, was six feet two inches tall and had a huge smile. He'd moved to the city because his girlfriend was studying at Leeds University. There seemed to be a team of good lads at the warehouse and we were all going out together and meeting girls. As young men this was our main priority and I seemed to be fairly good at. Deep down I wanted to settle down. It was hard for me as none of mum's relationships whilst I was growing-up offered an example for me to follow. Pulling girls of a weekend made me feel like I was achieving something but I always felt shallow when I found myself avoiding the girl the following day or week so really it was counterproductive.

George was another lad at the warehouse. He was forever up to no good. He was a white lad, two years older than me and he thought of himself as a bit of a fighter. George, Reggie, Stewart and I had formed quite a good friendship. Jerry was a lad who'd grown-up in Beeston. He was my age and everyone thought he was sneaky. He'd been friends with Miles, Ben and the girls growing-up but they didn't spend time with him these days. I'd met him a few times in *Uropa*. Jerry was now living with his girlfriend. He started spending time with us. Jerry told me one time that he'd tried heroin when he used to sell it in Beeston. He said he ended-up spending a short time in Doncaster YOI on remand for it. This made me feel I'd some shared experience with him which made us bond. Jerry was someone who'd been brought up by good parents in a stable environment but, for some reason, he didn't want to follow in their footsteps. They had recently moved to a nice area of Wakefield where his mother, ironically, had a job in a lawyer's office.

Jerry and I became close. When we went to clubs such as *Casa Loco* he would love the fact that I knew a lot of underworld-types as a result of being in gaol with them. I should have noticed this was due to him craving this kind of lifestyle. It seemed that he thought I was a way into it but, in truth, I'd little in common with these lads other than clubbing. I wanted to work, make a living and had simply found myself in prison because I was coerced into selling drugs and then got into a drunken fight, I wasn't a hardened criminal. I didn't have much going for me so I built-up my self-esteem by going out as much as possible and living for the moment. No-one other than a probation officer and a prison officer spoke to me about my future for which I was grateful to them. However I was getting the work-life balance wrong. I needed to enjoy life but I needed to look at my priorities which were unbalanced, just being happy to have a job that would fund my partying. At 20-years-old with a serious criminal record I needed to be more responsible. The truth is when you get out of prison you feel you have lost out, so you try to catch-up. I was catching-up on the wrong things.

The contract at the warehouse came to an end so Ben, George, Jerry and I arranged a night out. We went drinking all day and were planning on going to a club called *Spooks*. While we were waiting for it to open we went downstairs at *Big Lil's*. I met a girl and went outside to talk to her and whilst we were there a lad who I realised was Sinbad saw me and came over. I was drunk, with a chip on my shoulder and showing-off in front of the girl. I truly believed that girls who saw anything in me did so because they thought I was a criminal and a fighter. So I asked him if he could remember trying to rob me of my shower gel in prison. I then smacked him in the mouth. I was just showing off. The girl ran into the amusement arcade next to the pub and came out with a group of black lads. I always thought I was Superman when I was drunk and walked straight up to the group. I could see that Jerry, Ben and George had just walked-out of the pub and George swung for the nearest lad to me then he and Jerry got into a fight with the group. They felt overpowered, ran back into the arcade and I went after them.

What went on in the arcade is blur due to how drunk we were. Ben ran off and eventually the managers pushed us out and shut the doors. We were too far gone to realise it had all been caught on CCTV as we decided to walk to *Bar Cenza*. The police picked us up on the cameras and came in riot gear to arrest us for racially aggravated assault. We were bailed but I wasn't going to agree to the 'racial' bit as I'll explain.

I made an appointment to see my solicitor. 'It wasn't all that bad' I told him and he showed me the video at which I was surprised I could act like that. I was almost like another person, not only the instigator but willing to fight the whole group alone when they confronted me. It was a bad punch-up and I knew I was in deep trouble yet again. The group had tried to fight back but we overwhelmed them. Apparently, Sinbad had told the lads in the arcade that I hit him because I was a racist which is why they came out. I told my solicitor that I would plead guilty to assault, however this had nothing to do with race. I hit him because he stole shower gel from me not because he was black.

Jerry, George and I attended court a month later. When things like this happen it brings those involved closer together as they have a shared experience. The law calls them co-accuseds. Knowing that you're capable of this when together should mean you agree to go your separate ways, but this didn't happen in our case. I was given 120 hours community service, probation for twelve months and a four months curfew. They dropped the racial bit after checking the reasons I gave. We laughed at Ben for running-off that day, but he was the sensible one. When the monitoring company came and put the tag on my leg they didn't do it properly and I noticed straightaway. This meant that, although I was tagged, I could take it off and go out to *Casa Loco* and *Boilerhouse* where I got attention from the girls when they found out I was 'notorious'.

One day I was sitting on the window ledge looking out of the window and saw Adam walking down our street. I ran to the door as I knew he'd been about to be sentenced to prison. We were all thinking he was looking at around four to six years for a third strike burglary. My initial reaction was that he'd escaped but then I thought, 'Nah, I've been in Doncaster and it's completely secure. Adam told us that he'd had the burglary charge dropped and they'd released him free of any charges due to some technicality to do with the evidence. I was pleased to see him looking so well. His shoulders were massive.

Adam soon became friendly with a local woman. She was older than him and had a boyfriend with pots of money who drove an ageing Rolls Royce which looked odd when he parked it outside her council house. He must have fancied her enough not to care. It was rumoured he was involved in various rackets. He was always covered in gold necklaces and bracelets and way off his own patch. I think the woman used to flirt with Adam to make up for the fact this guy bored her stiff. One evening while she and her chap were out on the town they got into an argument and the guy slapped her. A group of men saw this and beat him up. As he was drunk, badly beaten and now back at hers sleeping it off, she came round to our place. I was pissed-off about it as I was due to work as a driver's mate and had to get up at 4 am.

I soon changed my tune after she told us that he had a large amount of cash in the boot of his car. When I said I didn't believe her she gave a key to Adam and he and Jerry went to have a look. I told them that if it was true they needed to remember using the key could mean leaving evidence so to throw the police off track they let off the handbrake and the car rolled down the street into a lamp post. They also smashed in the windscreen to make it look like vandals before coming back with a holdall. We took it into the kitchen, turned it upside down and out fell bundles of notes. Quite a lot in fact, just looking at it made my knees wobble.

There are always choices to be made when such things happen. However, the lives people live also contribute towards those choices. Given my life until then, I was always going to be involved in crime in some way and my initial reaction was to work out how we could keep the money without placing myself or my family at risk. Jerry wanted to take it and run but he wasn't in the position I was in. This man visited the woman who lived over the road. She told us he'd landed some deal that day but we didn't know if that was true or not. Having thought for 60 seconds, I told her that we should take a commission and she could have the rest and get as far away as she could. I thought that as long as she took most of it the problem would lie with her not us. Retrieving the bulk would be the man's main concern. I guess this shows that even when I wasn't under the influence of drugs I couldn't stop to properly weigh-up my decisions. We shouldn't have taken even a small cut but with my background I honestly believed I was being fair and sensible.

I told the woman to hide the money somewhere and as soon as her boyfriend left take the kids well away and use it wisely. Me, Adam and Jerry then took a taxi to Ben's house and waited for him to come home. When he arrived we showed him a wad of notes. The thing he was most unhappy about was that he hadn't left our house long before and felt he'd missed out so we gave him £50 for being a good friend. We shared out the rest equally between the three of us.

We decided it was best for Adam to go home and keep an eye out and to remind the woman to leave, saying, 'Be careful how you spend what you've got because we all need to keep a low profile'. Jerry and I slept on the floor at Ben's on some cushions. We didn't trust each other so we placed an envelope containing the cash between us and each kept a hand on it. It reminded me of the film *Trainspotting*. The following morning we went to town to buy new clothes. Combine having a little bit of money with the stories I'd heard from the likes of Clanger in prison and I felt I could make even more money. Jerry felt this was exactly what he would do now to achieve his sought after reputation as a gangster.

Having no other ideas we agreed to buy some drugs and try to double it. We figured that if we bought a batch and sold them we wouldn't need to work. We could party as much as we wanted to and wear flash clothes. On a spending spree we walked around with carrier bags from Harvey Nichols, House of Frazer and Accent. We ran into Adam and he'd bought a £10 pair of jeans from a cheap store. He just looked at our bags and said, 'I thought you said to be careful'. We just laughed and told him that we'd keep the clothes out of mum's sight. Bless his cotton socks. He didn't have any dress sense anyway.

By now, Jerry and Reggie were spending a lot of time together with George who was one of the dodgiest guys I've come across. We were going out nearly every night, taking cocaine at random houses, selling drugs and noticed George managed to do everything we were doing. It was because he had a scam going cashing cheques at a recruitment agency. I still don't know exactly how it worked but effectively he was getting paid for 40 hours work he wasn't doing and this freed him up to make money doing it in other areas. He was the most ruthless money-maker I knew. He would manipulate women into giving him cash by saying he had debts and leave them broke and with bills to pay. This was all while he was married. He was brave as if their brothers had found out he would have been in deep, deep trouble, but he didn't seem to care.

I was forever warning mum not to have the local woman round anymore. Although the rich boyfriend was no longer visiting her, I guessed he wasn't just going to walk away from his stash however dubious it was. I think the woman felt safe with Adam around. She had placed her family at risk and must have felt better with him close to her. He may have been telling her he would keep her safe and trying to sleep with her. His standards weren't that high. She was closer to mum's age than his.

I was now 21, Adam was 19 and although he was built like a bouncer he was still taking drugs. Verity was only 17 but chose to leave mum's and live with someone else as she didn't like it at home. Miles was 15 and probably learning no end of bad things from me and Adam and if

I say any negative things about Miles in this book it is my fault not his or Adam's if he got into trouble.

The drug-dealing idea didn't last long. Jerry had fallen out with his girlfriend before we got a hold of the money. As soon as he had fancy clothes he made sure he met her so she could see them. We'd both bought gold chains and Jerry and I were looking like gangsters. He wanted her to see him like this because he believed she would want him back. When I told him he was a fool he just said he wanted to make her jealous. I knew she wanted to have some control back when she asked what he'd been doing. They got back together and he starting spending more time with her. And, because I couldn't sell drugs, I would go to the girl's house if she rang me and give them to her. I was not the drug-dealing type.

Without Jerry, George and I were partying at every opportunity, going to *Casa Loco, Boilerhouse* and *Niche*. We were going out in Leeds through the week and drinking with student girls. It was only a matter of time before the bit of money we had ran out, but we were having too much fun to think about that. Adam was the one that had no idea how to keep cash in his pocket. He was taking kids out drinking and whilst drunk he bought a car from a guy in Seacroft. He thought it was a good idea to pay £500 for a Ford Mondeo with no paperwork and without being able to drive. He rang me one morning and told me it was in the town centre and I could buy it from him if I wanted. Me being the caring brother that I was, I offered him £100 so he took an overnight hit. I put £50 in and so did Jerry. Even though I couldn't drive I was being chauffeured around by others. Adam was due to get the paperwork from the man later. I didn't know much about cars and it seemed to run okay so I wasn't particularly bothered about that. After all it was only £100.

I met a girl in *Boilerhouse* and arranged to see her in the week. As she lived there I asked Reggie to drop me off in Bradford and said he could then take the car. Jenna was a model and although she was really pretty she was a bit strange. While we were chatting she told me that she had a little girl. She said she wasn't ready for a child so her mother was the child's main carer and that the girl called her grandmother mum. I suppose I was only looking to sleep with her so it didn't really bother me what her family life was like. I guess it was the way she explained it that made me feel she was unstable. I was excited about meeting her but after talking to her I knew it was only a fling.

I can't remember what time it was but at some point I received a phone call from Adam and he was panicking. 'I've just been hit with a gun,' he shouted down the phone and seemed to be running. After getting him to slow down I asked him to take a breath and be clear about what he was saying. He told me that he was in a woman's house who'd helped herself to the money and a group of lads had pulled-up outside. He said they ran into the house with guns and demanded the money. They'd hit him around the head with the butt. They took all the gold from around the woman's neck and told Adam to stay on the floor. I could tell he was shaken.

I immediately rang Reggie, Jerry and George and told them to get to our place as soon as possible. After spending a few hours there making sure the men didn't come back, Reggie came to collect me from Bradford. I couldn't believe it when I later returned that the woman was sitting in my living-room. 'Right, enough is enough. You didn't take my advice to move out, but you can't be in this house,' I said. Everyone was asking me to have compassion on her but all I could think of was that I encouraged her to take the vast bulk of money to not have these repercussions. Yet my stupid family thought that she could take money from someone and it not have any consequences. I was protecting them over this stranger and they didn't understand.

I managed to persuade the woman to get a private rented house on the next estate and get her arse as far away as possible. I felt sorry for her but I also felt the minute she made the decision to take this man's money she had a responsibility to keep her kids safe and use it wisely. The cash had started to ebb away slowly anyway. I had nothing left so I thought I might be able to get some back by selling the Mondeo. Me and George took it to this dodgy car dealer and tried to get him to buy it. He HPI'd the car to check its history and then rang George threatening him. I could hear him shouting that if he brought a stolen car onto his car lot again he would kill him. George didn't say anything back, so I knew the guy must have been serious as he never let anyone talk to him like that. The man told George that the police were looking for this car as it had been used in a robbery. We quickly found out where the guy was that sold it to Adam. George had no involvement in the purchase, but wanted to be involved. Reggie, George and I went to the man's house and we were surprised when George pushed him out of the doorway and walked straight into his kitchen. George told him that if we didn't get the money back we would take everything he owned. The man was scared but told us he'd bought the car from someone else and took us around to that guy's house.

We were close to finding the initial buyer but came to a dead end. I realised that I was best off asking Jerry to sell the car. He owned half of it and didn't know about it being stolen and sought by the police. I told him that I didn't want it. If he could scrape together £50 and sell it on he could take it. It took him a couple of days, but he managed to off-load it onto his girlfriend's brother. He'd only had it for three days when he was arrested driving it. The pulled him over and charged him with burglary as the car was used in one. Needless to say I acted surprised but he was known to the police. We'd used it to drive to different cities at all hours in the morning partying. He had it for three days and the police pulled him over.

Mum decided for reasons best known to herself that she was moving to a rented house in Beeston. This was a bad decision for the family but again she never seemed to think about that. Verity sensibly refused to move there and stayed in Seacroft. She was only 17, but more responsible and making her own decisions about where she lived as she'd done as an eleven-year-old. Being older, where mum lived affected me less but it did just the same. Gail and Miles were sometimes not attending school and this meant all five of us left school early. The longest we lived anywhere without a break was two-and-a-half years in Wolverhampton.

After the Mondeo, I bought a Proton with George for £300 and we shared it. Of course, I didn't have a driving licence, insurance or tax but I could drive now. I made it a rule to never wear striped jumpers or a hat in the car. I wore glasses so that I looked like a legit driver and I never drove faster than the speed limit. I started seeing a girl called Brenda. George had a wife, so he would stay at home and I would take the car in the evening and he would drive it through the day. I was so far down a road of anti-social behaviour it was like a roller-coaster I didn't know how to get off. One night I went to *Boilerhouse* and then back to Simone's house, a disc jockey I was friendly with. Simone was a lesbian well-known to everyone on the club scene. George was what I'd call a proper criminal and had arranged a commercial burglary for later the next day. As my money was down and I wasn't in work I agreed to help him out. How often did I identify as someone that said yes, especially to people like George? Was it my experiences as a child in care? Was it the identity I'd created by being led down a criminal path in Leeds and Wolverhampton? Was it the time I spent in custody that made me believe I was a hard man or just simply the choices I made? This is not for me to say, even though all the above probably played a part.

It was around 6 am on the Sunday morning when I realised I had to pick-up the car before I met George. The problem was I'd been taking drugs all night and wasn't in any fit state. I just wanted the car so I could get to George in time. While searching for the house I drove past a pub I thought I recognised. With the drugs I'd consumed I misread reverse, backed into some railing and the rear bumper fell off. I knew I had to explain this to George as the car was half his, so I forgot about the party and drove over to his place. He wasn't best pleased and could tell I was off my head on drugs but he had a van to use for a burglary of Wilton carpets from a shop. He knew there was a broken window at the back. It took us an hour to transfer the massive rolls to the van and I was panicking and sweating throughout whilst pretending it wasn't bothering me. We then took them to a garage in Armley where the owners were friends of George. I could tell he was pissed-off with me for crashing the car. This didn't get any better when the garage told us it was a write-off. I did say I would give him his half of the car in cash when we'd sold the carpets.

I'd a taste for driving now even though I still didn't have a licence. I thought I was one step ahead of the police. I used the little money I had left to buy a Cavalier. I'd lived life to the full for several months but now I was broke, back at mum's and my mood was low because the house was horrible, it stank and there was mould in the corners.

Days went by when I would ring George about the carpets. He kept saying the guy was on holiday. I'd a sneaky suspicion he was lying and went to the warehouse on my own. The guy there told me George picked them up the day after we dropped them off. This meant our friendship came to an end and I wasn't surprised. Times like this make you realise who your friends are and I didn't have many. Everyone wanted to be around when I had money. Now I was back to the old penniless Andi and it didn't feel good. Ben, Stewart, Miles and Jennifer had moved on while I was spending time with Jerry, George and Reggie, which made me feel even worse. I decided to sign-on for benefits after finding that the agencies seemed to be keen to take on more and more foreign workers. Maybe I'd taken the work for granted and these people were coming from places where there wasn't that much, so they appreciated having a job and worked extra hard. I didn't feel good going to the Job Centre, but I needed money. I felt like I'd done well not to be following in mum's footsteps but in the end the apple doesn't fall far from the tree!

CHAPTER 15

Addiction

Whilst cleaning the car I turned round and Jerry was walking up the street. 'Our lass kicked me out,' he said. I should have told him to get lost. He'd sold me out for a girl but as I didn't seem to have anyone else I gave him a pass. We continued by reminiscing as if the only reason we didn't share heroin before was because we'd become distracted. We were both down now, no money, no jobs and for some stupid reason we influenced each other to get high. I didn't have a reason to say 'No'. I was unemployed, an ex-smackhead, ex-prisoner and on benefits.

It wasn't long before we managed to get a guy's number and score. We took the bag to my bedroom at the top of the back-to-back house and smoked it. It was as if I'd forgotten all the negatives of being addicted. It took away my low mood and made things seem better. I always loved the process of smoking heroin and I'd missed it. I told myself I wasn't going to get addicted but might use it occasionally.

Reggie had fallen out with his girlfriend as he'd been caught cheating on her. He asked if he could move into the spare bedroom at the top of the house. I was spending time with a girl called Julie but the drug was killing my sex drive and that relationship soon broke down. When we met I probably came across as someone with lots to offer. I had a gold chain, my own car and lots of nice clothes. Now I was broke, my weight dropping and I was lying about drugs. She knew something had changed.

It wasn't long before both Adam and I were lightly addicted again. Jerry always smoked heroin but never seemed to get hooked. He had a decent home to go back to with structure and nice things. Adam and I were stuck in one which seemed to generate problems. We were creating more due to the decisions we were making. They were 'our' decisions, but our family was influencing every one. Everything around me was negative and I was struggling to stay positive when making choices. Mum was still going to bingo and none of us kids was doing anything useful. The family had begun to get a negative reputation in the area and this affected Miles more than anyone as he was being bullied for it.

I managed to get a job at a Gratton warehouse in Morley. It was the first time I'd had the opportunity of a full-time contract. The store was for large goods only and the agency I was with sent along twelve lads including me. The managers told us we'd be set on full-time if we got through the first 13 weeks. Lorries would come with furniture and we had to design the way products were placed in the building for picking which was new and bare when we started. I had experience of this so took the lead role. The managers noticed and disclosed that they were planning on training people for specific functions. I took one of them aside and said, 'I'd like to be the fork-lift truck driver'. Next day the main manager took me into a room with other managers and told me they wanted someone else to drive it. However, he explained that they wanted me to be the quality inspector saying this was more of a qualified role and better paid. They said they could see I'd the ability to manage a team and this would be wasted on the fork-lift truck.

Did I hear them right? A 'manager' did they say? 'Do they know who Andi Brierley is?' I thought. I didn't believe them, to be honest, and decided not to think about it because I wasn't ready for it. Although I used to get work soon after leaving prison, I would tick the box to say 'no criminal record'. I wouldn't disclose my offences unless I was required to produce identification. I only had one picture of myself and that was the one on my prison licence! I would often use this, but if ID wasn't needed I would keep my offending to myself. I figured that if they found out after I'd worked hard for them they wouldn't want to get rid of me, so it was a risk worth taking. Not having ID created issues for getting bank accounts, jobs and other things all the time. I never even had any pictures of myself under 14-years-of-age due to all the moves.

Jerry would often stay at ours. One night when we had work in the morning Reggie and I went to bed and left him and Adam downstairs.

Whilst I was tucked-up asleep, Jerry woke me saying, 'We've got some computers from over the road'. I didn't move and ten minutes later this changed to, 'The police are outside'. They woke-up all four of us and told us a witness had given a statement saying they'd seen two white men. This disqualified Reggie as he was black. The police made it clear that if no-one admitted the burglary they were going to arrest all of us. They told me that Adam's and Jerry's footprints were on a window sill, but they wanted an admission, otherwise they would arrest me. I was fuming as Jerry said he wouldn't admit the offence. I was wanted on warrant for not attending my community service from when we were fighting in town. Adam held his hands up and when Jerry said, 'I'm admitting nothing' I went for him. The officers grabbed me and placed us all under arrest.

We were taken to Bridewell Police Station in Park Street where I gave my name as Dwayne Cheetham. I knew this guy's date of birth and that he didn't get into trouble. I spent 16 hours in the cells before they interviewed me. When they did, I told them I'd no idea where the Playstation they'd found in the living-room came from. I was honest and just said it wasn't there when I went to bed. This might be seen as grassing, but the truth is Adam had already told them it was him that took the items, and Jerry had left me exposed. He didn't give a shit that I was likely to return to prison. He was trying to save himself, so I owed him nothing.

I was sick with withdrawing. I'd some money at home so I just wanted to get out, find some gear and feel better. Sticking Jerry in the frame meant I would do this sooner. I never mentioned that he told me he did the burglary, a step too far and after having to prove I didn't grass in Brinsford I was well-aware people might later access my interview notes. After waiting 24 hours for the police to open the cell door and say, 'The game's up, Andi' I was most surprised when instead they said, 'You're free to leave, Mr Cheetam'. The investigating officer walked me through the station and out of the door. Before I sped off he asked me if I would make a statement about the Playstation not being there when I went to bed. I said yes but that I needed to get some sleep and go to work. I walked-off talking to myself, clenching my fists and hurrying-up. The feeling in my weakened body can't be easily explained. I was rattling so

I got home after buying some gear on the way. I knew now that I was addicted once again. Damn.

I managed to get Adam his first job. He was now on bail and I told him this would help at court. I encouraged him and dropped him off there on my way to work. When I returned home that day mum was sitting at the bottom of the stairs crying. Even though he never admitted it, I knew Adam was injecting so we always had a lock on my bedroom door. He would wake-up early and go straight out to raise money and spend it on injecting which he did before he returned because we would smoke any that was left which must have started to frustrate him. He must have felt used. Mum told me that he'd left the job straightaway and returned home an hour or so after we'd left there. She said that when she came back he'd kicked the locks from the bedroom door and taken everything of value. This meant he wouldn't come home and probably start to associate with hardcore injecting addicts in drug houses. He identified and connected with them, something I never did.

Now I'd nothing to show for the money we had only months earlier I went from being a cool guy with material things and girlfriends to nothing but addiction in weeks. The dilemma I had was that I was working full-time and finding it difficult to lead a double life. Spreading my wage across the week to make sure I didn't rattle was hard. My tolerance levels were high so I needed three to four bags a day to stay well. Adam was better at making money when we needed it but was gone. I'd got past the initial twelve weeks' probation and we had all been given full-time contracts. It should have been a happy time in my life but I was starting to feel depressed. Over the coming months my tolerance level increased further. I started to need more and more heroin just to get through the day. I was having to go to the toilets and cry. I couldn't take the pain, but I couldn't keep disappearing off the job so often.

To make sure I didn't rattle during the working day I would save some heroin from the night before, but it was just enough to get me through the morning. Gratton had started selling small electric bikes for children and I saw this as an opportunity to make extra money. I would put one in my car and take it to the heroin dealer at lunchtime and swap it for drugs. The dealer was often still waiting for his batch, so I would get back to work late. I started throwing a bike a day under the ramp and the managers began to realise someone was taking stuff. Given that they could probably tell my health and wellbeing were deteriorating they told me that they felt I should leave voluntarily. I understood what they meant but it was the last thing I needed because now I'd no way of maintaining my habit. It was such a lost opportunity. I was the one person that stood out to the managers and here I was getting the sack.

Miles was still just 15 and I didn't want to go through my situation alone so I tried to drag my baby brother down with me. I would send him off to Tesco pinching razors. I was completely hooked again and the old selfish Andi was back. I didn't want to risk getting caught myself but I was in desperate need of a fix every day. I loved Miles but my morals were completely out of sync and it made me feel even worse. It's something that I must take responsibility for as the whole family's standard of living deteriorated further. I frequently asked mum for permission to pawn her mobile phone until I received my benefits. She tried to say no but I would persist. I would then have to pay ten per cent interest to get the phone back which made no economic sense, but it met my pressing needs. I was sneaking things out of the house to sell including pictures off the walls and even toiletries. You'd be surprised what you can flog when you need to. We never had much but the curtains were always closed and the house became cold, bare and unrecognisable.

I would often wake-up and Miles would already be back with heroin. I was the biggest influence in his life and this was how I was showing my love for him. Just like I felt I should have been looked after better by adults when I was his age, I should have been doing the same for him. I'd become a horrible adult and it was leading to a life of crime. Because of me he was arrested on multiple charges of shoplifting and, being 'prolific', was sent to Wetherby YOI for two years. It was down to me. Miles had little choice about being involved. So before judging the adults that exposed me to negative behaviour I first need to judge myself.

Even though I was heavily addicted I'd stayed away from burglaries or robberies. Now Adam was gone and with Miles locked-up I'd no choice but to steal from shops to pay for my habit. I would wear a black suit and take aftershaves from upmarket stores. It was the quickest and easiest way I could find to support my habit without getting into more serious trouble. Jerry was still on the scene and working at Louis Vuitton getting good wages but one day neither of us had any money and I was ill. He told me he'd been to Stewart's place earlier that day and he knew Stewart had cash in the house. He persuaded me to go and see if we could get it. Jerry never liked or respected Stewart so this was nothing to him, but Stewart was my friend. I knew it was doubly wrong, yet I allowed Jerry's voice to influence my decision.

We arrived at Stewart's in broad daylight and he wasn't there. Jerry decided to kick his door off, but I was too ill to get involved and didn't want to anyway. He kicked it several times but it wouldn't give way. The bottom was damaged when we gave up and walked away. Later, Stewart rang me and asked if I knew what had happened as someone had told him I'd been there. I denied it of course because I knew it was a deal breaker. Stewart had always been a friend and I let him down in a way that was unforgivable but all I could think about was my next fix. Withdrawing broke me in every sense. I was extremely depressed and neglecting my health and appearance. Heroin addicts walk everywhere and I was no different. I had a small Citroën that I'd bought for £170 but rarely had money for petrol due to prioritising drugs. I was a smackhead who wanted to hide from the world and pretend no-one else existed.

Jerry struggled to hold down his job so we needed a new way of making money. He'd taken a batch of heroin from a local dealer with the intention of selling it. I kind of agreed to go along with this as I needed to find a way of feeding my addiction. I hated committing offences such as shoplifting because I felt embarrassed by it and selling heroin seemed to be the most logical way of making money for a heroin addict because it was one step away from using. It seemed to be low risk, but it also brought lengthy sentences if dealers got caught and I knew all too well what the consequences could be. Jerry used his contacts and I sold my half of the heroin quickly. I took the money back to the dealer but Jerry decided to smoke his half and it wasn't long before this guy was sending threats our way. He only lived two streets away and at one point mum told me there was this big guy outside my house. He was a tough bare knuckle fighter from a travelling family I'd heard all about. I didn't know him personally, but I knew who he was. I told him through the door that I'd paid back my share and he needed to talk to Jerry. He made it clear that he knew where I lived and that I needed to pay-up Apparently, the dealer was using him for protection. 'Get the money or I'll break this door down and your jaw with it,' he said as he walked-off down the street.

Later that week Jerry and I saw the dealer in a doorway. I wasn't scared of him as he was only a small guy. Jerry obviously was because as soon as we recognised him Jerry shot off down the street. I continued to walk past the guy. When he came towards me I just smacked him in the face before he could hit me. One thing I didn't notice was that he had three other lads in his van and when they saw us fighting they jumped-out. The dealer tried to grab me but I managed to run off down an alleyway. They jumped in the van and chased me up and down for 20 minutes. I felt as if everywhere I turned they were right behind me, up one street and down another and I could hear brakes screeching. At one point I ran past a heroin user I knew. He tried to grab me because he probably thought he would get a treat. I pushed him off as I didn't have time to argue. I was absolutely knackered by the time I ran into a back street and jumped over a wall, coming to terms with the fact that if they found me I was in for a beating. I tried to stop breathing so heavily as the steam from my mouth was rising above the wall in the cold. My heart was pounding. I just lay there thinking how I hated life. I could hear the throttle of the van as they drove into each street. I just stayed there as long as I could and prayed they wouldn't find me. After half-an-hour they must have gone and I slowly popped my head over the wall. Walking to the house I watched at every corner and each time I heard an engine my heart dropped. My life had involved drugs, alcohol and violence since I was born. Here I was at 21 and there didn't seem to be an end in sight.

The Citroën was now worse for wear. Driving it when I was wanted by the police was a risk, but so was everything I did at the time. Eventually I was caught using it and taken back to court for breach of my community service and driving without proper documents. Just my luck that Judge Foster was in court that day, the one who'd sentenced me to the community order I'd now breached. She said, 'I gave you a chance although I thought you should have gone to prison. You didn't take it, so I'm sentencing you to 16 weeks' imprisonment'. It meant I would do eight. Not bad I thought as I'd hardly done any of my order because I was out most weekends after they didn't fit the tag correctly!

I was now back on the prison bus but this time heading to Armley Gaol which everyone called 'The Big House'. Being brutally honest, I'd started to think that a prison is just a prison which in some way meant the system was beating me. By the time I got there I was already withdrawing. I felt shocking and this was becoming a recurring thing. Every time I went through this process it was more and more demoralising. Rattling has a way of making you feel utterly worthless. Add to this the fact that I was entering prison and it just stripped away any sense of self-worth. I couldn't blame anyone but myself because my own decisions had led me there. No-one had ever told me what the root causes of my offending were and that I faced all of them as a child. As far as I was concerned everything was completely my fault.

This time I decided I would tell the officers about my addiction. I didn't want to go cold turkey like I had before and hoped they could help me. Had I gone backwards in that I was less willing to hide it now? Was the drug getting the better of me the same way that prison was? I was placed on D-wing for induction. Although I'd been in YOI it was intimidating as most of the cons were a lot bigger and hairier than me. The wings were massive with hundreds of prisoners to each and the whole set-up was different. Not that I let anyone know I was worried, no I put a bounce in my step and pretended I was comfortable.

I noticed the gaol wasn't overly clean and nothing like the tidy YOIs I'd been in (other than the one cell covered in blood at Onley). My cell didn't have hot water or a pillow. In YOI you go to the officers with this kind of problem, so I went to an officer on the landing. He just replied, 'What do you want me to do about it?' I asked how I was meant to sleep without a pillow and he said that if I really wanted one I would have to steal it from someone else. I couldn't believe the prison was almost encouraging crime and the risk of violence but as one of my neighbours looked like a smackhead I nipped into his cell when he went for his food and hoped no-one had seen me take his. Problem solved. The pillow was no real use anyway as I wasn't sleeping due to leg pains, back pains, headaches and stomach cramps. The prison doctor issued me with DFs, tablets that reduce the pain slightly but don't really help you to sleep. I was in prison clothes, the worst I'd worn over the years. I knew some people on the wing but one thing stood out. Instead of being surrounded by young lads in stylish clothes who seemed to think they were the next Charles Bronson, I was surrounded by drug addicts and no hopers. Life and prison was grinding all optimism out of these men.

Eventually I was moved to B-wing on the top landing, known as Breezy B because there was a draft and the heating pipes didn't work. Even when you closed the window shutters it felt cold. Fortunately, it was nearly mid-spring but I can't imagine what it must've been like in winter. I know prison is not supposed to provide comforts as it's meant to teach inmates a lesson but the issue for me was that I didn't iden-tify as a criminal. I was more a fool that kept finding his way to prison because I couldn't control my own life choices. Most inmates said they would get out and commit crime, but I always knew I'd work, yet here I was. 'Am I a criminal?' I would ask myself. 'Society thinks I am but it doesn't feel like it'.

Armley is a prison like those you see on TV with landings, metal doors and mesh between the floors to stop people falling, throwing each other all the way down or committing suicide. YOI does prepare kids for adult prison but it is still a completely different ball game. I was padded-up with an inmate described as a buddy meaning a prisoner trusted to spend time with other prisoners finding it hard inside. Like a prison Samaritan. He was trusted enough to have his cell door open all day. I didn't intend to leave anyway and it was not as if I desired to wander around. The screws told me I'd be moved when a cell became available. Moves hap-pened a lot and it pisses you off when you feel settled but I was starting to feel a bit better and the DFs played a big part in this.

When we were sent out to the exercise yard I saw Clanger. Remember my old friend from Doncaster? I wasn't entirely surprised until he told me how long he was out. He was released after doing his three-and-a-half years only to be recalled and returned to Armley within days. He told me he was caught doing a ram-raid. He wanted me to believe that his friends told him he didn't need to go with them. That they would do the crime and 'take care' of him, but he'd wanted to be involved. This was him justifying the fact that he'd been plain stupid. Then who was I to judge? I was a smackhead doing my third gaol term. He was a good kid but had some real issues. He got something from everyone in gaol knowing who he was. Yet he clearly had nothing going for him outside. I met quite a few people like him. I admired them in the beginning, but was starting to see it was all false. The life they spoke about sounded entertaining compared to my working life. However, I started to think that if their lives were so exciting why were they always in gaol? There were a fair number of east Leeds lads in Armley and they walked around together. I didn't really have any allies so I went with that group. You're not too picky when you're desperate to feel safe. It was weird listening to the same old stories these guys were telling.

An officer came to my cell later and said it was time for me to go down-stairs. He told me where to and my pad-mate said, 'That's Royston's cell'. He took me outside on the landing and said, 'Look down there, that's your new pad-mate'. Even from three stories up I could see it was a large guy with dreadlocks. The sheer size of the man sent shivers down my spine. It was almost like a comedy as I swallowed my spit and said, 'He looks like Predator'. 'Rather you than me,' my now ex-pad-mate replied as he walked-off laughing to himself. 'Prick,' I said, under my breath.

When I got there Royston wasn't in the cell. 'He's at gym,' the screw said, as he shut the door. 'Probably eating the weights,' I mumbled to myself. One bed was made up and one wasn't but I thought I'd wait for him to come back before I lay down. I sat on the chair for what seemed like hours but it can't have been. When the door opened and Royston came in he stood for a moment with a look of disappointment on his face. 'Just say something, you big bear,' is what came into my mind. He then asked, 'How long you been in'. When I told him two weeks he went into his drawers and took out tobacco and shower creams for me. I asked him why and he said, 'You're new in and you're going to need them. This way you won't want to steal from me, so stay out of my things'. I certainly wouldn't be stealing from him! It turned out within a few moments that Royston was an easy going man. He made it clear he would much rather be in a cell with a white kid he didn't know than a black kid from what he called his ghetto. His reasoning was that black kids would know him and assume that he should look after them. I later found out that he was a property developer who'd lived in London before moving north. He was well-respected by most inmates and screws and his gaol time seemed to be as easy as anyone's.

Out on the exercise yard I found that Clanger had managed to get hold of some cannabis and he asked me if I wanted some. By this point the aches and pains had almost gone but I was still not sleeping all night after three weeks so when he asked me I said yes. I did say that I wasn't sure if Royston would appreciate me smoking in the cell. Clanger's response was, 'Stuff Royston, if he starts we'll just rush him'. Rush him meant several lads running into his cell with weapons and beating him up, a gaol term that you would rarely hear outside of prison as with most gaol language.

During my time with Royston I learnt a lot as he was an influential person. He offered me a job which I turned down and he told me that I needed to think bigger if I was to 'make it'. His view was that I needed to get into property and working for him I could make enough money to do it. I just thought that he'd be like Malcolm and take advantage of me. He didn't know about my heroin use and I didn't tell him. I wasn't sleeping but I didn't make him aware of this, so I would just lie there staring into space all night. He had three visiting orders per month. However, he had several women coming to see him, which was his biggest dilemma. One was his baby's mother, one was a Russian girl and the other two were also both foreign. He had pictures of them and they were all amazingly good looking. Even though he was in prison this guy's life was better than what most people had. He had co-accuseds on other wings and they would come to the window to talk. I would listen as he chatted about getting a Ferrari when he was released. He'd been sentenced to five years on gun charges. Some of his co-accused were sentenced to ten to 15 years for drug offences. Not long after I was released I saw in the newspaper that he was sent back to court because the Crown Prosecution Service had appealed against his 'over-lenient' sentence. The court increased it to nine years after agreeing he was the ringleader. I know this would have hurt him as he wanted to get back to his daughter.

By the time my eight weeks were up and it was time for my release, I could tell I'd put weight on. Although I was still not sleeping through the night I was getting at least a some sleep. Being released from Armley was a little strange as it is in the centre of Leeds, so I got my £40 leaving grant and off I went. By then Adam had been locked-up and released again. We didn't fall out as he looked a little healthier and who was I to judge given the things I'd done for drugs. The flipside was that he and Jerry were still taking heroin, so when they told me they had some upstairs I was too weak to say no. Eight weeks was simply not long enough to prevent me from starting all over again. I was just a recovering addict and I hadn't yet fully completed my withdrawals. Let's face it, I didn't stop taking heroin through choice. Walking into the two of them taking it was the worst possible situation for me to be released into.

I was now back to square one though I didn't look like a smackhead because prison meant I'd got healthier. I'd known how bad I looked which is why I avoided contact with everyone. Now I was looking better I felt more comfortable going meeting people. I wanted to see Jennifer and the girls to see how they were doing. One of her friends had a new boyfriend. Brendan was a skinny, bald, mixed-race lad from Bradford and we knew each other from clubbing. We instantly hit it off as like me he loved to party and, as I was feeling good again, I wanted to get back into that life and be my old self. I was looking for something in life and although partying wasn't positive it was better than the heroin lifestyle.

One Sunday a friend of Jennifer's held a party at her house. Although I didn't want to take Adam I felt guilty as Jerry and I were going so I allowed him to go with us. Me and Adam were never close unless I was taking heroin a lot, which none of us were but just dabbling occasionally. Jerry and Adam were close which tended to pull us back together. Adam didn't stay at the party long and left with one of his friends. Brendan came and told me and Jerry he had a drug deal going and wondered if we would accompany him. It all seemed a little strange as the person he was supposed to be meeting kept telling him to go to various places. It soon became apparent that Brendan wanted to buy drugs off this guy to sell. I started to think the guy would know Brendan would have a lump sum on him and probably wanted to rob him. When Brendan told us that we had to stand at a given location, I said, 'No'. I might not have been some big time drug-dealer but I knew when things stank and this certainly did. Brendan was eventually persuaded that he was being lured into a robbery. He was simply a wannabe dealer and quite gullible.

The next day we met Brendan and he told us that he and Lizzy had fallen out as £10 had been stolen from her house. I rang Adam and told him to meet me. He point blank refused to accept that he'd taken the cash, but of course I didn't expect him to admit it. He never admitted anything and was a good liar. I told him that I didn't normally take him around the people I mingled with and this was the reason. When I said 'Who else could have done it?' he made me feel guilty for accusing him.

Lizzy and Jennifer had a barbecue and Brendan took the blame for the money going missing. We all went to it with the idea that we'd just eat and leave, and Adam wouldn't go inside the house. I'd got another job in a warehouse due to start next morning so I couldn't stay. The problem was that although all the girls were there so was a lad called Scott who was with Lizzy's sister. He was ginger haired and skinny and didn't know any of us. The combination of Brendan, Jerry, Adam, Scott and another lad called Jamie who was a friend of Adam's wasn't good. It felt like they were whispering in the kitchen the whole time but, as always, I spent it with the girls. I'd no idea what they were saying and wasn't that interested. It turns out they were discussing how to make some money. I think both Jerry and Brendan wanted to be criminals. They thought Adam and I were good ones as we'd been to prison. This was far from the truth as we were really dysfunctional young men after constant exposure to adversity. I'd go even further and say if someone wanted to learn about crime we were the last people to ask.

Somehow the conversation went further. I was just ignoring them and when Brendan approached me with an idea I shrugged it off. Although I still took heroin occasionally, I'd done what I always did and got a job. I said, 'I'm at work in the morning so I'm off home'. They took no notice and kept planning their money-making scheme. They agreed that when the beer ran out they'd get more. The problem was they didn't have any money. Scott, Brendan, Adam, Jerry and Jamie got straight into the car leaving me standing on the grass bank. It was full so I said, 'Tell you what, you boys go do what you're doing and I'll wait here'. It was at this point Brendan said, 'No way'. Brendan didn't like Jamie and as he was only 17 he threw him out of the back seat saying to me, 'Get in'. Every inch of my body told me not to. Even aged 22 I wasn't strong enough to say 'No'. I should have done because I knew it wasn't going to end well and I didn't really know what their plans were anyway. I wanted to go home ready for work. I don't think I would have got into the car if I hadn't just come out of prison and was partly back on heroin. The expectation the lads placed on me more than anything else was far too much to shake off. They were looking to me as their leader and I crumbled under the pressure. If I'd been stronger, I would have told them I didn't know anything about crime. All my prison sentences were down to bad choices and here I was faced with another. There is no doubt that we make our own choices, but it seems that they are based on our individual experiences and environments. I was craving to be re-accepted after being stripped of self-confidence, so I was vulnerable. Drugs, crime and my childhood affected me in these pivotal moments and I was failing yet again.

The car was full with five young lads who'd all been drinking so adrenaline levels were high. Scott drove to a retail park near Batley. Brendan got out and tried to smash a shop window with a shopping trolley. Brendan and Adam then tried to kick one of the windows in but when that failed they got back in the car and we drove off. I thought, 'This isn't a crime, it's a joke' but I didn't know how to get myself out of it.

Next Scott reversed into the glass door of a Co-op store. It didn't make sense and they had no a plan. It was just a case of wanting to cause chaos. It made me feel stupid knowing I was involved yet I was still not saying what they were doing was daft and walking away. All I was thinking was, 'Let them do what they are doing and then they can drop me off at home for work'. I didn't believe for one minute that they were really going to raid a shop. Scott then drove the car forwards, then reversed it at speed into the shop doorway catching and making a mess of the shop front. Adrenaline kicked in all round as the alarm went off. After Scott drove the car forward again we all ran into the store where it was difficult to see given the window shutters were down. Adam and I ran straight to a counter and grabbed two bags. I got him to hold them open whilst I filled them with bottles of spirits and cigarettes. Back in the car I noticed that others were eating ice-creams. They were laughing saying, 'We just went straight to the fridge'. This was all their idea but it just seemed like a fun thing to them. This was soon going to change.

Our white car wasn't hard to spot on the way home and before long a police car passed us on the duel carriageway going in the other direction. It immediately turned round and followed us. I started to worry as Scott had been drinking and he clearly didn't know where he was going. We were swerving in between parked cars and Scott was screaming, 'Where shall I go?' I was panicking by this point and so was everyone else. How Scott didn't hit another car I'll never know. He eventually managed to lose the police and not knowing where to head drove onto a rugby field. To make things worse it was surrounded by the rail that stops fans getting onto the pitch. The police were right behind us, so we got out and ran, falling over because we couldn't see the holes in the pitch. We picked ourselves up, but Jerry fell down and stayed where he was. The rest of us hid in a garden and hoped to stay there until things calmed down. We told each other to be quite but we were breathing heavily and uncontrollably. After a couple of minutes, a light came on in the house. We automatically made a run for it. The police helicopter was out by now which made us worry more. We ran into a main road, which probably wasn't the best idea, but with adrenaline still pumping we just followed whoever was in front. Clever ideas were few and far between.

The helicopter came right above us and seconds later we were surrounded by the police. We tried to stop and blend in with people out clubbing. This didn't work for a second as we were covered in mud. The police shouted, 'Stop lads and lean against the wall'. We were seconds away from *Frontier* nightclub which had just closed for the night. The clubbers stood watching and at least got some entertainment on their way home. We were all knackered and couldn't have run any more if we'd tried. The police went down the line and asked each of us our names and I became frustrated and said, 'I've forgotten with all the running around'.

The truth is I was furious with myself and this was how it came out. All of us had mud on our faces and grass on our clothes so it wasn't difficult for them to know we were the lads they'd chased across the field. The officer got right in my face and said, 'I'll only ask you one more time lad!' This just made me angry, so I told him 'Fuck right off'. He grabbed me with his mate and threw me in the back of one of the vans. I landed in a way that nearly snapped my neck. It's not that I wanted to be rude. I didn't really know what to do as I'd messed-up real bad.

We were taken to Dewsbury Police Station where we were interviewed and all went 'No comment'. We'd agreed this as we didn't have an alibi or version of events that would explain being in Batley. We were kept in the cells for 24 hours and the police took our clothes for forensic testing and collected fresh ones from our homes. Why hadn't my last prison sentence helped me? Although I'd put weight on, my addiction, lack of self-confidence and identity were still crippling me. Four weeks inside simply wasn't long enough. We were released on bail in the early hours pending enquiries. Courts often give you credit at sentence for an early guilty plea, but when you get arrested your focus is on getting out of the cells not what sentence you might get and going no comment often gets you bail. Professionals say it's not taking responsibility, but I think it's self-protection. If we took responsibility we often wouldn't be in a bad situation to begin with, so talk about stating the bleeding obvious.

The police collected my trainers for me but they couldn't for Adam due to him being homeless. He was sent out onto the streets in some foam slippers the police gave him which we naturally thought was hilarious. None of us had any money and it was around 3 am. It meant we had to walk the eight miles back to Beeston. The slippers lasted five minute so Adam went barefoot and this kept us entertained all the way home. We were constantly talking about how we would get out of the mess we were in. We didn't know what evidence they had yet so we pretended they didn't have any. It took us around three hours to get back and when we did Jamie was at the house. He must have felt relieved that he was thrown out of the car earlier even though he wasn't happy at the time. Jerry was also there and he told us that he just fell down and had stayed hidden by the changing rooms. He said the police spent a lot of time looking but couldn't find him. He could fall in shit and still smell of roses. I on the other hand seemed to get caught every time. There was a message in this for me somewhere. The question was, would I ever hear it?

As I missed work I told them I'd been robbed of my mobile phone. Stretching the truth I said I'd spent the night at the police station which is why I didn't get in touch. They accepted my reason and I started work the following morning. I bet they wouldn't have allowed me to start if I'd said, 'I attempted a ram-raid last night'. It wasn't a coordinated crime which the courts would no doubt think it was. It was just more evidence of the fact that, although I didn't consider myself stupid, I didn't know how to function in society. I always got jobs and yet gravitated towards negative peers and self-sabotaged any positive progress.

When I went to the police station to answer my bail I was charged with aggravated taking of a vehicle without consent (TWOC) and burglary. I was in an Excel jumper (the company I was working for) and the police asked why. I told them that once I'd signed for bail I had to get to work. They laughed and said, 'It's not very often we came across people doing ram-raids that hold down jobs'. My obvious reply was that I was never involved in any ram-raid. I was told that there was no forensic evidence of me being inside the store; however, I had glass from the shop on my tracksuit bottoms.

A few weeks later, Adam went further off the rails and was injecting again. He went off to live homeless which is what he did when things got on top of him. I couldn't inject and certainly couldn't live on the streets. I spent time with heroin addicts when I was scoring gear but then I would leave because I didn't feel like them. Adam would build relationships and do what they did. I always felt they were different to me as they would live in smack dens and inject. I'd destroyed mum's house, selling everything, but I couldn't have lived in the places I'd go to buy drugs. They were disgusting. No matter how much I was rattling I would go home to take my drugs even if it meant doing it alone.

It wasn't long before Adam offended again and found himself in custody on remand. There was evidence that he was in the Co-op, so he wrote and told me he was willing to plead guilty. He would say I drove a different car to pick up the group. That the glass found on me was in fact from them. This could mean I would only get sentenced for TWOC and not commercial burglary. Scott had been in a car accident and found himself with brain injuries. I don't know what happened as none of us really knew him. It meant that he never faced trial.

My addiction gradually worsened. I lost the job at Excel due to taking time off when I was too ill to go in when I was withdrawing. Miles was supporting me and was strong enough to know his short time in Wetherby YOI was more than enough for him. He didn't want to return to the same lifestyle and this made me proud of him. I had a heart to heart with him. I cried and told him I was ashamed of myself and needed to get my act together. I would wake-up of a morning and as soon as I started to withdraw I would focus on getting money for drugs.

All of my friends and family were now aware that I was taking heroin as I was in bad health. My teeth weren't brushed, my hygiene was disgusting and my hair needed cutting. It wasn't only long, it had enough grease in it to fry chips. I was going to town every day in a suit to steal aftershaves and perfumes. I'd become more sophisticated. I cut down one side of a cereal box and placed it inside a shopping bag. This meant I could put perfume inside it and if I was searched the security man would only see the outside of the box. I would sometimes go to Wakefield or Castleford. The problem was they would see me everyday, which meant they'd automatically follow me. The more I rattled, the more risks I took. The earlier in the day the less likely it was that I would get caught.

Jerry was now unemployed and leaving to go back to his mother's. He was starting to piss me off. I was so addicted I was selling everything I had. He on the other hand wasn't and just smoked drugs with me. I wanted company so that I wasn't alone. He would return home for a few days and get away from the drugs which meant he never became fully-addicted. I think I was jealous that he still looked well and had a nice home with parents that supported him.

One day Jerry and I were out scoring gear. On the way home we passed a large crowd of people and stopped to take a closer look as we noticed the police and ambulance were there. When we got close enough we saw a body on the pavement. We found out it was Ozzy, a young lad we knew on the estate. Apparently he'd been chased down by a gang of

Asian men and they'd beaten him to death. We found out on the news
that he'd also been stabbed. His friends all said they were going to kill
the perpetrators. I watched as his mother tried to get to him but the
ambulance men were attempting to resuscitate him so they wouldn't
let her through and she broke down on the floor. We stayed for a while
but even faced with these events I still needed my fix. I did however feel
that this put things into perspective. I was only talking to him a day
or so before about my charges. Ozzy had said if it was him he wouldn't
plead guilty and would say he stole the tracksuit bottoms off someone
in the street. I couldn't work out if he was serious, but either way I don't
think that would have worked. I knew I was going to custody. I wasn't
quite ready for it yet because I was more concerned about the drugs. I
didn't have anything to lose and, let's face it, I was more than prepared
for prison by this point as I'd already done three sentences.

I'd no choice now but to keep stealing from shops as I was all alone
and I couldn't any longer expect Miles to do it for me. I'd a serious habit
to feed which cost me around £40 a day and this was difficult to keep on
top of. I spent as much time avoiding people that I knew as I did stealing. I hated the fact that by now everyone knew I was a smackhead but
I didn't want people seeing me shoplifting. I have always been a reflec-
tive person and I would often sit in my room and think, 'How did I get
so low?' I asked myself all the time if I could I pull the situation round.
One night before I dropped asleep I was so off my face I sat and talked
to myself. 'What's your future going to look like you loser?' I would also
talk to Miles and tell him that I was just a smackhead. I wanted him
to know he was better than I was as he was strong enough to say no to
drugs, yet here I was dependent on them. 'Sorry I let you down kid,'
I told him. I did take responsibility but I was stuck. Still no-one had
helped me connect my childhood to my adult behaviour.

I was spending time with a girl called Natasha. She had no idea I was
on drugs, but I think she liked the idea that I was on my way to prison.
She would talk about crime and people who'd been there. She was a lovely
girl and had a similar childhood to myself. She was good company. But
because my sex drive was again none existent we would often just talk.
I hated it when she came round because I couldn't get out my tin foil.

I would have to go to the bathroom and smoke there. When I was too high to speak to her I would just say she had to go. She was either very naïve or she knew and chose not to mention it.

Brendan had started spending time with known drug-dealers and I saw little of him. He knew full well I was a junkie. One day mum shouted upstairs that he was there. I was smoking heroin alone and I rushed to put the drugs away before he came into the room with two girls. One was extremely pretty and the other skinny. Brendan had met them in town and had nowhere to take them as he was still living with Lizzy. He asked if he could use Reggie's old room. Reggie had left when Adam stole all his stuff. Reggie met me when I was full of life and slowly he saw my life fall apart. He saw all the stealing and me avoiding him so I could take drugs in the next room. I think he eventually moved back to London. This left a large spare room as Adam was still in prison.

I did what was expected of me and started kissing one of the girls. I picked her up and put her on my bed but it was all wrong and I couldn't do it. By the time Brendan came back from the spare room we were just sitting there staring at the walls. This was more pressure I didn't need. I was stripped of my self-esteem. Where was the confident chap that would approach girls he didn't know? Brendan said, 'Let's bounce' and literally left giggling on the way out. He knew what was going on. The room was stripped of anything of value and didn't smell too great. I knew he would tell everyone and it made me feel ashamed.

What Brendan did was go back to Jennifer and Lizzy and tell them that I was taking smack. Stupidly in return I told them he brought two girls to my place. It probably wasn't the right thing to do but my first line of defence was attack. I point blank denied taking smack as I always did if confronted. I never openly admitted it and why would I? A few weeks later he collected two new robbery charges and was keeping Adam company in Doncaster YOI aged 20 and looking at a long sentence.

I was given a trial date in May 2004. I was 22 by now and had deteriorated to the point that I didn't even recognise myself. I'd done three prison sentences and any bulk I'd put on through the weights sessions was completely gone. I was withdrawn, smelly and although not medically diagnosed I was extremely depressed. Most heroin users can be seen at the doctor's first thing in the morning collecting their doses of morphine. I was that embarrassed that I never told the doctor.

Before my trial I sat the family down. We had a heart a heart and I said I was sorry for all the problems I'd caused. I was straight with them and said, 'I'm going to change my plea to guilty'. I had to change the road I was going down but even with my intention and motivation I couldn't do this alone and needed help. The most ironic element was my view that only the Criminal Justice System could help me. There were services to help I knew but I'd no idea what or who they were. It wasn't just me that needed help, but mum, Gail and Miles too, to deal with the impact of me living with them. Social Care weren't involved enough in our lives which seems strange given the dramas we went through year after year.

I managed to save some benefit money for the night and morning before court. I even had Natasha come around and keep me company right up to the last minute. Jerry also came. I don't think for a moment he cared, he just wanted to see someone go inside. It was horrible and rainy and Jerry and I went to get some gear. While we stood at the phone booth I told him that this was the last time I'd do it. He said, 'I think you will get a long enough sentence to get clean'. Words of wisdom and support as ever! If you spend time with an insensitive, selfish, self-centred person don't expect compassion. It hurt even more that he should have been walking into court that day with me. We went back to the house and had one last bag to mark a new beginning. I'll never forget how good it tasted. I cherished every draw. I kept skipping and telling Jerry he could buy more which led to an argument.

CHAPTER 16

Here We Go Again!

Mum, Gail and Miles came to court. Before I went in I hugged them and said, 'Now we're going to prison and no drugs are in the house this is a fresh start for all of us'. Our family home had become a place with nothing of value and the curtains were shut all the time in case the police came. Drugs had taken a family with not much and destroyed the little self-confidence it had, which was well short of most. They promised me they would stop pawning their belongings and mum would stop playing bingo. It was a sad but beautiful moment with each of us accepting that we'd made mistakes but that this had now ended. I for one meant every word. I knew something better lay ahead if I took responsibility.

In the courtroom I was taken behind the glass screen where Adam and Brendan sat waiting. As I'd changed my plea to guilty and because they'd done so earlier there was no need for a trial. It meant we could get on with being sentenced. All the professionals had to do was explain the offences to the judge. It was difficult to listen to the prosecutor who made it sound as if we were hardened criminals executing an organized plan. We were asked to stand. The judge told us he'd no alternative but to send us to custody. He sentenced Adam first. He said, 'You're a prolific offender and a nuisance to society. You sir have accumulated over 50 convictions leading to over seven prison sentences'. He handed him 18 months. Taking account of remission and the two months he'd spent on remand he would be out in seven. The sentence was made up of twelve months for commercial burglary and six for taking a car without the owner's consent (TWOC). The judge then sentenced Brendan and gave him the same. However, he'd also picked-up two robbery charges, so he was given a further 18 months for those. This meant he would serve three-years altogether less time off. He was pleased as like me when I went to Brinsford everyone had said he was looking at five to six years.

The judge then asked me to stand. He said that although I'd entered a guilty plea at court I'd wasted everyone's time and money. I should have admitted the offences earlier and then I could have been sentenced at the last hearing. He gave me twelve months for burglary and twelve for TWOC. He wasn't prepared to give me six months off for a timely plea of guilty so I got the full two years plus a two year driving ban. All I listened to though was the length of my sentence and I didn't really take in anything about the ban which affected me later. 'Here we go again,' I thought, 'About to face the prison system and I must try to stay out a fourth time. Can I do something about it?'

We were taken down and placed in a cell. Adam and Brendan took their tops off and showed me how big they'd got since being banged-up. Brendan was still skinny with a few extra muscles but Adam was enormous. When I unveiled my skeleton-like body they both said in unison, 'You looked knackered, Andi,' and started laughing. If they were trying to make me feel good about myself and my masculinity before I started my sentence they failed miserably. They looked at me with pity in their eyes. I hadn't realised that I looked so bad. They were both put on the same wing in Doncaster as they were still under 21. I was 22, however, and as last time I went back to the horrors of Armley Gaol. Brendan said he would to try get shipped there when he turned 21 which was soon. Adam was in a similar position. Sometimes inmates can request specific locations for special reasons, so it was possible I'd see them again inside.

On the prison van I heard a loud individual shouting about how happy he was that he was on his way to Armley. He was shouting and banging on the windows to the point that the officers threatened to take him back to the court cells. Apparently, he and three other lads on the bus had spent a week in Manchester Prison due to Armley being full. All I was thinking was that I would start withdrawing soon and I was scared.

The induction process was the same as before, however this time I looked as rough as the smackheads so my worry was how I could hide my addiction. I was concerned that people I knew were going to see I looked worse due to the length of time I'd been addicted. I'd been on heroin for three years now. After this sentence it would be three-and-a-half years in custody. They'd decided to kick me out of high school aged 15 and the years since I'd spent in prison or taking heroin. How much of me being a 22-year-old addict led back to my childhood and was there an answer? I had no choice but to tell the staff I was a heroin user because my habit was that bad. It would have been dangerous to try and go cold turkey on my own. I was worried about how bad the rattle would be this time given the amounts I'd been smoking. I'd heard stories of smackheads dying when going cold turkey if they had severe addictions so I wasn't going to risk it.

When I arrived on D-wing I was placed in a cell with an alcoholic. He'd been sentenced to several weeks for smashing an ashtray over his brother's head, or so he said. He didn't smell good and when he spoke the saliva stuck between his lips. Not that I needed to feel worse, but this was absolutely disgusting. I just wanted to get settled so I thought I would get on with it and talk to the poor lad.

When we were released for association, I didn't really know anyone on the wing so I sat by the pool table. I said I was last on and spoke to anyone who wanted to listen. It was at this point that I saw a crowd gathering around my pad-mate asking him questions and taking the piss out of him. I felt for him because he was gangly and well over six feet tall, so stood out, but he was obviously simple-minded. Someone asked him who his pad-mate was and he pointed at me. Great I thought, attention I really need. They shouted, 'Yo, are you in with the big thin lad?' Not exactly the way I wanted to be identified but I replied, 'Yeah. He's in with me'. One of the lads said, 'That pad must smell of roses'. I didn't know if he was referring to me too, but I hadn't the energy to get into conflict.

That night England were playing soccer on TV and I was looking forward to watching it. My pad-mate had his tablets for his alcohol use and went straight to sleep on the top bunk. That would have been great had he not snored like a pig. The thought of breathing in this guy's air was making me feel worse so I placed the blankets over my face, leaving my eyes clear to view the match.

The DFs worked for an hour or so. The rest of the time I lay there begging for the next day to begin as my body was aching. I was sweating but freezing and I couldn't stop thinking about how messed-up my life was. The fact that a smelly stranger was above me snoring his big head off made things worse. I got about 20 minutes sleep all night. As before, days turned to night and then the lights came on, visible through the windows. It felt like a never-ending rollercoaster that you hate but can't get off. I was depressed, poorly and enclosed in a space where I'd no control. I tried to focus on my new beginning when I got out but it felt a million miles away. Had they asked me if I wanted to leave now and return to heroin I would said yes and gone straight back to the gear even though I'd handed myself in to get off it. I knew it and it made me feel weak and I almost accepted defeat before I'd even given it a try.

Eventually the officers opened the cell door and asked us if we wanted to go to the gym. I thought, 'As I'm here and it's not going to change let's get back into it sooner rather than later'. When I'd been released from Deerbolt I'd been able to bench press 90K. I was struggling to press 40K now which was a disgrace. It reinforced what Adam and Brendan had said. Weight and heroin have a funny relationship. You can't see weight disappear, you just watch yourself in the mirror one day and you don't recognise the person looking back.

I managed to get through the session without being sick. As soon as we got back to the wing and they opened the door of my cell the smell hit me in the face. I took the officer by the arm and said, 'If you leave me here for long I'll likely kill this chap'. I didn't mean a word of it, but I knew the system by now. If I said I was going to kill someone they would need to log it and do something about it. There had been recent incidents where prisoners had killed their cell mates. Prisoners find out about these things and use them to scare officers. Maybe I was manipulating the system but I had to use what little power I possessed. 'Go back in and we'll get you to another wing this afternoon,' the screw said. Later he told me to pack my kit as I was going to E-wing. I was happy because E and F were the new ones which meant I wasn't going back to Breezy B. When I arrived on E-wing it was new but still had the same set-up as others in Armley. Three levels in a rectangle with mesh between the levels and hundreds of cells. I was taken to the top floor and my pad-mate there was a chap called Nipper. A tall, older man with a bald head who asked me straightaway if I was getting DFs. He seemed happy when I said yes. In fact, he welcomed me with a coffee and a roll-up, so I instantly felt at ease. I knew we'd get along but also kind of knew straightaway that he wasn't to be trusted. He was no Royston from B-wing, let's say, but a typical smackhead. Someone who is friendly but at the same time you know will take advantage if they get half-a-chance.

Some people in prison have no intention of getting off the heroin and try to get DFs whenever they can to tide them over. This never happened in YOI because not many of the inmates were on heroin, but in adult prisons lots of the population were addicts. This explains the difference between young lads in YOIs being full of life and criminal aspiration like Clanger was and the older prisoners that have failed time-and-time again, lost family members, realised where they are in life and virtually given up. I wasn't there yet but worried it could be me in the future.

Nipper had a stereo and liked baseline music so I guess this was as good as it got in an adult prison. He was around 35 but acted ten years younger. When I was let out for exercise, I found that there were a few lads I knew of such as Jimmy Johnson and Sam Price, whose names I'd heard many times. Jimmy was a big mixed-race kid and we'd met at lots of parties. We didn't know each other well but had mutual friends so that was where I would focus my energies as he'd been in for a while. The problem was that I didn't want these guys to know I was taking heroin as it would affect how they viewed me. I wanted the right reputation and being known as a smackhead wouldn't get me that.

It was a hot summer's day and I walked around talking to the lads I knew like I was on top of the world. This wasn't easy as my stomach was churning with the fresh air. I was putting on a front when all I wanted to do was lie down on my bed. I was so glad when the officers blew their whistles to make us aware exercise was over and as soon as they closed my door behind me I ran to the toilet and threw-up everything I'd eaten. Nipper made me a coffee. He'd stayed behind and told me he didn't like mingling on the yard as there were often fights and he avoided the youngest lads which was great for me. He knew I was taking DFs and I'd rather he didn't have chance to tell anyone. I told him that we could sell them. I thought the quicker I got the drugs out of my system the better. Nipper was still taking them and Subutex as well whenever he could obtain them and had been inside for a year. I didn't want to be in his position. He did all the running and I just wanted tobacco and shower gels in exchange. DFs were worth quite a lot in prison as people like Nipper were everywhere, still with addictions through the tablets the doctors provided them with and the heroin that somehow and inexplicably got onto the wings now and then. The price was high and people would get into serious debt. Not a good advertisement for prisons rehabilitating addicts but how do you stop someone that refuses to take opportunities? I was ready to stop but these guys seemed content with the lives they'd created. Those like Nipper seemed to like the hustle and bustle of the lifestyle just as much the drugs.

When I went down for dinner I saw a mixed-race kid who I knew was the father of Tara's baby. He spotted me but we didn't greet each other as we weren't quite sure. On one occasion he was beating her up and we nearly ended-up fighting when I tried to protect her. He'd walked into a pub when I was asking her to give me a chance after my last sentence. She just sat there looking me over because she liked gangster-types and I didn't fit the bill. Pete walked in as I was trying to tell her how I felt and slapped her round the head. He didn't know what I was doing with her but must have been jealous. I hoped he didn't kick-off in here.

That evening I was let out for gym and heard someone shout me over to their cell. When I looked at the name on the door I knew it was him. We had a discussion and there didn't seem to be an issue, so it seemed all was good. At the gym I worked-out with a guy called Roger. He had a good physique but was about the same size as me so we exercised together. I guessed he was a heroin user so asked him and he said he used everything but mainly crack. He was bald and looked like he'd done a few years inside. He had gaol tattoos all over his forearms and knew the system inside out.

I was two weeks into my sentence before I got a decent night's sleep. The aches and pains were horrific for the first few weeks but I managed to get my tablets daily and sell half, but those I took did help. This meant I could buy the things I needed and hide my habit. The tablets were handed out in the morning before inmates were unlocked, so I managed to get them to Nipper and no-one saw me. I collected shower gels, tobacco and other bits and bobs in exchange. I was slowly starting to feel better, so it seemed like a good decision.

I spent quite a bit of time with Pete when we were on the exercise yard. He would come and spend time with other Leeds lads even though he was from Bradford. He'd lived in Leeds with Tara before he was locked-up and he was planning on returning there. He was forever trying to get information from me about her. I knew she was seeing another lad but I didn't tell him and I certainly didn't mention that I'd always had feelings for her going back a long time before he arrived on the scene. The truth was she and I had moved on, so he didn't need to know that, but it made me feel uncomfortable. Pete's pad-mate was shipped-out and he asked me if I wanted join him. I think it was because he felt he would find out more about her, but I thought it would be a good move anyway as he was well-respected. Apparently, she then asked him why he was in a cell with me saying I was nothing but a smackhead. This hurt when he told me. I knew we weren't going to get back together but I felt it in my stomach when the words left his mouth. I hated the fact that girls knew I'd been taking heroin. I refused to admit it to Pete. Instead I said I was taking crack as he'd also done as that was a little more respectable. Something I'd quickly learnt from Roger. Pete had a gambling habit and I know I've no room to talk given my addiction but he would often sit and watch horse racing on Channel 4. I just couldn't get my head around it. We were in gaol, not in William Hill's and even though he couldn't gamble in prison he got something from watching the races.

I stopped having aches and pains but I still wasn't sleeping regularly four weeks in. I felt this was the worst rattle I'd had, but I felt the same every time I came into prison. The frustrating thing with Nipper was that he'd been able to keep the TV on because he understood my situation. I was hiding it from Pete, so I was back to just waiting for the morning light to come flooding through the window. When it did I would know that we were at least close to company. It wasn't the worst part of the rattle, the physical side and pains were, but it made me feel extremely lonely. It wasn't too bad when you were open with your pad-mate but when you were hiding it you felt isolated. Pete requested to be sent to a prison in Preston that dealt with prisoners in a restorative and thera-peutic way. Apparently, the inmates were responsible for each other. If they were caught taking drugs they would instantly get shipped-out to an ordinary prison location. Eventually he was successful. When you lose a pad-mate it's always a worry because you never know who will walk through the door next.

A lad from Beeston who I knew came onto the wing so we asked if he could come into my cell. It was a mistake as he was strange, so I obvi-ously didn't know him that well. He told more lies than I could keep up with. He constantly contradicted himself. One minute he had two children and the next he had five. He made out he was the best criminal on the streets of Leeds. Lots of people knew him and they didn't give me that impression. After a few days I'd had more than enough of his bullshit. He also had a lad on F-wing sending threats over because he was saying things he shouldn't have. He tried to convince me they were true, but I didn't care. I didn't want to be involved. The move happened within days of the threats.

My next pad-mate was Dick from downstairs and we got along well. He was from Halton Moor and knew a lot of people I did from when I lived there. I was able to use the constant moving to good purpose in building relationships. I always knew someone from an estate, so I would drop their name in conversation. Why not, the way mum raised us was so unconventional I guess I deserved something from the experience. Dick was skinny and quite open about the fact that he would take any drug at all so he had me worried.

Dick got into an argument with a screw and lost his rights to the TV. The officers asked me if I would give-up mine for him and I point blank said, 'No' so he had to leave. Remember Roger Ambler who was the same size as me when he came in? Well he was 13 stone of solid muscle now. When he found out I was in a cell on my own he jumped in with me. Now the funny thing with Roger was that he had always taken steroids and he told me many stories about how flash his life was on the out with money and cars. I was naïve enough to believe him, partly due to his size, but he wasn't that size when he came in. We worked-out together and he was lifting 130K which was loads for someone our size weighing around twelve-and-a-half stone.

In September, Roger was shipped-out to Lindholme Prison and Dick came back into my cell. The morning Roger went I was on the landing waiting to be taken to education. There was a Jamaican called Noddy and another lad that seemed to be quite strange called Greaser. They were arguing about something and I seemed to be in the middle as they shouted at each other. Having had enough and being still half asleep I stepped back and said, 'If you're going to argue, do it to each other'. Almost as soon as I did so, Greaser smacked me in my eye. Before I'd realised it he flipped on me, punched me several times in the face and the officers had run over and grab him. I'm not sure whether I was more pissed-off at the fact he'd punched me or that I didn't manage to retaliate. It all happened so quickly and I couldn't have seen it coming. All I got from the rest of the lads on the wing was that I'd been chinned by him. He wasn't seen as a lad that should have been able to beat me up. I felt the need to say, 'When I get him, I'll really get him'. I didn't mean this as what I was thinking is, 'I hope I don't run into him again because I can do without the hassle'.

Even though I didn't want to get into any more fights it pissed me off that someone was able to do this to me for no reason. I made a promise to myself not to let it happen again. 'Be quicker next time,' I thought whilst cleaning my face. Violence and crime had been a part of my life from birth and I didn't even know how to protect myself in these situations even after three years in prison. Although I was telling myself to be a prisoner, the truth is I wasn't one. I didn't think he'd hit me but I'd let my guard down and should have known better. People like Greaser and Noddy were always a threat. 'I must be tougher,' I told myself.

One morning when mum came to visit I was in the waiting room. The lad that I mentioned who was being loud on the prison bus was there. He said, 'You're from Beeston aren't you?' When I told him that's where I was living he told me that one of the lads in the room was amongst those that had killed Ozzy. Everyone looked at me as if it was my duty to do something about it. I knew that some of the Beeston lads had been fighting in Doncaster YOI with some of the those they suspected had attacked Ozzy. This is another example of not being strong enough to say no to peer pressure as I approached the lad and asked him, 'Where you from?' He had heard the entire conversation, so I wasn't surprised when he said 'Ilkley'. I liked Ozzy, so it wasn't just peer pressure. Emotions were getting high and the pressure of everyone in the room was intense. I walked over and said, 'If I find out you're from Beeston, I'll become Ozzy's fists'. Don't ask me where this kind of talk came from. I must have been watching too many movies. The truth is I didn't want to do anything about it just to sound tough.

While I was sitting with mum I saw the lad's visitors as I had on many occasions, which meant he was lying about Ilkley. I could have just left it at this stage and not mentioned it again. Instead, knowing he feared me, I took the opportunity to rebuild my status in gaol after the Greaser incident. In the holding areas at visiting time there was a camera. Once everyone had come back into the room, I told the lad, 'I know your visitors … How can I know them if you're not from Beeston'. He still refused to accept he was from there, so I told him to go into the toilet area where there were no cameras. He just kept saying that I was wrong and that he wasn't who I thought he was, but now I'd control of the situation my adrenaline was pumping. I think in situations like this, at the same time as the tension increases, you get encouraged by others wanting to see a fight. Instead of walking away I got more confident and less humane.

He was pretty much standing by the door which made him feel safe. I felt strong and after Greaser taking that away from me this felt good. In one swift move I darted across the room and punched him a few times. He covered his head and ran past me and out of the room towards the staff. I was bundled to the middle of the room by those trying to protect me and they quickly surrounded me. This was the perfect way for me to get some pride back and I now felt like a celebrity.

The screws came with the lad and he blatantly pointed me out to them. As soon as he did so the atmosphere changed. I think everyone wanted to hit him as this broke prison rules. The screws shouted, 'Come on everyone'. One of the officers whispered to me that I was lucky as the camera wasn't working. When I returned to the wing I made everyone aware. Not directly, but by making sure they'd ask what was wrong with my hand as it had swollen-up. This was, of course, because I'd been feeling insecure in an environment that only placed value on violence and masculinity. Really, all I'd done was pick on a young man that I knew didn't want to fight me. I guess he was involved in a bullying incident himself. Although I did it to rebuild my reputation, I also liked Ozzy and therefore it was a successful event for me at that time.

Two weeks later I was returning from the gym and while I was waiting on the landing the same lad walked-out. When I saw him I told him to turn around and face the wall because I didn't want to hit him again. At this point an Asian guy that must have weighed 16 stone and was built like The Incredible Hulk went over to him, then to me, and got in my face. I stood straight up to him as he said, 'If you have anything to say, say it to me'. I replied, 'What has it got to do with you, you big muppet, I'll chew your face off'. A lad I knew got between us and I was thinking, 'Please stay there'. The last thing I wanted was for this meathead to hit me like Greaser had since he would have taken my head off. I'm also sure you wouldn't have been able to tell I was scared given I was making out I was ready to fight him. But I was shaking inside. His biceps were the size of my thighs. The situation calmed down as the officers came to take us back to the wing. I found out he was in for serious violence. The funny thing is that I saw him several days later at the gym and approached him and asked why he got involved. He said that he'd asked the lad why I was telling him to face the wall and he'd told him I was racist. When I told him what the lad was in for he said, 'I won't be getting involved next time'. We shook hands and that was that.

Adam had at this point been on F-wing for several weeks and trying to get a move to E-wing where I was. Eventually he did and it felt strange to be with my brother in prison again. The only time this had happened before was in Brinsford and I hardly saw him there. E and F-wings were connected and while we were walking around the exercise yard someone shouted out of the window, 'Brierley, you're fucking dead'. Within seconds Johnson and the rest of the group started shouting, 'Are you mad, who are you?' which meant I'd achieved a good status in prison. The lad then explained and said that Adam had taken his tobacco before he was moved over. The group of lads I was with just said, 'So what, there's nothing you can do so get your heads down'. I can remember seeing the look on Adam's face as it must have felt like he was being protected, a unique experience for him. The difference between me and Adam was that he drifted towards the homeless and the junkies. I would spend time with respected lads. I did this for good reason and Adam had just seen it.

Prisoners would speak about burglaries, robberies and car crime, talk about spending time together on the out at clubs and taking enormous amounts of drugs. I on the other hand didn't live a glamorous life on the out. If I wasn't taking heroin I was working not committing crime. I think it was picked-up on as one guy said he could imagine me working in the market. He even did an impression of me pushing a wheelbarrow shouting, 'Mind your backs'. I'd learnt not to expose myself as prisoners respected crime not working. I didn't lie or say what was on my mind or that my first stop when I got out would be the recruitment agency as always. The guy said his dad owned second-hand shops and he would put a good word in for me when I got out. There are prisoners that encourage those who want to change, but few and far between.

In October the officers came to my pad and told me to pack my kit as I was being shipped-out to Lindholme. I was ready for it this time. The months had started to drag and it felt like the longest sentence I'd done. All I wanted now was to get out and have another go at a crime free and drug free life. I knew Roger was at Lindholme and Brendan told me he'd also been allocated there. The bus ride felt like a day out and when we arrived I was placed on H-wing which was their induction wing. It also held long-term prisoners and there were some Leeds lads there which I was buzzing about. The first thing I noticed was that H-wing had the same set-up as Armley. However, A to F-wings were spurs. There were ten lads to a spur and the officers just locked the landing at the end, so we could move from cell-to-cell. There were no bars on the windows of this Cat-C prison. Roger sent a message over to me to try and get onto F-wing as this is where he was. I thought he was a good person to have onside. It is always an adjustment, getting used to a new prison, but after being in Brinsford, Onley, Doncaster, Deerbolt, Armley and now Lindholme I thought I'd seen it all. How little did I know!

CHAPTER 17

Sportsperson

I persuaded the officers to get me put on F-wing using my ability to get screws on side without putting myself in jeopardy with the inmates. A lot of the lads saw officers as the enemy and gave them abuse at every turn but it didn't make sense to me. I tried to use my social skills with the officers to make my time in prison better. An officer told me there were two cell spaces going, one of them with Roger, so needless to say I was over the moon when the move was approved. I wasn't kissing bums, just getting what I wanted and needed in a bad situation.

The spurs each had five two-man rooms. Roger told me he could get anything I wanted and that they had lots of gym. He was even bigger by now and I was happy about being padded-up with him. I'd just six months left to put on as much weight as possible. A lot of people say prisoners should have books and not weights. I can't disagree but all I thought about was getting big for my release. Prisons are institutions that seem to promote aggression, violence and bullying. All prisoners tend to think about is how big they can get. I can assure you the main reason is not to be able to work on construction sites on release. It's to gain respect from other inmates and prevent people wanting to fight you. Also to look good when you get out. Most inmates head off down to the Jobcentre on release, so it is understandable.

After tea Roger took me for a walk. It was 6 pm and the middle of November so it was pitch dark outside. The thing I noticed straightaway was that everyone walked around in prison issue jackets with hoods. This meant you couldn't see who they were as they all looked the same. It worried me as people could walk up beside you and you wouldn't know who they were. You could see gangs of lads standing in one place and looking shifty. No screws were around because it was a low category establishment, and I felt unsafe. The wings were on the outside of the yard and inmates could walk on and off it as they pleased. Dodgy dealings were happening right in front of me and fights could happen unnoticed by officers which I thought was dangerous.

Those on our spur seemed to be good lads. At the end of the landing there was a Jamaican guy called Cedric. Remember Noddy who was arguing with Greaser in Armley before he punched me in the face? Well Cedric was his co-accused. Apparently, they were involved in selling most of the crack and heroin that went into Harehills, the area where I spent a lot of my childhood. So they must have made a few quid. Everyone loved Cedric because he'd converted to Islam and would walk around saying, 'Bless up the place', 'Bless up the officers' and 'Bless up the prisoners', making everyone's day go a little better.

Roger gave me an overview of the gaol telling me there were quite a few Nottingham lads there. 'They all think they're black'. From what I could figure out what he meant is that they were loud, boyish and acted streetwise. I adapted well given I could act mature. This transition can be difficult for some, as adult cons don't like loud kids and some lads don't mature quickly enough. Roger told me he and some of the older Bradford lads were sick of the Nottingham guys, that if they kept on they were going to shut them up. He often said stuff like this in Armley but didn't follow through. Yet I did think he could hurt someone.

It wasn't a month after I was transferred to F-wing that I found out Brendan had landed in the closed part of the gaol. On Christmas morning we arranged for him to attend chapel so we could get together and have a chat. He was sent over but instead of chapel we walked around the yard. In the daytime it looked a lot better and you could get a pleasant view of A, B, C, D, E and F-wings. There were ducks all around, walking everywhere. The prisoners were forbidden to touch or play with them. The ducks didn't seem to mind about being in a prison environment and it was quite therapeutic for the inmates.

When the guard shouted for inmates to go back we walked past F-wing and saw a large group of prisoners crowding together. I said 'Bye' to

Brendan and noticed that Roger and some other lads I knew were in the group. Greg and Banjo were two I knew from Chapeltown. They told me that a lad called Flick on their spur had been beaten-up by some Nottingham lads the previous night. As it was Christmas Eve, the Nottingham lads had decided they wanted to play a prank. They told Flick, who was the most vulnerable lad there, to throw a cup of urine over an officer after they rang the bell for attention. Flick refused, so they beat him up and one of them did it instead. The gathering was due to Flick being from Sheffield and, let's face it, this was a South Yorkshire prison. I think the Nottingham lads just pushed their luck too far and the South Yorkshire lads weren't having it. The problem was that the Bradford lads were already at a point of wanting to beat them up too. They had too many enemies and were about to reap the consequences.

Greg, Banjo and I walked onto the landing with no intention of getting involved but not wanting to miss the action. Their cells were on Flick's spur so we all stood in Greg's cell doorway. We wanted to make sure we got an unobstructed view. Whenever anything like this occurred I was always in two minds. Should I leave and make sure I was safe or stay and see what happened? This time I felt comfortable being there as it had nothing to do with me. Two of the Nottingham lads that weren't involved walked past us knowing something was wrong. I didn't blame them for not staying around to find out what.

From the doorway of Greg's cell we could see that the three Nottingham lads were on the spur watching TV. We could also see the group preparing to come onto it. Suddenly, I heard Roger say to Flick, 'You're going first Flick and we're behind you'. On that note, Flick came running onto the spur. The Nottingham lads jumped-up and one of them instantly took out his self-made blade. The rest of the lads came running onto the spur. As Flick got there first, he received a cut down his cheek. He fell to the floor holding his face, screaming. I felt for him as I think they used him as an excuse to show what they could do.

I just stood and watched as a dozen mature men beat up three lads aged between 21 and 24. The three didn't just lay down. For the first few seconds they gave as good as they got, but inevitably the bigger men overwhelmed them. It got to a point where two were holding one and others were punching at will in the face and body. In amongst the chaos, Flick picked himself up off the floor. One of the men asked him, 'Who threw the piss?' Flick, clinching his cheek, pointed to the smallest one. The man told the two men holding him to put him on the floor. He shouted, 'Hold him down,' then picked up the buffer used for cleaning. He was a big man and he struggled it was so heavy. While the lad was held down with his back on the floor and his arms down, the man dropped the buffer on his face. I couldn't look. Just knowing what was about to happen made me feel sick. I heard a thud and everything went quiet.

The men didn't even run away. They just dropped the other two lads that had been beaten and strolled-off. As they did so they told the lads, 'You're in a Yorkshire gaol now'. Greg, Banjo and I just slipped into the cell. We knew it was only a matter of time before the officers arrived. We acted as if we hadn't seen or heard anything. The lads managed to pick themselves up and go to the front office. Their group was quickly shipped-out. Nottingham lads were not easily seen after this and they didn't spend time together in big groups anymore. I can remember thinking it was Christmas and although no-one would admit it they were missing their families. Something always happens in gaol at this time of year.

Over the festive period I was told that in the New Year I could take part in a PASRO course. This was a target of my so-called sentence plan, although I can't remember seeing any plan! PASRO stands for Prisons Against Substance Related Offending. This was my fourth prison term and only now was I being offered a course to tackle my substance misuse. All my offending was related to it. I sold drugs when I'd a heroin habit and fought when intoxicated by drink. My current offence was also whilst drunk. In between I was a heroin addict twice. I'd never committed an imprisonable offence whilst sober. Not once had anyone offered me this type of support until now.

I was also told I could re-sit my Community Sports Leader Award, which made me particularly happy. Firstly, doing the courses would take me through to my release date. I was currently working in the stores, but I hated it partly because Roger worked there and we were spending too much time together. Secondly, I wanted to use one of the certificates I got in custody to obtain a better job when I was out. Mr Bannister in

Deerbolt gave me the idea that I should stop making excuses and ask someone to give me a chance. Was it possible that I could use certificates to make a living in a decent job? Would someone offer me, Andi Brierley, smackhead criminal, a chance to be something more than a warehouse packer? Maybe not but I decided I'd nothing to lose. I had to at least try, otherwise I would be watching people get their heads smashed in when I was 40 and that was the last thing I wanted.

On one of my last days at work in the stores I got into an argument with Roger. He was becoming frustrated with me and this meant he would shout at me. He had a short temper due to using steroids over the years. The heroin and crack cocaine and whatever else he'd taken didn't help him to stay calm either. I'd taken these drugs, but I wasn't like him, so it was more the steroids he'd taken than anything else I guess. He treated me a bit like a little brother. This made him think it was acceptable to boss me around. If I said anything back he would shout and intimidate me. Let's face it, he was almost ten years older and at least two stone heavier. His strength couldn't be disputed, not by me anyway. It probably made it worse that he hadn't had any heroin for a while. At this point he was still smoking with his friends from Bradford, but I was only taking the drug when he brought some back.

He shouted at me in front of the lads at the stores. Although I was pissed-off I just went to the area at the back. They all came there because we had a delivery of prison clothes. I jumped into the van to unload. Roger then said, 'Get out you little prick, I'm unloading'. I'd taken just about as much as I was willing to as he was making me look like a child. I calmly said, 'Look, if you think you can take me out Roger crack on. Believe me when I tell you it won't be as easy as you think. Get on with it if you want and I'll give you a run for your money'. It went quiet. No-one said anything for about 30 seconds until Roger broke the silence with, 'Fuck me Andi, what you on about, you're like my brother so why would we fight'. Then he said, 'Sorry lad, I don't know when I'm doing it'. I felt quite proud of myself as I'd shown everyone in the stores that I was willing to fight if I needed to. It was an impulsive response due to frustration. I was still shaking an hour afterwards. The funny thing is that even though Roger made out he was a big man and could fight, I don't think that's so. I remembered the skinny lad that came into Armley at the same time as I did. Putting muscle around your bones can make you more confident, however it doesn't make someone more able to inflict pain on others. In my experience tough people tend to be those that don't mind hurting other people, They do exist. Cyclops and Jeremiah were certainly two. If, like me, you're conscious of hurting others, you'll struggle to be tough, think too much about the consequences. Looking at the violence I was involved in it would be easy to think I was tough but I think I just lived in a tough world and that's how it taught me to act.

I began the PASRO course and it was lengthy and intensive. I couldn't wait to get on with it as it would give me something different to do, but I found some of the information difficult to take in. I felt patronised by the two young, educated women delivering it who seemed to prioritise their research findings over my personal experiences. They certainly knew what they were talking about when it came to their field. The problem was they struggled to get it across to those like me. I knew as well as anyone in that room that they'd faced nothing like I had or many of the other people there. It was as if we'd something wrong with us and they were going to fix it if we listened to their point of view.

I've always liked a debate and I wanted them to acknowledge they didn't know what it felt like to tread in my shoes. They said I was try-ing to justify my actions and avoid taking responsibility. Ironic, as all I did was to try and obtain their personal views, but they avoided giving them. It felt like they were saying that if we embraced what they said we wouldn't re-offend. Although in some ways this maybe right, it failed to take account of environmental factors. I couldn't do much about Gav being with my brother smoking heroin in my house when I was last released from prison. Nor could they explain how to change the view I had due to a home around negative adults and peers rather than positive ones. They didn't once ask about my childhood.

Nowadays I understand that a lot of the information on that course was good. However, I still believe that tutors need to open their ears and listen. Prisoners have genuine experience and I believe listening and learning can make course leaders better practitioners. I challenged them regularly and, as a result, they referred me to a separate Thinking

Skills course to straighten me out. I was trying to get them to help me overcome my personal hurdles because I was reflecting. They felt that as I was being disruptive. That I believe is one mistake that professionals make. If you don't play to their tune and say what they want to hear they think you have problems. I was sincerely trying to make sense of the situation I was in which was a positive thing, surely? Had they allowed themselves to listen to me, I would have met them in the middle and we could have had a discussion. If they wanted to effect change, I was at the perfect point. But they couldn't see the wood for the trees and seemed more worried about being right than effective. I've learnt a lot since as I mention later but I hope this still resonates.

By the time the course ended I was nearing release. The facilitators now told me that I needed to complete an Enhanced Thinking Skills course for my licence because I still had thinking deficits. They claimed that although I was an intelligent individual I was unwilling to take on board other folks points of view about the factors that lead people to prison and they knew 'what works' to prevent people returning there. I couldn't get my head around the language as how can anyone know that. I'd grown-up with the same people in prison year after year and yet the tutors were telling me they knew the solution. Give me a break!

I'd been speaking to my socially adept sister Verity and found out she now had her own house in Seacroft. She told me she had a spare room that I could move into as getting away from Beeston was going to be important if I was to stay out of prison. She also said Adam's ex-girlfriend had fallen pregnant so I was going to be an uncle. It started me thinking about the type of uncle I wanted to be. How would I influence the next generation of kids in the family? I couldn't think of anything worse than being a bad role model for my sibling's kids. I didn't want to be a Benny, Geoff or Sid and encourage them not go to school or take drugs. I knew I could be a good uncle and really did have a reason to be responsible.

I reached my release date in May 2005. This anniversary has became important to me. I knew from then on I had to work out how I was going to go from a being a prisoner to an achiever. I aspired to be something in life. Walking-out of a prison aged 23 the big question was could I turn things around. Was I, Andi Brierley, capable of such a thing? The one thing I knew was that I'd get work, then see where it went. Heroin wasn't going to be a part of my future, or crime and violence. I knew anything like that would ensure my aspirations meant nothing. It was to be an exciting time for me for many a reason.

CHAPTER 18

Release

I had my Lacoste jumper in property. I'd sold every decent piece of clothing I bought when I was earning but kept and loved that jumper and was so glad I hadn't parted with it. A lad in the holding area commented, 'At least you're getting out looking well'. Twenty-three and feeling good because a fellow prisoner tells me he can see I've been in the gym and am wearing a nice sweater! The truth is that I'd take on board the smallest compliment. Let's face it, since being born I'd faced domestic violence, severe substance abuse, aggression, school exclusion, kidnapping and a variety of father figures in the absence of a real one. I had to find confidence from somewhere.

I made my way to Leeds city centre and was greeted by mum, Adam, and Miles. The role of released prisoner meeting the family was becoming all too familiar to me by now. They wanted to go to *Hoagy's* again. This time Gail was working there. It wasn't long before I'd had enough and left them to their boozy afternoon. They weren't really celebrating my release but using it as an excuse for a drink. Now Gail was in the bar they had a permanent one, but at least some of them were working for a living.

I made my way to Verity's house which was to become my home while I sorted myself out and had a fourth go at life post-prison hoping things would be different this time. Verity had done well for herself. The house was clean, tidy and more than presentable. She'd got herself into college and progressed while I'd been away. Maybe I could learn from her. Although just 19, she'd done the sensible thing in not moving to Beeston like the rest of the family.

I was optimistic because I was starting to realise that my problems lay at my own feet and only I could do something about them. Yes, I'd had it tough but I was an adult now and could create the environment in which I lived. In the past, every time I tried to take positive steps forward I was held back by the family one way or another, whether it was visitors with drugs or ill-gotten gains. Being at Verity's gave me the opportunity for time out from my downward spiral.

Although I lived in the Seacroft area, north of the city, all the recruitment agencies I'd worked for before were in south Leeds. It meant I needed to travel to the south each day to seek work. The agencies were becoming more specific on their application forms concerning criminal records, but I would still tick 'No' as to my mind they didn't need to know. I wasn't a risk to anyone unless I'd been drinking. Lying to them didn't seem to be the biggest offence given my experiences and if it meant getting an opportunity it made total sense to me. I started to hear stories of agencies not giving ex-prisoners jobs for insurance reasons and the risk if anything happened. I couldn't help noticing the level of foreign workers had gone up massively, meaning they could be more choosy.

I never let go of my belief that I was just as deserving as anyone else. Some of those I'd been locked-up with had given up on this. Their way of dealing with their situation was to operate on the margins of society and its laws. They believed they were rejecting society and therefore didn't need to accept that it had rejected them. If prisoners believe they deserve less than others they become their own barrier to success. Most prisoners, however, had that belief placed on them through their family and life experiences like I did. Who taught me about education? Who taught me about aspiration? Who was patient with me as a child going through adversity after adversity? When I was growing-up I felt that school, social workers and the police blamed me for everything, or disappeared when I needed help. I took this on board and started to blame myself.

I'm sure one of my key qualities is drive. No matter what job I've done I've always tried to do it well. Environmental factors such as family and drug-use would get in the way, but I was a hard worker. If I was given a task I would get it done to the best of my ability. This is what I needed to focus on, not my past. I didn't want to forget or deny what had happened but dwelling on it too much would hold me back. So here I was with a clean slate and a bit of support.

I got a job fettling joints on engine parts in a warehouse after they'd been moulded by the engineers. It was a dead-end job on the minimum wage, but it paid the bills. I stood at the same spot chipping metal all day long with thick gloves on to prevent splinters getting into my skin. There was a team of six doing this unskilled work. One of lads was my age and we got along well but most were middle-aged and so negative. I can honestly say I saw far more positivity behind bars. Believe me when I say that I listened to a lot of moaning. I remember one man continually saying he'd given-up on becoming rich. He thought the only way he would ever have money was if he won the lottery. Don't get me wrong, he was no spring chicken as he was around 40. However, he still had more than enough time to improve his lot. I had to accept I'd just come out of prison and that my life wouldn't change quickly. I was younger and happy just having a job, so I was a little more optimistic about the future.

Things went fine. Yes, I was living with 'my little sister', which didn't make me feel like a grown man, but I was making changes. I had to slow down and remember that change takes time and I wasn't able to demand it immediately. The other thing was that I was living with her for £40 a week plus a little extra for food. So I had it easy. Then, however, as she was in a relationship and the house had three bedrooms she decided to move her partner in. A week after that his friend joined him as this meant extra money. Although I liked to go out of a weekend I still preferred my own space and now two grown men were invading it and they weren't friends of my own. There was little I could say as it was not my house, but I did find it hard to keep my opinions to myself. It wasn't long before the atmosphere became strained. I mentioned to Verity that I was thinking of moving out and finding my own place as I'd been there for four months. She must have thought she was messaging someone else when a text came to my phone saying she was 'Buzzing as Andi is moving out'. I can understand this, like anyone else living in someone else's house I'd outstayed my welcome, so I'd no choice but to go back to my mum's. It was the very worst time for this to happen as it was winter and mum's boiler had packed-up during the summer. The landlord had allowed her money to fix it but, as it was good weather, that wasn't a priority and mum had also let a cousin and his girlfriend stay rent free in what was a deprived household. Neither of them seemed to contribute to running the house. It wasn't just a doss hole, but a freezing doss hole.

Mum went to Scarborough one weekend with a friend who turned out to be Adam's dad. Remember Stan, yes he was back on the scene even though at this stage I didn't know the connection. Then one of mum's more distant relatives turned-up after not coming to see her for years. Archie was overweight and looked like he'd been sleeping rough. She had an open-door policy and told him he could stay while she was away. When I came home from work one day he was sitting in the living room with no top or socks on. He needed somewhere to stay as he had nowhere else but he was always picking his nose and he stank. I was disappointed with mum and rang her after the others started whispering that they didn't want him there. They wouldn't say anything to his face though, so I made my feelings clear to mum. She said, 'It's my house and he's one of us'. There were too many people in the house anyway and as I was trying to sort my life out this was something I didn't need. I put the phone down and told Archie he wasn't welcome, that he needed to leave. I'm quite big and he didn't like confrontation. He just gathered-up his clothes and took off down the road. We all watched him not knowing where he was going. It was difficult and we wanted to call him back, but we didn't. Was this me being selfish? Possibly, but someone needed to be a leader in the house and this was now my role.

The situation with no boiler was completely out of hand. When I woke-up in the morning the bedding was cold and damp. My head was frozen and I could see my breath in the air. The walls of the middle floor were black with mildew and I couldn't invite anyone in to see this, especially girls. Miles was only 17 but I managed to convince him he would be better off living somewhere else with me. He'd got himself a full-time job and contract at a firm that manufactured kitchen furniture. I was still fettling but, as it was agency work, I asked him to see if there were any permanent vacancies at his works. We managed to find a house to rent half-a-mile away. It was carpeted and they didn't want a massive bond so we were able to move in straightaway. It was a step in the right direction. Just after we moved in he told me that his manager had asked if I would come in to talk to him about a possible vacancy. I felt this was my big break as I needed a full-time contract now we had our own place. I arranged to go down and speak to him as soon as possible. Although I was confident of obtaining employment through agencies, this never made me feel stable and I think getting laid-off from work regularly contributed to my bad decisions. 'If I can get a full-time contract maybe I will be able to build stable relationships,' I thought. I'd had one once at Gratton but I was on heroin so that was never going to work out.

I had an interview with Simon the warehouse manager. He told me he was looking for an edgebanding machine operator. After telling him about my work ethic and aspirations he told me that I was over-qualified. This didn't make sense as I didn't have any relevant qualifications or skills. He then offered me a trial through a recruitment agency and said if I was successful after 13 weeks I could have a full-time contract. I had to sign on at the agency but this was great timing.

When I told my existing agency I was leaving they offered me a pay rise to a little more than I would be getting at my new job. I told them that I appreciated this but as the new firm was offering me the chance of a full-time contract I couldn't turn it down. I didn't sit and think about how this was building my confidence, but it was. Since I was working hard I was being presented with opportunities. I was going out at weekend, but this would have to stop as I now had bills to pay.

One day while I was taking the 40-minute walk to work I bumped into Matthew, a lad I knew from Doncaster Prison, well-known for fighting back then. I remember him being one of the toughest lads on the wing. One of my pitfalls was that I cared about the thoughts of people like him. Selling drugs for Malcolm, getting in the car for the ram-raid and fighting in prison are all examples of my misplaced ideas about what others thought of me as a bad guy mattered. Probably from being brought up by people with similar values. I was wearing a long trenchcoat as it was freezing. He asked me where I was going looking like a workman in dirty clothes. I said, 'Grafting' thinking this would make it seem more glamorous than saying 'To work'. It had the opposite effect. He looked at me puzzled and said, 'Legit?' in a way that made me feel small. I said, 'Yeah mate, I'm late, I have to rush' and walked-off feeling embarrassed. Working wasn't what he or most of the people that raised me felt was cool. It wasn't their social norm. This may be difficult for most people to understand but growing-up like I did there were norms, just not the same ones as those for most of society. I still needed to shake them off and what Matthew said affected me. I didn't care about what he thought but it made me realise I wasn't following my predicated path and I had to understand that this was okay, something I'd failed at repeatedly.

I quickly moved on because I knew I had to focus more on my future and less on my past. I told myself that I wasn't a criminal anyway, so it didn't matter. I wouldn't now be doing anything but working, so anyone who thought otherwise didn't really know me at all. The labels society gives us do have an impact on how we operate within it. I was taken into care because mum couldn't for whatever reason cope. This gave us children the label 'hard to manage'. I was sent to prison which labels people inmates and criminals. I was a smackhead which labels people as less deserving than others, including offenders and the poor, the very worst label I ever had. Poverty is bad enough without being called poor. It would be incredible to think that these labels didn't affect my self-esteem. I wanted to prove to myself that none of them defined who I am. They may have been what some people believed but I knew who I was and what I stood for.

After working at the warehouse for my probationary period I did manage to get myself that full-time contract. So again things seemed to be looking-up and after being employed there for a while Christmas 2006 was a stable time. But I was partying, and stupidly I didn't make it back to work after the holidays. I woke-up in a friend's house when I was supposed to be doing my job. I was in a low mood when I went home and realised Miles had gone to work. I knew my manager might be thinking about getting rid of me due to a few earlier attendance issues, mainly after bank holidays or big events when I'd been out drinking, occasionally sniffing coke and forgetting my responsibilities. It may not have been crime but drink and drugs were still playing a part in my life.

As I'd done in the past, I went out to score a bag of heroin to deal with my mood. I don't know why I felt this was a good way to cope with my emotions but I did. I had the money and I knew it would be easy, and heroin had never left my thoughts totally. It's a drug that can pop-up in your mind at any time. If you are in a good mind-space it is easy to talk yourself out of taking it. However, if you feel down you're vulnerable and this is when it grabs you by the balls and pulls you further down.

I closed the curtains, locked the door, sat down alone and smoked the heroin. It felt awful because I hadn't done it for so long. I threw it on the floor half-way through and screwed it up. I was so angry with myself and I just sat with my head in my hands and cried uncontrollably. I was an emotional mess. I felt as if I was doing things like this to spite myself and prevent my life moving forward. I talked to myself for several minutes. 'This is you wanting heroin Andi, because you're weak'. I sat and thought about where I wanted to be and how I didn't want to be a prisoner, smackhead or bad uncle.

Now was when I had to make the right choice. One motivating factor was the professionals who delivered the PASRO course. Not because I thought they had equipped me to deal with this situation. No, it was that they felt I needed to do more courses to improve my life. If I allowed them to be right and returned to heroin, it showed I was weak and they were strong, and I wasn't going to have that. I wanted to prove to myself that I was right and I was strong, not them. I was old enough now to understand that I'd had a bad childhood, but did it have to affect my whole life? Only if I allowed it to. Only I could stop me smoking heroin, not some course or sentence, but *me and now*.

This was without doubt one of the most defining experiences of my life, well, in a positive sense anyway. If there was a lightbulb moment, this was it. I got rid of any trace of heroin so Miles wouldn't see it because he didn't deserve this in his life again. I walked into work the following day expecting the sack, but I took responsibility. I went straight to Simon and told him, 'I know I've been slipping but I give you a promise, I won't have a day off for the rest of the year'. He looked at me and winked. He knew I was a young lad with a lot on my plate. I think he liked it that I hadn't shied away and had approached him first. I meant every word of that promise as that job was the one thing which would keep me focused and out of prison for a fifth time.

By this stage Miles was starting to spend his earnings on other things and not having money for bills. He wasn't at the stage of maturity that I was. He was working full-time but just wanted to have a good time. Mum allowed him to go back home as she was hardly staying there at the time, so Miles and Gail had her place to themselves. I tried to explain to her that although she believed she was helping them she was in fact making it easier for them not to take responsibility. She would agree then do nothing at all about it. I was old enough to understand now how this was having a negative impact on their development and learning.

Identifying the things that held me back in life was one thing but changing them was another. Drink and drugs were always going to be difficult given they'd played such a big part of my life until now. Miles had taken the easy route and gone home because he saw my support as oppression. The family would talk about me forcing Miles to pay bills as if I was the bad person and he needed rescuing. This left me to pay for everything, which meant no parties, that as it happened was good timing and probably exactly what I needed.

If I was to have a new plan I had to think about what I needed to do and how I would achieve it. I then worked backwards. What was the outcome I wanted? I needed to make my own decisions that didn't involve my family or the people they brought into my life. I'd never been abroad, so this was something I knew I wanted to do. In fact, none of my family had even had a passport or any form of identification. Another important achievement would be to get a car and a driving licence. I wanted to buy my own house so I didn't have to pay rent to someone else but I also knew that this would take a while, so that was a long-term goal. The ultimate achievement would be to have a settled partner and a family of my own, so I could be a better dad than I never had. This would be the most difficult aim because, coming on 24, I'd never even had a stable partner.

Financial stability would underlie everything. Living alone in the house and paying £360 rent per month when I only earned £900 was difficult. After bills, it left me with hardly anything at all and what little

I did have I'd spent on partying. Not now though, now I was going to make sure I saved money, even if it was very little as I had to start somewhere. I focused on spending time with people who worked and didn't spend all their money on alcohol and drugs. This wasn't easy as changing social groups can be one of the most difficult things to do. However, I managed to use my childhood as a positive by remembering how I was able to mingle in different circles and adapt due to moving from pillar to post and change being forced upon me.

I found the perfect example at work. John had just started there as an agency worker. He was from Ghana. He'd been in the UK since he was 18 and was now 25. He'd been living in Buckinghamshire and moved to Leeds to live with his girlfriend in Wortley, one of the better areas. He didn't drink. He spent his money on clothes and saved for his family back in Africa. One thing I noticed about him was that he was athletic looking. We eventually got talking and we agreed that we could start going to a gym together. This was important for my plan. It would also make sure I took care of myself and was more constructive with my time.

By this stage, I was in a relationship with a girl that worked upstairs in the firm's offices. Zoe was great and from a good family. I would sometimes visit her parents' house and seeing them support her made me realise just how much I'd lacked this. They would give her the right help at the right time both financially and emotionally. She had always lived in a stable environment which I was now starting to realise makes a massive difference. It helped me to understand that, although I'd been to prison and done negative things, I was disadvantaged and there were explanations and I shouldn't beat myself up about it.

Zoe asked why I hadn't looked for a job that paid better. My response was simply, 'What could I do?' She told me she felt that because I was intelligent and reliable I would be able to get a better job. I told her that I never applied for good jobs because of my criminal record and the gaps in my employment. But I was starting to build my self-confidence and view myself in a more positive way so it was an exciting time for Zoe to ask me this question. It wasn't part of my plan, but it would certainly help me to achieve everything in it if I earned more money. I recalled the guy when I was fettling engine parts who just moaned about life and

I didn't want that to be me in 20-years' time. Every relationship I'd had in the past never progressed to an emotional stage. I recognised that not having a serious girlfriend was one reason I was out partying. I needed to do something about this, so I tried hard with Zoe because I cared for her. What she didn't know was that she was helping me and how much. She was the first girl that really knew me and I valued her opinion as she was a headstrong girl with good values.

As for my family, I was spending less and less time around them. I was frustrated with how they lived their lives and I wanted us all to see what I was starting to see, but it didn't work like that. Every time I met them there was yet another drama. One minute Adam was being accused of stealing a drug-dealer's dog (yes, dog!) and his friends were threatening to smash up the house. Then Miles was sent to prison for pinching a handbag after getting drunk in a pub. All my family seemed to do was bring problem after problem and I felt I had a responsibility to help them out. Every time it hurt me, and I couldn't allow it to affect my life as I was going through this delicate time. I had to make sure I achieved my own goals, so I decided that I would give advice but if they didn't take it that was their business. I can't explain how difficult I found it to disengage from them. They might have been the most dysfunctional group I knew, and I have met a lot, but they'd been with me for my whole life. I didn't need them now, but at least I felt I belonged to something and I loved all of them dearly. So I focused on my plan. I now had John and Zoe who were going to help make it happen. I started to understand the difference between my choices now and those I made as a child when I couldn't control what I wanted to. Now I had the opportunity to construct my own world and hopefully make better choices at the same time.

Things were looking good. I'd been working at the firm for two years and this helped to build my confidence. One incident knocked me back a little as I was unloading wagons. I was doing this when a Polish agency girl walked by the fork-lift I was driving without looking and I nearly hit her. I slammed on the brakes and she screamed. One of the coordinators looked over, screwed up his face up and yelled, 'Andi, get off that truck now'. I immediately went into prison mode because all I saw was that he'd made me look stupid. It was an instantaneous response and I said, 'Here, who do you think you're talking to? If you want to talk to me like that let's go outside'. It meant that I was still recovering from childhood experiences like Benny fighting in Halton Moor and telling me, 'Never walk away' or Malcolm showing me how to defend myself with violence if it threatened. My imprisonment had compounded my aggressive experiences through daily fights and violence.

I took myself off to the toilet and cried, partly in anger with the coordinator and partly at myself. I didn't know if I could shake off the past even though I wanted to. I knew I was close to lashing-out but then I realised this wasn't prison. I could deal with a situation like this differently. I explained to the coordinator what had happened and said sorry. I learnt a lot that day, including that they respected me for this. He also apologised and I felt better straightaway. I always felt bad after fighting, whether I got the better of the person or not. When I was beaten-up I felt like a victim and was left frustrated. When I attacked others I felt guilty. Saying sorry and receiving apologies gave me closure and it felt good.

I was having the occasional night out but able to keep myself away from drugs most of the time, simply down the fact that I wasn't spending time around people that weren't at all interested in doing drugs. Every time before when I'd ended up going out with friends that did snort coke, I'd ended up doing it myself. Then I would forget that I had a job, commitments and bills to pay. I'd stay out spending every penny. This affected my self-worth too. I would feel down in mood when reality came crushing in and I was sitting at home, broke and alone. The party scene and cocaine can itself be extremely addictive. It's not as intense as heroin and is more mainstream and acceptable but for lots of people it prevents them developing and if it keeps them unemployed it can lead to offending to maintain their lifestyle.

Whenever I spent the weekend with John, however, I would get to Monday morning with something left in my pocket and to show for my wages such as clothes or things for my home which made me feel mature and responsible. I didn't miss a single Monday at work and I was more focused on the job. Until then, no-one had shown me how to spend or value my money constructively or responsibly. I was trying to learn positive traits from the people around me. To stay away from negativity, even if this meant from my family. Family habits are often passed from parent to child and it leads to learnt behaviour. Although people can learn to make bad decisions as a child they can also learn to make good ones as an adult. Children offending is often a result of negative thinking and, although parents may not teach their children to do it, they may pass on to them the negativity which leads to crime. As a child I absorbed that claiming benefits and taking drugs and alcohol were normal, stability and education not a priority. That it wasn't a sin to get into debt and not pay up, the type of people to associate with. It didn't mean I was being taught to offend, but my environment certainly contributed to this. Now I had to find people who would teach me different things.

As John had a girlfriend, he couldn't always spend time with me which left me vulnerable to seeing my old peers. He would sometimes come with me to meet them but it was obvious he didn't feel comfortable. He didn't say so, but he never came if he knew it would be this type of atmosphere. He couldn't relax in an environment where tension was high. I'd made steps forward but my wider social circle was still not productive. I needed to feel some sense of belonging, so I occasionally spent time with old peers, but less and less.

My good relationship with Zoe petered out due to looking in different directions. I hadn't been fully ready for it. I had to solve my own issues first. To put it simply, I had issues, and this meant I was struggling to build a real relationship. The constant moving and changes had left their mark on me. I did care for Zoe. However, the timing just wasn't right. I took some positives from the time we spent together as I was starting to think about my future, but I wasn't ready to bring someone else into my life full-time, mostly because I wasn't happy with myself and felt that if someone got too close they would see me for who I was and leave.

By now, Adam had a son and Verity gave birth to a boy a year later. This was yet more reason for me to succeed as I knew I would now be a role model for both. I didn't want them to face the same adversities and hurdles I'd done and wondered what I could do to prevent this. I knew that they would face some of the things we did as children. I remembered Mr Bannister in Deerbolt saying, 'A picture paints a thousand words'.

I knew what he meant and this applied here. I needed to show the lads how to be a responsible adult by actually being one.

In 2007, I reached the grand old age of 26. I wanted to pass my driving test and go abroad as planned. They are things that most people do or have but something none of my family had thought they could achieve. I'd never saved any money or had ID with a photo in all my life. I didn't believe this kind of thing was important, even though by now ID was necessary for some things. I didn't know who my dad was, and I hadn't had a stable place to live. I hadn't long left home and, other than in Wolverhampton, living in the same house for a year was already one of my longest residencies. In relative terms, I'd already achieved more than I thought possible. But I'd higher expectations of myself. I'd made one momentous change thanks to John. I was using my money more wisely and this meant that I was able to feel secure and pay my bills, making an enormous difference to my life. Some friends were going to Greece that year and I realised I could pay to go with them and still have money left in my account.

When I was sentenced for the ram-raid I received a driving ban but didn't know the details. When judges sentence you in the Crown Court they seem to make a long statement. They did with me each time. If these are matters have an impact on our lives surely they should be conveyed in words we understand. Anyway, I switched off. So I went to the police station and asked them for the details and they told me to ring the DVLA who told me that there was no record of any ban, that it must be over and that I could have a provisional driving licence. So I had that and a passport now. There is no doubt I was becoming my own person and not the poor kid that went into care and got excluded from school. 'I'm Andrew Brierley and I can prove it,' I told myself. I felt important, 'normal' and that I deserved it. I was making better choices.

CHAPTER 19

Youth Justice Volunteer

Early in 2007 whist sweeping the warehouse floor I heard on the radio that the Leeds Youth Offending Service was seeking volunteers. It was the late shift and I was alone in a massive building. I thought about my conversation with Zoe and ran to write down the number whilst it was fresh in my mind. I didn't know anything about the service. I just felt working with young people that offend would be an excellent thing to do. I guessed it would pay more than my current job. It was incredibly hard to keep on top of the bills living independently, even working full-time. Next day I called and arranged an interview. I was pretty nervous as I knew I couldn't lie to these people about my criminal record.

I knew I didn't want to work in a warehouse forever so I figured they would probably be happy for me to leave. My attitude wasn't always great but it had improved over time and I'd now worked there for 18 months, so it was a stepping stone for me to learn how to operate in the work-place. I'd had lots of jobs before but all short-term. I'd built relationships with staff but in the beginning would often treat them in the same way I did those in prison. Although unacceptable, it was completely normal for me. Other ex-prisoners told me that they'd struggled to adapt in the same way, so why would I be any different?

I didn't tell anyone I was going for the interview, partly because I couldn't know what their response would be to me planning to join the system. I'd only done one real interview before, at my present firm, and that was more of a chat with Simon. I can just talk my way through so I thought, 'I'll smile and tell them how hard working I am'. I went to a smart building and sat in reception staring at posters raising awareness of drugs and crime. 'If you see a crime call this number,' one of them said. 'Whatever are you doing, Andi?' I thought. I was greeted by two women and taken to another room. One thing I noticed straightaway was that young people were nowhere to be seen. This came as a surprise as I'd pictured a building full of kids. As I found out later, I couldn't have been more wrong.

I was asked why I felt I would make a good volunteer. I told them that I'd been to prison and believed I'd lots of experience to pass on to young people in trouble with the police. I told them about my sports and weight-lifting awards, but that I'd no idea how to put them to good use. I explained that I'd held down a full-time job for two years and hadn't been involved in crime for nearly three. I'll always remember one of them saying, 'I'm interested to see where it will go' but I think they believed me when I said I'd changed. The different volunteering roles were explained to me and they said I would need to attend and complete training. Then that I'd been successful and there was a place for me. The training sessions would be at a weekend which would test my commit-ment. 'Welcome aboard,' they chimed.

Although I was now living alone, questioning my relationships and starting to make changes, I still lived in an area surrounded by my past. Two girls down the street were forever drinking, taking drugs and bring-ing people back to their house to party. I'd had a short relationship with one of them, Brenda, before. The night before training started I saw them walking-up the street with someone I thought I knew whose nickname was Massive. I'd partied with him in the past and we'd had an interesting debate around whether crime pays. He was a drug-dealer, so he felt crime was worth it. However, I was never a successful criminal, so things were different for me. As I knew it was him and the girls that knocked on my door I gave Massive a ring. He told me he was with them and asked me if they were good girls which sounded creepy. I did respect him due to the attention he got and the reputation he had, none more so than from Tara. Although I was making positive changes, this shows how fragile they were. I still felt it important that someone like Massive had gone out of his way to knock on my door so I arranged to meet him round at the girls' house. When I arrived he was with friends.

They'd been partying since Friday and it was now Saturday evening. My mistake was in going there at all when I'd an important next day to face but it shows how easily influenced I was.

As soon as I arrived I was offered cocaine. As I wanted to be accepted, I said yes, as usual. When I was high I talked a lot and made everyone aware of what was happening next day. They were going out in Leeds and I was back to the old Andi, so I said, 'I'm coming'. Massive said, 'You've important things to do tomorrow so I don't think you ought to'. But he told me that if I insisted I should go home and get changed.

By the time I got back there was only Brenda in the house. She told me they'd left as soon as I did because they knew I wouldn't make training next day if I went out with them. I've since written Massive a letter to thank him for thinking about my best interests. The reason I did this is that he's now serving life in prison for murder with a tariff of 30 plus years. Although society deems such people monsters, this is not all they can be. He had compassion for others, regardless of the terrible crime he became involved in. Bad decisions can lead to bad outcomes but don't inherently make bad people. I know this view won't be a popular one. I wrote the letter because I wanted to make sure Massive understood that his actions could have a positive impact on others. He doesn't need me judging him on top of everyone else and he will be ancient when he gets out. Not the plan he had in mind. He thought he'd retire 20 years before those who worked for a living. I bet he'd swap places now. I doubt he still thinks crime pays. That's the thing with it. To maintain an income risks get taken. I didn't think they were worth it.

I managed to make it to the first day of training. I turned up empty-handed, looked around and thought, 'I need a man bag, pens, paper and a diary as this is what everyone else has'. I was making progress on the road to a better life and if I wanted to be accepted I needed to act in a positive way. I felt myself looking around at those on the course, students, professionals and pensioners in the main who wanted to give something back to society. I knew none of them would have my experiences and that left me feeling vulnerable. I thought, 'If I'm going to complete the six weeks training I'd better make sure I don't stand out!' I needed to blend in. I knew feeling out of place wasn't down to how others saw me but more how I saw myself, something I could deal with and control. I thought, 'I'll get myself a man bag and they will never even dream I've ever been arrested'.

On the course I met Dylis from Chapeltown, a petite black woman, and we seemed to get along well. As we were both open and opinionated we got into a conversation about the word 'Nigga' being something no-one should use whether they are black or white. We were told by the facilitator not to have 'inappropriate conversations'. We laughed that we'd crossed the line and that the person who complained was a middle-aged, middle-class white guy in a club tie and a blazer. 'White people feeling uncomfortable with black people talking about their culture,' I thought but we accepted the telling-off.

Life was moving in the right direction. I remember that when I'd completed the training I told my good friend Jennifer that I was volunteering and showed her some of my paperwork. She was someone I thought a lot of but when she said, 'Where's my Andi gone?' I felt the relationship start to deteriorate. It seemed that she didn't see me as someone who could work 'for the system' which wasn't cool in her eyes. It taught me a lesson about how hard it is to leave friends behind. I had to be ready for more friends to do what she did once they found out. Working for the system meant being against not just crime but bullying, violence, drugs, negative role models and certain behaviours. As my life had been swamped by violence, drugs, negative role models and poor behaviour I couldn't expect my old circle to accept it.

By this point I'd moved in with a friend of a friend in Morley as I was struggling to pay the bills on my own. Amanda was older than me and she was pretty. It worked well as she went out with her boyfriend and I stayed in most nights. She was struggling financially and Tara thought it would makes sense for us to share. The flat was brand new and I'd never experienced anything like it. It made me realise that it isn't that much more expensive to live to a good standard, you just need to believe you deserve it. It cost more than the house in Beeston but it was in a lovely area. I knew this is what I aspired to. I would work hard and have a lovely home one day because it was what I thought I deserved after my childhood and all the years of crime, prison and heroin. I'd literally started to view myself in a different light and this was most of the battle. It didn't matter how some others saw me. I knew who I was.

The flat sharing arrangement didn't last long because Amanda went back home, and the flat was more expensive than my old house, so I had to find somewhere else. I moved in with friends in a nice part of Rothwell. They had four kids and three girls and let me have a room for £250 per month. This meant I could save every other spare penny I earned towards a mortgage. Getting one in a warehouse job might be a big ask but at age 26 I couldn't keep depending on people to let me live with them. I needed stability more than ever to make positive changes. Instability had created much of the mess up to now, so this was a fantastic opportunity to see if my dreams could become a reality.

During training I'd requested to be put on a list of volunteer panel members. This meant I would sit on a panel with two other community members and a professional to create a plan for a young person that had received a referral order at court. These orders given to young people for a first conviction and low-level offending set out a plan. I would get sent a report by post marked 'Confidential' so I could prepare myself. I managed to sit alongside professionals (we all received training). This was important to me as I got exposure to people I wanted to emulate. It was good to know how the YOS staff worked too. I took part in 15 referral cases. Although I'd experienced a disruptive childhood, care, heroin, prison and abuse, I was now being given responsibility within society. The burning question was could I go further?

CHAPTER 20

Golden Opportunity

I was now getting a bit of respect from those at work. They knew I was volunteering to help young people with similar experiences to myself and that I was trying to improve my life. The managers had it too good to move on and as it was a small company no opportunities were going to arise. There were some who said almost every day that they hated their job. The funny thing was that they were unwilling to do anything about it. They would just moan, which made them even more unhappy. I knew I couldn't be one of them, so I had to do something.

One day I got home from work to a letter from the YOS sent to all volunteers offering a part-time opportunity to undertake paid work for £10 an hour on a sports programme for six hours per week. I gave them a call straightaway as this felt like fate. I had my sports qualifications from prison and this would be a fantastic way to use them. Karol who interviewed me told me he would need to speak to his manager about my criminal record. This did feel ridiculous as I was already working with young people face-to-face for the same service. But I went along with it as I had to. Ten pounds an hour was £3 more than I got at work.

I couldn't have been more excited. 'Is this really the chance for me to achieve something real and not just do warehouse work?' I asked myself. The buzz it gave me was like that in the days when the police would arrest and bail me. I received a phone call later that day to let me know I'd been successful. Karol said I would need to stop doing referral panels in the meantime. I couldn't believe that I was going to get £10 an hour working for a professional organization. I knew I'd created the opportunity with my drive to make something of myself, but now would be the time to see if I'd the ability to make something come of it. I managed to persuade Simon my manager to allow me to leave work early to get to the programme. He was supportive and I think he was impressed by the growth he'd seen in me. He must have seen something in me from that first interview when he said I was over-qualified.

I'd been taking driving lessons throughout this time and successfully obtained a full licence. I was scheduled to go to Greece with my friends from Beeston before the programme started. It's fair to say things were looking pretty good by now and I was well on the way to achieving my targets. The heroin I used at Christmas was the one lapse that saved me, even though it didn't seem so at the time. Whilst I was going through all this I was living in Rothwell and avoiding old friends. But I made sure I went away with them so I didn't feel like a loner. They were still friends. I just needed to create a life where they wouldn't have influence over me.

I was spending a lot of time alone in my room when not working at my two jobs. But this also meant that the money going into my bank account was increasing and for the first time in my life I felt I had control of my finances. When I'd got my hands on money in the past I didn't know how to be productive with it. I would have put it into a mortgage if I'd had it now. I managed to buy a Fiesta which helped me get from job to job. It was taxed, insured and completely legal which was another step forward.

It was as if nothing could go wrong. However, as we all know, there can always be something lurking around the corner. I had to be ready to deal with anything that did come up in a positive way now as I'd so much to lose. Growing-up, it hadn't mattered as I never had anything to lose, financially or emotionally. Mum would hardly ever disapprove of my behaviour, so I never felt as if I was letting anyone down. I now had material things and I didn't want to disappoint those who believed in me.

The manager at Leeds YOS overseeing the sports programme found a discrepancy between my criminal record check and car documents. The record showed that I had a driving ban, but this wasn't reflected in the insurance paperwork. As I've already explained, the DVLA told me that I didn't have a ban, so I didn't declare it to the insurance company. I was told I must sort this out before getting any paid freelance work with the YOS. I knew that if I declared the ban now my insurance would be cancelled or the cost would dramatically increase, but it would be worth it in the long run. I also rang the DVLA before I went on holiday. They told me straightaway that it was my responsibility to tell them I had a ban. I find it hard to believe that it is down to an offender to disclose their own ban to the authorities but anyway they said they would get back to me, so I just tried to forget about it for now.

I got Stan to take us all to the airport. By now mum had come out to tell us they were in a relationship having kept it secret because she knew it would upset Adam. Then he made the connection by chance. It upset him because he felt he'd found his dad and wanted to build a relationship with Stan but it left him thinking that she'd just taking an opportunity to get onto the next relationship. I'm not sure how concerned she was about Adam's feelings. He was in trouble again and had gone missing. So I don't think he was setting much of an example to his new son. His own bad childhood was now affecting the next generation. He had to keep out of sight because of the incident with the drug-dealer's dog!

On the plane, my friend Jimmy was kicked-off and arrested for being disruptive. He was messing about but deemed to be a security risk. We flew out without him and it was everything I'd always thought it would be. Sun, parties and lots of young people there just to have fun. Jimmy rang me the following day and said he'd spent the night in the police station and was now at Manchester Airport. He was on his way and would be with us in six hours. I know he was a crazy guy, but he was scheduled to share my room and he knew how to have a laugh, so the news made me happy. I didn't really get to see Greece because we were out drinking all the time but it was a big step for me as no-one in my family had travelled outside the UK. I just had to get my own place and girlfriend now, sort out things with the DVLA, and I would have achieved my targets.

When I got back I found a letter saying my driving licence was invalid and that I must send it back to them and sit an extended driving test which cost double and took twice the time. To say I was upset would be an understatement but I understood that I needed to take responsibility even though the judge had spoken to me in a way I found hard to follow. I rang my solicitor and he said I wouldn't have a leg to stand on if I tried to challenge this. Despite it making my progress difficult I had to follow the proper legal route.

Remember Dylis who did the training with me when we first volunteered? She was the person coordinating the sports programme so I had connections. I told her about how I would now find it hard to get to both work and the sports programme and received her textbook response: 'Isn't it just a consequence of your own actions?' When you've committed a criminal act anything that happens from there on is deserved in the minds of some people. I loved Dylis to bits but I could have stood on her toes when she used the same words to me that professionals do to challenge young people. Just like PASRO did at Lindholme. You'll hear later on how I had problems adapting to being on the side of authority.

So I lost my transport and had to leave the car in a neighbour's front garden. It meant that I had to get several buses to the programme, which made it hard to be on time. I worried because I was trying so hard to prove to the service that I was punctual and reliable. It was incredible to think that, whilst trying to improve my life, the system was making it more difficult than it needed to, especially at a time when I was doing so well. It would have been far too much for some people. Nonetheless, I realised there was no point moaning and just got on with things. The system had done little to help me all my life, so it didn't come as a surprise. It gave me some certificates which in some way helped, but, on the other hand, it took me into care, to prison and it had now taken away my driving licence and become a barrier rather than supporting me.

Now for some good things. I couldn't believe it when we were delivering the programme at Headingley Stadium when a couple of famous Leeds Rhinos players, including Ben McDermott, came to speak to the kids. It made me realise what a privileged position I was in. Ben gave the kids advice on how he always attended any appointment ten minutes early. This meant that he would avoid being late and if he was later than his ten minutes he would be quite upset with himself. He was talking to the kids, but he was also giving me advice without realising it. I have always worked this way since hearing him say that.

Senior YOS professionals attended the programme to see how the kids were getting on. At one point Dylis pulled me aside and told me she knew they were 'looking at me' and this made me feel great. Let's put this into perspective. My day job was loading and unloading wagons in the freezing cold. I'd get shouted at if I didn't get it done in time and all for £7 an hour. I was then coming to be a part-time youth worker for £10 an hour and enjoying myself doing sports. The kids were easy for me to engage with even when other staff found them difficult and this seemed strange but natural to me. The one thing I spotted straightaway was that when they said these kids were 'hard to engage' they meant that they behaved the way they did at home, meaning like I did. So instead of changing the children they needed to alter their behaviour or to accept their individual behaviour but help them. Change doesn't happen over-night and I was the perfect example of that. So I would accept the kids unconditionally and offer guidance and advice.

If Dylis was right and they were really looking at me then maybe, just maybe, I could do something like this full-time. I knew I could. I'd experienced adversity, care, prison and indulged in drugs since the age of eleven. I didn't believe this meant I should face a life of disadvantage as an adult. I could offer more and it meant so much that my friend Zoe and manager Simon had also thought so. Validation from someone you know matters. Neither was a professional from the system being paid to tell me I could do more or how I should behave.

One of the hurdles I faced was how to fit in with the professionals. I often felt uncomfortable around them as they were in the main edu-cated and middle-class. Not that I didn't have life experience, but most of theirs was extremely different. They would have conversations about politics or society which I struggled to follow. I didn't know the differ-ence between the political parties, left or right, and I certainly didn't vote. Our house never had a single book in it other than a mail order catalogue and it's safe to say I felt out of my depth in most discussions. But I could walk into a room full of kids that had offended and build relationships immediately, which other professionals sometimes seemed to struggle with or at least take time and caution over.

Some of the staff knew I was worried these differences were an issue and would pile on the pressure by asking if I'd done things with the kids they knew I didn't understand in their professional terms. But John was a massive help, talking things through with me. I would have struggled without him urging me to stay positive. He even completed the volunteer training, but things didn't move quickly enough and he didn't progress to volunteering.

I had conversations with old friends about the fact that my licence had been taken from me. When they knew the reason I needed it they told me that I must be daft. Some of my closest friends questioned my decision to volunteer and work for the service. I was on a journey, but still especially conscious of saying, 'I work with the police'. After all, at the time, it was just six hours in a sports programme, so that's all I told them.

The programme was due to come to an end so I went to speak to Karol to discuss how it had gone and to say I wanted to return to referral panels as soon as possible. When I arrived in my work clothes on my way to the warehouse he told me everyone felt I'd done well. He asked if I knew anything about a team called ISSP. Of course I didn't. He said their managers wanted to talk with me about my future. Apparently, ISSP stood for Intensive Supervision and Surveillance Programme. The ISSP team dealt with the most serious and prolific offenders, either on release from custody, on bail or as a direct alternative to custody. Some of the kids on the sports programme had been sent there by this team. It meant that some of the staff I met on the programme were also from the ISSP.

I was taken through and greeted by Wilfred and Josephine who were the managers. I instantly felt nervous as it seemed like another interview. They asked me questions such as, 'Why do you feel you would be good at working with young people that offend?' 'What would you bring to a team such as ours?' I was unprepared and just gave off-the-cuff responses. But they were easy questions for me really. I'd relevant experience of coming out of prison and getting a job, though I don't think I impressed them when Wilfred asked about my writing skills. Although I didn't get through school, I'd managed to grasp the basics. I was in the bottom class throughout high school due to behaviour rather than ability. So I said, 'Pretty good' and hoped for the best. I didn't have the skills to sell myself.

He said, 'Tell me about your offending'. They'd completed a Criminal Records Bureau (CRB) check when I joined the YOS and I'd been up front and honest. Yet there was something different about this interview compared with the volunteering interview. I think it was because, at the volunteer stage, I just thought, 'Either you let me in or you don't'. This, on the other hand, felt like there could be a real job opportunity so I had to get it right. My cheeks went red and I struggled to articulate my answers. I didn't want to sound like I hadn't taken responsibility. At the same time I didn't want to go into detail. At this stage, I hadn't fully bridged the gap between my upbringing and my offending. Wilfred knew I was struggling and said, 'Just relax, all we need to know is why you won't return to that type of behaviour'. That made it a lot easier and I talked about wanting a better future.

Wilfred then said that ISSP were delivering a summer school and that he wanted me to be a part of it. It would mean I'd be working with the most serious young offenders from the Leeds area. It meant I would get £10 an hour for 37 hours a week. He said if it went well there would be opportunities for me continue to work within the ISSP team full-time as a sessional worker. I walked-out of that office and jumped as high in the air as I could. I couldn't believe this was happening to me. Andi Brierley, the junkie smackhead convict that always managed to mess things up!

This I thought could be my opportunity to be a normal person and maybe I could shake off my past. I could make some decent money and maybe, just maybe, I could get a mortgage and own my own home. I'd only been released from Lindholme Prison in 2005, yet I was close to achieving all my targets and more and it was still only 2008. 'This shit could be a story,' I thought, walking-off shaking my head. 'Calm down Andi, you're getting a bit carried away,' I laughed to myself.

I had to agree the arrangement with the warehouse as my shift work there was 6 am to 2 pm and 2 pm to 12 pm. It meant they would have to allow me to stay on the late shift over the summer period. Simon was happy for me to work 5.30 pm until 12 pm for the period concerned. This meant I would leave the house at 8 am (as I didn't have a licence and things were going too well to drive my car illegally). In fact, I had to walk past the car in the neighbour's garden and get the bus every morning. I would start work at the ISSP at 9 am. When we'd finished at 4 pm everyone else would go home and I would go to the warehouse until midnight. Yes, this might seem demanding, but there was an end goal, so it was an obstacle I just had to overcome.

Face-to-face work with the kids wasn't difficult for me. They were labelled as hard to reach due to their disengagement with services and their persistent offending. However, to me they were simply kids from the estates on which I grew-up. They were not difficult to be around and opened-up to me as I gained their trust. They knew I was a local lad who spoke in a similar way to them, so they didn't view me as authority. I was told by Wilfred that senior managers had decided not to allow me to talk to the kids about my past.

I wanted to be taken seriously so I got myself a better man bag and a professional looking diary. I was also conscious about the clothes I wore. I'd always placed value on designer clothes even though quite often I couldn't afford them. I would spend money on clothes I knew were expensive to cover-up for the fact that I'd been brought up on the breadline. It was certainly insecurity but when you're young you don't see things that way. I believed that wearing such clothes was going to help me build better relationships with the kids. For this reason, I would come to the summer programme in Nike tracksuits and expensive trainers. The kids were attracted to these things due to their negative peers on the estates, so my thoughts were that I would try to do the same but in a positive way.

I could understand everything the young people were saying even though they would talk in code quietly when they didn't want staff to know something. I would often do it myself in prison. As I said, I wasn't to tell the kids about my offending or prison and the kids weren't aware of it, but they knew I was from a similar background to them. This meant that when they were talking about stealing cars or beating-up other kids I could interpret what they meant. I would just quietly say, 'I can understand you boys' and hope they didn't wonder too much why.

During the summer school I did a lot of activities such as visiting art galleries, museums and sports competitions. We would debrief at the end of each day which meant I would spend time in the office. I would listen to the professionals but didn't understand a lot of what they were saying. It was a confusing. I'd spent my entire life around offending and offenders. I'd offended several times and spent several years in prison with, guess what, offenders. Yet here I was in a room full of people responsible for helping people like me, but I couldn't follow their thinking.

This was in the main because they were educated and saw offending through the sphere of learning and research. It made me think that, if I felt this way, the young people must feel detached from many of them too. I felt I could help to build bridges between the kids and the professionals. A skilled professional will hide special language, but this can be difficult when speaking to other professionals much of the time. Some I think seemed to use their education to bamboozle offenders and even each other. Being concerned with winning an argument doesn't make you right. Children may have been wrong in their behaviour; they were always right when they described the circumstances in which they lived.

When the summer school ended Wilfred and Josephine told me that I should think about giving up my day job. The issue for me was that I didn't have a contract with the YOS. They said I would get 37 hours every week and when a permanent job became available I would be able to apply for it, and I would be a strong candidate with my inside knowledge. They also made me aware that there was an interview panel for workers coming-up next month. So that was it, I went back to see Simon and told him I wanted to make a full-time commitment to the YOS. Although it was a risk, given I'd a full-time contract with the warehouse, I couldn't afford to not make the leap as this was a potential career and it might only happen once. I'd created the opportunity through my drive, determination and application. I had a lot to learn but what an opportunity I was being handed.

CHAPTER 21

The Professionals

I was put in the ISSP office and given my own small desk, a computer and a modest pay rise. I couldn't quite get my head around it, but I needed to and quickly. I felt that I was being thrown in at the deep end and I needed to show I could swim. I remember several conversations with Wilfred. I told him I felt I wasn't as clever as a lot of those in the team which was predominantly made up of what I thought were middle-class, well-educated people, mainly women whereas I was from the uneducated underclass. I felt normal in a warehouse but here I was surrounded by people who talked about politics and culture and I couldn't keep up. I felt alienated and, without consciously knowing it, excluded, isolated and somewhat on the margins.

Wilfred could tell this and helped me by saying I was one of the cleverest in terms of intelligence but that I needed to develop my knowledge of youth justice, that I had the ability to learn what it was all about. I left his room wondering if he was right. Was I as clever as these people but just needed to catch-up? I'd never had a father figure and Wilfred was a black man, so he wasn't automatically what I would see as one. Having said this, I was embracing his words, building my confidence and he was able to get me to view things from an unfamiliar perspective. It was the start of a long haul as my first impressions slowly adjusted.

After a few months and reading as much as I could about the work, I went home and sat down on my bed. I placed my head in my hands and told myself, 'You can't do this'. I'd gone from being an uneducated employee to working in an educated service. I was taking on board heaps of information and couldn't stop thinking about work even after I left for home. Things like supervision, legislation, intervention, evidenced-based practice, effective work, social exclusion and such were swimming around in my head. I thought I was great with the kids but this simply wasn't enough. The service was made up of intellectuals and if I couldn't take in all this information I wouldn't be taken seriously. The problem was that it seemed like too much at once. But I couldn't let anyone know.

I did manage to retake my driving examination and complete the extended test. When I explained what had happened, the examiner asked me who was responsible. When I explained, as I had now learned to do, that it was all down to me he felt this was ridiculous and said, 'Just drive'. We had several chats and he wasn't really examining me. He hardly wrote anything down. To my way of thinking either the courts or DVLA made the mistake and I was paying the price, but it didn't matter any more, I now had my licence back. Just another hurdle overcome.

When I went into the office next morning everyone was happy for me which made it feel as if I was one of the family and I hadn't really experienced this before. Was I now being included? If so they must like me and my work, I thought. Wilfred threw his arms around me. He was a naturally tactile person and him doing this made me feel uncomfortable. I know he picked-up on this and quickly let go. I sat down with him afterwards and explained that no man had ever shown me affection and not in that way. Although I knew it was from a good place, I just hadn't expected it. He understood as he said his father hadn't shown him love and he recognised that I'd never had a proper dad at all. He told me he made a conscious effort to be this way with his baby girl. I remember thinking that I might one day do the same.

Wilfred asked me if I wanted to go on a residential week away in the Lake District with a group of kids that were struggling at school and said I would get an extra £200 for the week. I said, 'Are you joking? Of course, I'll take that'. I had to meet with the Safer Leeds police officer running the programme, called Guy. He knew all the kids and his job was to prevent those in school getting criminal records. 'Andi Brierley working hand-in-hand with West Yorkshire Police only three years after being released from prison,' I thought. This wasn't a handout, nor did I get support or help from anyone else. It was something I'd created myself and boy did it feel good. I got one of the kids to take a picture of me in the driver's seat of a police van. I couldn't help myself.

The week away was by Lake Windermere. The seven young people were hyperactive but a lot better behaved than ISSP youngsters. The ironic thing was that the programme was designed to expose kids to new experiences. Other than my recent holiday, I'd never done anything like it either, so it was doing wonders for me too. I kept wondering how on earth I'd managed to get myself into this position, being paid to go camping (when I wasn't speaking to players from Leeds Rhinos). It was as if someone was going to jump out at any time and say, 'Andi Brierley, you've been framed'.

The ISSP kids had to be with us for 25 hours per week. One day I was running a group of eight with a colleague on victim awareness and I was creating imaginary victims of offences and encouraging the kids to discuss how they would feel. One of them suddenly asked me directly, 'Have you ever been arrested or to prison, Andi? If you have, it gives us hope that we can get a respectable job like you'. Thinking of what I'd been told I replied, 'If I had I wouldn't tell you, but I know people that have offended and work for the YOS'. This was the best I could do even though the lad was really asking for some something more and I could have given it to him. However, I couldn't risk my job by telling him. I could see my response left him flat and uninspired as he thought he'd cracked it that I'd been in trouble and was inwardly deflated.

People from my previous social circles were now starting to hear about my work. When I occasionally saw them, they'd say, 'How have you managed that because I'd love to do it'. I always wanted others to follow me, so I would give them the details and say, 'Volunteer like I did'. Not too many followed this up because it was just words to them, an easy thing to say but harder to actually do. Most people didn't make the strides forward I was making. It was still an insecurity of mine to not view myself as unique or special and instead believe that anyone could do what I'd done given the opportunity.

After working for Leeds YOS for eight months a vacancy came up. I was interviewed by Wilfred, Josephine and Rosamund and I did more than enough to get the job. The problem was that when the contract was being formed by Human Resources they refused my appointment due to my offending. Wilfred and Jim, who ran the service, then had to have a meeting about it and make a solid enough argument for employing me. Wilfred's case was simple. 'We say we are promoting young people that have offended to get them to make positive changes. We now have an opportunity to promote someone that has proved he made that very change and then we don't take that opportunity'. This must have been enough as I was offered a full-time contract which meant I could try to get a mortgage. It didn't make me feel that good to know this was all going on behind the scenes. I felt that I'd sacrificed everything for this opportunity. I wasn't spending time with my old peers. Hardly ever seeing my family because most of what they did jarred with the values of the YOS and what we advised the kids to do.

Now I had a contract, Jim was happy for me to share my experiences with the young people. I felt I'd learnt to do the job without that so far so I decided that I would use it when it was required, like when asked directly whether I'd been in trouble with the police. I wouldn't ever talk about specific offences as this wouldn't benefit anyone and indeed I have disguised or fictionalised these in this book. I got the mortgage and help from a government scheme. It meant I didn't have to use the money I'd saved for the deposit, so I could buy furniture for my new apartment. I kept expecting someone to ring back and say, 'Sorry Andi, you can no longer have the mortgage,' but that call never came. I kept driving over to the flat to look at it as it was being completed. I got to choose my own kitchen units, fittings and tiles for the bathroom. So yes, from 2005 and watching my pad-mate take a shit a metre away within four years I had two toilets! Oh, and just for good measure, I bought a suit.

Taking my family to the flat wasn't the easiest of things. They were now starting to have a 'He thinks he's better than us now' mind-set. I would simply point out that there are some things children should not know about or be exposed to. They would counter by saying they didn't misbehave in front of the kids. Miles would want to borrow money off me now I was stable. He or they didn't understand that I was saving it for things that mattered to me. It started to grind me down. To get him to stop I asked him to pay back double. He didn't stop even then and I quickly realised I was contributing towards his lack of budgetary skills. I had to say the same to the rest of them because they would always pester me. They felt I wasn't supporting them. Miles and I stopped speaking to each other for a time.

Things like this didn't just happen with family but my entire former social circle. Two incidents stand out which made me realise I couldn't continue to work for the YOS and keep-up my previous relationships. One was when I arranged to meet a friend in a pub we used to drink in. While we were standing at the bar, he said, 'Let's sit and talk to these two while we wait for the other lads'. They were older lads from Beeston and they were talking about crimes they'd done the night before. It was difficult for me. I spent 40 hours a week at work with kids talking about crime, victims, consequences and the community. These two would have probably smacked me in the face had I gone down that route with them. I just said I was going to the toilet and took-off out of the back door.

Another time I met a bigger group in another pub who hadn't gone home from partying the night before. A girl I knew well, although I didn't always like her, walked in. She was sleeping with a lad who wasn't the most compassionate person. As she walked through the door he said, 'Shit' so the whole group stopped and looked. He then said, 'Err, look at the state of the spots on your face'. She told him to shut up and some of them laughed while others probably thought, as I did, that this was completely out of order. Not one person said anything due to the status this lad had within the group. I walked upstairs with the girl to give her some comfort. As soon as I got the opportunity I left.

Both these incidents made me realise I had to make a choice whether I wanted to commit to the YOS or to continue spending time with my old crowd. Partying brought me some good times but ended-up taking me back down a negative path. My work was a different world for me and I didn't always feel fully accepted yet, but it offered me an opportunity for a career, so it wasn't a difficult choice. The one thing I had to convince myself of was that not all of these friends were close. Most of them I'd started partying with just before I began working and weren't friends I should hold on to. It was a simple decision but I got a lot of my old confidence from going out and getting girls and the respect I got from that social circle. I was now pursuing a different type of confidence. Knowing I would be viewed differently by my peers made it difficult. I'd tried my whole life to be accepted by certain types but this was a complete change and it now felt uncomfortable to be with them. Leaving them behind was a risk though as if my YOS career failed for any reason I might find myself lonely, but it was a risk work taking. I'm sure this applies to most people when they decide to change country or job for example but probably more intensely for me as most people don't make such a dramatic change from prison to profession.

In 2009, an email came round all YOS staff asking if anyone wanted to commit to studying for a four year long youth justice degree. I was in two minds so I asked Wilfred what he thought. He said I should do it as I might want to be a qualified youth worker later on. I didn't have any appetite for it. I thought, 'It's just paperwork the qualified staff do. I want to work with kids'. Wilfred said I should have the option 'just in case'. I committed to it and was given the go ahead. It would at least help me stay away from partying as I wouldn't have the time. The problem was I'd never passed any test or exam at school. My first assignment was a complete mess and I needed other staff to support me, but it wasn't long before I started to pick up on things.

By this stage, I was having my nephews every Friday night, killing two birds with one stone. I wanted to stay in and I wanted to be a good role model for them. I knew they were facing issues at home and wanted them to see a different way of life. Both of them knew what weed meant and talked about seeing violence in their neighbourhoods. I didn't live far away but it was quiet and sometimes I took them to Roundhay Park and other places where they felt safe. Miles and I (we were by now reconciled) agreed to take on a team for Hunslet Club under sevens. This was voluntary and the owner knew about my history but that I now worked for the YOS. It meant I would train Tuesdays and Saturdays and we would have games Sunday mornings. It was a perfect way for me to occupy my time and also great for lads to develop and learn.

I wasn't drinking much and really struggled on weekends and evenings when I found myself on my own. I'd built some good relationships with people at the YOS, however I kept them at arm's length due to a feeling that they were different to me. Peter was from London and, although he was born and grew up in Peckham, he was clever and had managed to get a scholarship to a private school. He supported me with my studies and wasn't the typical academic. I knew then that sometimes those more clever than me could make me feel deserving.

I was asked by Wilfred to be reparation champion at ISSP, responsible for encouraging young people to undertake recompense to victims or the community as a way of 'paying back' for their offences. ISSP were quite good at getting the kids to litter pick or do gardening, however the kids viewed this as onerous or demeaning and it wasn't meaningful for them. I attended a meeting with Karen who worked for Leeds City College and together we came up with an idea for a project. We wanted to engage kids but in a positive way. If I got the go ahead from management we felt we could work together and use reparation to get kids into learning activities.

I attended regular meetings with all the YOS reparation champions in the area where we would share good practice. It was here I felt like a success. People sometimes spoke in a way I couldn't fully understand but I would make notes. I felt a million miles away from heroin addiction or prison. This was the first time I'd had the opportunity to discuss multi-agency working. The chair of this meeting was Felicity, a woman who looked strikingly familiar. After the meeting I asked Wilfred if Felicity used to work for the Probation Service. When he said she did, I immediately realised she was my probation officer! I couldn't help but email her to make sure she knew. I guess it must have been nice for her to know she played a positive part in my journey and here I was working for the same service.

Karen delivered a screen-printing programme for young people not in education, training or employment. She agreed to allow us to use her machinery to create items to be sold for the Martin House Hospice charity (see martinhouse.org.uk). I agreed to take a group of five young people on a six week programme to design and create reusable shopping bags. Karen also had a link to someone at Pudsey Market. We designed and made bags and sold them cheap for the hospice (which is for children with life-shortening conditions). We managed to get a charity number to ensure the young people knew why they were raising money.

ISSP kids had to attend on a Sunday which wasn't the easiest thing to persuade them to do. However I had great relationships with them and had earned their trust so they did. After five cohorts, these so-called hard to reach young people had raised £750.65. They attended the hospice and handed over the funds and they saw how difficult some other young people's lives are. This was a humbling experience for all of them and gave them a different perspective on life. I was frustrated that we didn't make the target of £1,000 I'd set.

Senior management were impressed and asked if I would mind being put forward for a Leeds City Council award for personal achievement. I wasn't going to say no and believed that, by now, I perhaps deserved a little bit of recognition. I took one of the girls that had completed the programme with me to a YOS briefing. She had to stand in front of the whole service and shame them into buying bags. Most staff avoided this kind of public speaking and yet here I was in front of them with a young person by my side. I felt more comfortable with the young people than I did with the staff. I could take kids with me on my journey.

The awards covered seven categories such as Children's Services, Adult Services and the Financial Sector and the second was for category winners going head-to-head for the Leeds One Award. My seniors wrote this statement in support:

> Andi is an excellent role model for all the young people he works with. He supports the most serious offenders known to the service and always goes the extra mile to help them to turn away from crime and develop successful futures.

> We are very proud of Andi and he should be very proud of himself. He is ambitious and he deserves to go far. He has overcome a great deal and has applied himself to changing his lifestyle and developing a successful career. The YOS knows about the challenges he must have faced but his determination and 'stickability' have paid-off—against the odds. That is why he truly deserves this award.

It came as a pleasant surprise when my name was read out as the winner for Children's Services. I was given a glass trophy. However, when I got back to the office, I returned to comments such as, 'We could all have committed crime when we were young'. This is something I frequently faced. Although I'd raised all that money and sacrificed my Sunday's to ensure kids got something out of the project, what I found was that some people still wanted to view me as an ex-offender. I knew then that I had to work that little bit harder because of it and I didn't need other people judging me for my previous mistakes. It was confusing as well. Professionals paid to promote children that offend and yet here they were quietly judging me and not seeing who I'd become. I should stress it wasn't everyone.

I had many conversations with Wilfred about the fact that I'd lost all sense of my previous identity. I wasn't speaking to friends or family because I couldn't be sure what they were up to. I was struggling as, although I had my own place now and a career, I felt as alone as I did on heroin. I would spend my evenings studying and my phone stopped ringing altogether. Even in prison I felt a bond with the people around me. Yet working for the YOS reminded me how different my experiences were to most of the staff. I kept asking myself whether this was due to them or me over-thinking things.

Wilfred kept telling me, 'It will get better with time'. I think my biggest problem at the start was due to my experiences being so far away from theirs. I felt they didn't want to listen to my simple chatter and, to be honest, I struggled when they talked about their supportive families or travelling the world. I'd only been to Greece for one week and spent most of my time at the bar or in the pool. I guess this is how any minority feels when working alongside the majority. I'd experienced this when living in Chapeltown, but at least people spoke the same basic language. I was slowly learning that language through my studies and it was then that I began to realise that although I disagreed with much of what they thought about working with kids I needed to approach it in a different way. I'd got into heated discussions and was never one for holding back my opinions and, given my background, I often felt I was the defender of service users. Maybe I shouldn't have but when professionals said, 'These kids' or 'These families' I always felt they were talking about me. A welfare worker once said, 'Love is all these kids need'. I took offence as I knew my mother loved me deeply. He disagreed with my view and felt that if parents loved their kids they wouldn't neglect their needs. I thought this was a naïve view as most parents do love their kids but some don't have the tools required to meet their needs. Two very different things.

Likewise I recall mentioning something that happened to me in prison to a manager. She told me, 'Forget about prison, move on' and walked away. This was like telling someone to forget about their time at university. I never felt ashamed about my journey and I think she only said what she did to shut down the conversation because she didn't want to engage with me concerning my own life events. I tried to tell myself I was different and they didn't understand. This seemed to leave me in the middle of nowhere. My old group didn't understand me and neither did my new one. I'd two strong allies in Peter and Wilfred and without them I don't think I could have continued. 'Time,' Wilfred kept telling me. I couldn't see me changing enough to make this work. 'Should I change?' I thought. 'I no longer offended and would never. Shouldn't that be enough?' But I realised that I had to.

I didn't manage to complete the Enhanced Thinking Skills programme that the PASRO facilitators referred me to because they weren't running it during my licence period. The YOS had been given the go ahead to deliver it to young people. Seven professionals were selected and I was one of those chosen. Although I didn't feel accepted, the service seemed to recognise that I was working hard and going the extra mile. They asked me if I wanted to train to deliver ETS. I wished I could sit them down in a room now and tell them just how wrong they were in my case when I was in prison. I didn't need their referral to make positive changes. Yes, I still had some confidence issues but I'm pretty sure their courses didn't help to reduce these. But I was learning to keep quiet and listen.

The seven of us were sent to a five star hotel in Peterborough for two weeks to train how to deliver the ETS programme. I felt like I was in the movie *Curly Sue* which features a poor kid in a posh house. When we went to eat I was given cutlery that I didn't know how to use so I watched the others and tried to copy them. The whole thing was a far cry from a prison cell. I realised my true situation when we watched a music video. Two women told me that the girls were being exploited. I said, 'It's just what girls do' and the whole group turned on me. Mine was an uneducated statement, but I meant the girls had a choice. The group felt they didn't and told me I didn't understand women's struggles. Whether I was right or wrong, I learnt that in this type of environment I couldn't always be open or I would be labelled a racist, bigot or just odd.

I opened-up to Peter about my old addiction whilst we were walking around Peterborough one evening. He said that he saw me in a different light now as he didn't think offending is a choice, however he understood how hard it can be to come off drugs. I realised I shouldn't be quiet about my experiences because, like him, I could educate them just as much as they could me. I could give them an understanding of how it's often not just a simple case of bad choices. Many of the kids we work with are stuck. We are there to offer advice and guidance, but we shouldn't get frustrated if we have little impact. Like I did, they respond to their environments and we challenge them, but we do little about the environment itself and need to do more.

The second part of the city council awards ceremony, a really fancy event, was in November 2011 when I was two years into my studies. Peter came with me as we were really getting along by now. We were in the Civic Hall, one of the prestige buildings in Leeds. It's protected by golden owls outside as they are a part of the history of the city. I saw that the trophy was a miniature golden owl. Up until this stage, it was all a bit of a laugh. However, once I saw the trophies, I said to Peter, 'I want one of them bad boys for my new living room'.

They called out the winners and I was up against a disabled woman that hadn't had a day off work in 16 years. There was another woman that had broken lots of bones in a car crash and yet was back at work within 18 months. I felt that the disabled woman should have won but the nominations were called out and they announced that the winner was Andi Brierley. It was embarrassing but, you know what, I believe this was more than deserved. I'd sacrificed everything I had to work for Leeds YOS. I was fully committed and most of all I think I was good at the job, able to convince many young people I worked with that they too could make similar changes and choices. I'd been flattered when they asked me to deal with some of the most difficult to engage kids. I worked with many who weren't engaging with their workers and I got them to complete their orders. The award gave me a new found motivation and quickly afterwards Peter and I created a further programme. We wanted similar success to Karen's screen-printing project. I didn't work in the same way as many YOS practitioners, however I like to think I was effective and connected with the kids without being too unorthodox.

I was given the name of a prison officer at Armley Gaol. Peter and I between us felt we could use prisoners' experiences to deter children from following a path into adult prison. It meant I could work with a prison that I'd been in, which would be another milestone. Peter and I met with the officer who was called Dick. We got on great and all of us felt we could work together to benefit adults and children to change. Dick liked the fact that I'd been in the prison as a prisoner. We agreed a five week programme. This would allow the young people to attend the prison and the undertake community work with adult prisoners. They would work in the community for the St George's Crypt charity for homeless and vulnerable people and those suffering from addiction (see stgeorgescrypt.org.uk). The young people were able to have unmanufactured conversations with the prisoners who would be honest with them about the damage crime had done to their lives. They were handpicked to ensure they gave out the right messages and the scheme was an unqualified success.

The four young people who completed the programme didn't want it to finish. This was unusual for ISSP youngsters as they often said YOS programmes were 'boring'. The adult offenders got a certificate stating that they had been involved in volunteering with young offenders. This was a personal goal of mine. Although I like working with young offenders, I also liked to help adults as they can be motivated but lack opportunities. The St George's Crypt charity also got some free labour so they paid for the celebration event at the end when all family members came in as well as the heads of services. It was a great day for all concerned.

Dick asked if I would come and do a motivational talk to prisoners in Armley a few weeks later. He wanted me to discuss how I'd managed to get my job after being released from prison and to focus on having a criminal record and how to deal with this. I would go onto the wings, which made me nervous, but I wanted to take the opportunity to help people in prison. I wrote a timeline for my talk for which they told me they were expecting 40 inmates which made my stomach turn. It got worse when they walked in and I saw two I knew.

'Just get on with it,' I told myself. They weren't my friends at any stage, but they knew who I was and started whispering. I just had to remember that the message I was giving out was a positive one. The speech went well and I didn't really need to look at my notes. I felt that to bring it to life I just needed to go with the flow and I knew how to tell them about my life anyway. After I'd finished most of the inmates came and shook my hand. They said, 'Thanks for that'. They said they felt like I was talking about their journey and they recognised every word. It was nice to speak in a way that allowed them to recognise how they may have been exploited as children or failed through drug abuse. These are not the conversations prisoners normally have but are necessary so we need to try and make them acceptable.

The prison officers then shouted to the inmates that if they wanted to ask me any questions they could do it on C-wing for ten minutes. I wasn't prepared for that. It made me nervous again given I was wearing skinny jeans and brogues and this wasn't a prison look. Some inmates came and said, 'I'd love to do what you do, but what can you do for me'. I said, in simple terms, 'Did you miss the point of my presentation? No-one will do things for you mate, you have to make things happen for yourself'.

In my experience, this is the problem for most prisoners. Many end-up where they are and lose confidence in themselves and in others giving them an opportunity. They believe something external needs to happen for their lives to change. The truth is that they are the ones with the power to make the changes and, once they realise this, change will follow. Whether I was 17 or 23 the minute I walked-out of prison I took it upon myself the get a job. What we need is opportunities for prisoners on their release because part of our job is to build their confidence. As it's fragile, they need to be given that opportunity to prevent further offending. In my experience, it works and prevents offending, not simply education or programmes. We can advise, but in the end they need to be able to feel they are valued members of society and that doesn't come from sitting in a room and using only words of advice.

While I was on the wing I bumped into a lad called Martin. I knew him from the clubs when I lived in Seacroft. He told me he was in for non-payment of fines. He always worked when we were younger so it surprised me to know he was in gaol. He said, 'Look how different our lives have turned out' which didn't make me feel great but sad for him. There is a fine line between offering experience to help other people and gloating, saying, 'Look at me'. I have to be mindful how I come across.

CHAPTER 22

'Me, promotion?'

It was now 2012 and I was re-thinking my situation. Up until now, I'd simply been thankful for the opportunity the YOS gave me. I was starting to ask myself if I should think about progressing further. I was a youth justice worker, had created several successful projects and won an award. I was a year from completing my degree, so was starting to build my confidence further. I was able to hold my own in conversations with practitioners about youth justice. I was just as good as anyone else, I thought, at building relationships with the young people and their families.

I looked on the Leeds City Council careers website and saw a vacancy as a deputy manager for their Family Intervention Service. I applied for the position and, although it was a change in direction, it meant a rise of £5,000 a year. I'd a mortgage to pay and was a saver now, so money was becoming really important for my future. I'd changed my behaviour and was not spending time with people that committed crime, so I wouldn't be involved in it. I'd made lots of what might seem less important changes. I'd almost stopped drinking and smoking and I'd become good with money, all linked to looking ahead.

I was successful in getting to the interview stage so I now called on my friend Peter to help me out. We prepared my presentation and two hours after the interview they called to say I'd been successful. As soon as I put down the phone I shit myself. In 2005 I was released from Lindholme, seven years later I was about to supervise practitioners working with vulnerable families. I couldn't work out whether I was moving too fast or if I'd lots of skills that had been hidden by my life experiences. I kept telling myself, 'Keep your feet on the ground and focus on finishing

your degree'. One thing I didn't know was that one of the job require-
ments was holding an NVQ Level 4. This meant I would have to finish
the final module of my degree, complete the Level 4 and learn about this
new role as a deputy manager. Twenty-twelve was going to be a busy year.

When I was introduced to the team I instantly noticed that they were
all nearing retirement. I did learn from my time with them, but the culture was one of 'We've done and tried everything before'. I was a young
and enthusiastic practitioner but they seemed to challenge most of my
ideas. My manager felt I shouldn't tell them about my past. She gave me
a risk-assessment form and told me that because of the theoretical risk I
posed to families I needed to complete it. It made me feel like I should
be ashamed of my past. I also felt she didn't know how to deal with me
or my background. Even if she did feel I presented some kind of risk, I
shouldn't have been the one doing the assessment, so I reasoned. I just
felt bad about being there so needless to say this wasn't going to last
long. I kept consoling myself that I'd been given a pay rise and at least
some of those I supervised were great to work with. Maybe also that I
had still a lot to learn about engaging with the views of others and this
was somehow helping me with that.

Deep down I now wanted to be a qualified practitioner at the YOS so
I would try learning whilst at the Family Intervention Service and apply
for a YOS position if one came up. One important milestone did happen while I was in my then role. As a deputy manager I was expected
to spend time with other deputies at different offices. When I went to
one office, I sat down to have a meeting with a woman called Lucy. We
went into a room and before I said anything Lucy said, 'Can I just stop
you there and say I know who you are'. Not the best words for someone
with my background but I thought, 'Okay'.

She went on to tell me that she was related to Benny. Remember him?
I hated that man but, from what I can remember, he did come from a
good family and Miles and Gail would sometimes go and spend time with
them. Lucy told me that she could remember pretty much all our story
from Benny meeting mum onwards. I was intrigued so work went out
of the window and we took a walk. Lucy told me that I could access all
my social care files. All I needed to do for this to happen was to contact

a friend of hers and he would tell me how. I immediately contacted her friend, Darren, from the Care Leavers Association and found out that obtaining my documents was pretty straightforward. No-one had ever had this conversation with me even though I'd often told people I was in care. I called a number he gave me and was told they would send out my care files within 40 days. I became nervous and excited as there were questions I'd always needed answers to. The big one now was whether I would be ready for what could be in there? I thought I'd a good grasp of most of what happened, but what would be in the files?

Darren, a Yorkshire lad, worked in Manchester but wanted to do some work in Leeds, so I gave him my contact details. He worked specifically with people that had been in care and to prison. He interested me when I spoke to him as I could tell he was passionate about this work. He told me that he had a group I could join made up of people with care experience working in services. I took the details, but it didn't sound like my kind of thing.

Sure as their promise Leeds Children's Social Work Service sent the files to me. They landed in my postbox on a CD so I could transfer them onto my laptop. They didn't ask if I had mental health problems or whether I was living alone, etc. Not that I think this would have meant I shouldn't have been entitled to see them, however I might have needed support to deal with their contents I figured. If I wasn't ready for this information, surely someone should have supported me to read them. Access to them was something I felt I should have had well before then, especially since I'd spent years in the adult prison system. The system aimed to support me to deter me from offending. However, they had never until my last sentence linked my crimes to my drug-use. If they had, they would have learnt it was linked to my thinking and my thinking was linked to my childhood experiences. It was great to finally be able to make sense of some of the decisions made way back when we were children.

The files gave me all the information this story started with, such as Adam lighting fires in the house and injuries to him and Verity. He had always convinced himself that he was the reason we were taken into care. Not because he was a vulnerable child unsupervised and getting access to lighters. No, he thought it was because he was a child arsonist. Just take a second to consider the impact of believing this for 25 years. Not only that but it was your fault your family were separated and your siblings taken into care. I have tried several times to discuss this with him as an adult. He refuses to accept my point of view about our childhoods influencing our adult life being of the impression that I'm making excuses. He wants to take responsibility. The funny thing is, by blaming himself and not considering other factors, he identifies himself as a bad person. This has followed him around his entire life and it's something he has not been able to shake-off. I can't speak on his behalf, however. I'm sure not many of the professionals who have tried to help him understand the link to his childhood or have told him it wasn't his fault.

Surely it is important to help kids that not only go into care but that have Social Care involvement to understand significant factors in their offending. If, like Adam, they believe they are fundamentally bad and that's the reason they went into care, it seems obvious that this will lead to them having a negative identity. Adam needed protecting but his version of events is that others needed protecting from him. I appreciate that he can't understand or remember this from age five. However, he seems not to have been given any later opportunity to explore his development. He has never understood the trauma he faced and how this links to and impacts on him and his decisions.

One problem that did arise was that all my siblings knew I had the files. I couldn't show them to them but they can access them directly if they want to. I made the decision to leave that responsibility with each of them apart from what I say here. I did have a discussion with mum, but she seemed to brush it off. 'It's all in the past, Andi, why do you always bring up the past? … I did my best'. I love her to bits and she has the right to her view of course, however these are my experiences too and they impacted on me, so I think its okay mention them.

CHAPTER 23

Back to My Youth Justice Roots

In 2013, the YOS advertised for two youth justice officer positions and, needless to say, I wanted one of them. I'd finished my degree and had my NVQ Level 4 so some might even argue that I was 'educated' by then. Yes, that last year was hard work. However it was worthwhile and I could now speak the language of those around me. Not only had I got educational status, I'd demonstrated that I could study and work at the same time. When the interviews came around I didn't tell anyone at the FIS. I had to say I was going to the doctors. I immediately found out that I was successful for now and had made it through with three others to the second round. This was with a panel of young people, so I felt comfortable with that. The competition was tough. Two of them were experienced probation officers. Take a minute to consider the fact that I was on probation in 2007, yet by 2013 I was competing in interview with those from the service that supervised me!

I waited at home for the phone call having convinced myself I'd be happy no matter what the outcome. If I got the job, I'd return to the YOS which was a great service. If not, I'd remain in my existing senior position. When I received the call to tell me I'd been successful I jumped high in the air. I realised I would have to become a part of the system I previously felt was process driven and with maybe too much of a focus on academia. I also knew that the officers in that service were skilled and took on a lot of responsibility. I became extremely anxious about going back. The question was, did I deserve it, or had I just blagged my way back in?

Telling my FIS manager I was leaving was awkward. I'd only been with them for eight months but I knew it wasn't for me. I thrive on innovation and to my thinking there was little for me to grapple with in that service. Maybe they didn't feel comfortable with me. One time I was told they would have to 'clip my wings'. Basically, I think they were worried about how quickly I was moving and felt I should soar elsewhere.

I wanted to improve services for young people such as myself as a child. It wasn't about the money. I'd already achieved far more than I could ever have hoped for and was 'rich' by my standards, earning a decent salary for someone coming from where I had. So my return to the YOS happened and I worked my backside off to quickly establish myself as a member of my new team. I was no longer in ISSP but now part of an area team. The first thing I noticed in this role was the amount of paperwork I had to complete so that I was unable to spend as much time with the young people as I would have liked. My success had always been based on the relationships I built with the kids. When you start to progress in services you spend less and less time with them. This inevitably impacts on your ability to build those relationships. I would often spend more time writing about a child than I did in their company.

Whether I agreed with this way of doing things this is the way services operate and I had to accept it. One thing I really struggled with being someone that had come through the system to working within it was perspective. I felt lots of things they did were ineffective and unlikely to engage kids. I also looked at the flaws within the system and focused more on them than the positives. I needed to work on this because although I felt I could make everything better the reality is that I couldn't. I didn't have the knowledge or the ability and I had to recognise that my perspective didn't always make me right.

It was a gradual adjustment. Initially, I would sometimes get into heated discussions with other staff and convince myself those who disagreed with me about how to deal with kids did so because they hadn't the experiences I had. This was an easy way of persuading myself I was right and they were wrong. I'm sure this happened with other issues like race and gender. I had to reflect more and make sure I changed my approach because it was going to get in the way of feeling included rather than isolated. The truth is that everyone's views on offending were relevant, not just mine. If I didn't change my attitude I would be out on a limb.

One thing I'll never forget is getting to stand-up in court as a professional. I loved writing reports for judges and magistrates now I was able. I still got nervous. On two occasions I stood before judges who had sentenced me in the past. Her Honour Judge Foster sent me to prison for not completing my community service. His Honour Judge Greenwood sent me there for the knife offence, so it was strange for them to see me as a professional. I got some kind of kick out of the fact that they had no idea who was. Not, I guess, that they would have cared, but I cared and that's what seemed to me to be important and it would have been nice to tell them my story.

One day Adrian who had been my own defence solicitor was representing a kid I was reporting on. He would often come to the cells in the morning when I'd been held overnight. I looked at him and he said, 'I know you, don't I?' I asked him to guess but he tried and couldn't place me. After several wrong stabs I had to tell him. 'Well, Andi, now you say it, but I would never have connected up the dots with you in a suit. I would have thought it was a work connection not that you were once a client!' Adrian remembered I had a brother but was disappointed when I told him Adam had been back in prison. All these experiences were doing was making me feel more and more confident. I was being recognised for positive things and my successes. It felt great.

I knew casework alone wasn't going to make me feel as if I was making a difference. Remember Darren who helped me obtain my care documents? Well he'd met with Felicity and wanted to undertake some work with adult prisoners. It was user led, which meant those with care and criminal justice experiences would facilitate the group. He was the only person allowed to work directly with them due to his own background. As I'd experienced both, he was happy for me to work alongside him. Clear Approach was a six week programme to build looked after children's confidence. We trained them to deliver a presentation to senior managers. It was based around what young people felt services could do to improve. It allowed me to have more contact with young people so I was happy.

We started the work in 2013 in Leeds to weigh-up how effective it might be. I got on great with the young people who were amongst the most disengaged youths. When we started, less than one per cent of children in England were 'looked after', however that tiny percentage encompassed up to 50 per cent of children in custody. These numbers just made me want to undertake this work even more so as to improve outcomes for vulnerable children.

We completed the first group with four young people using exactly the same model Darren had used in Manchester. Manchester wasn't ready for the feedback from the young people, so they'd discontinued the work. Child friendly Leeds were open to new ideas and committed to an inclusive approach so it wasn't an issue there. In Manchester the youths had spent five weeks exploring their own experiences of care and looking at what similarities they had. They then created a DVD and two members delivered presentations. They were quite critical of the system and some of the professionals within it. In Leeds senior managers wanted to actively listen to and engage with the young people's voices to improve their practices. Darren and I were pleased with our first group so we immediately arranged more and widened invited managers to those from care homes, Social Services, the police, housing and drug services.

By autumn 2016 we'd completed five groups and the referrals were coming in thick and fast so the groups got bigger. We always invited members from the previous group back to be mentors for the following ones. All engagement with Clear Approach was completely voluntary. The young people's motivation was based on how passionate they were about improving the system for other young people. Most of those who came to YOS from care felt they had the skills to help others. Darren and I working with them in such a positive way was evidence that as long as they stopped offending they were probably right.

While running these groups I got to spend time with some of the most amazing young people. Quite often they had extremely troubled lives, however we were a group of people with similar backgrounds empowering ourselves to make change for others. It was an encouraging three years and the YOS recognised our success by creating the role of Care Leaver Specialist which I was successful in getting when I applied for it. It meant that instead of having a caseload and working on the Clear Approach programme twice a year, I would focus solely on all looked after children in Leeds. My object was to profile those coming to us from care and see if we could implement a policy to reduced that number.

This work highlighted many areas for improvement within Children's Services and it made me aware of the limitations when dealing with traumatised children. I started to view services as failing by not doing enough for vulnerable kids. This made me feel isolated and negative about my working environment and sometimes my colleagues. It wasn't healthy because from this narrow perspective I burdened myself with trying to change and improve everything. I quickly worked-out that I had to do something to correct myself. I would argue a lot with colleagues and go home feeling drained and frustrated. I would often take the work home with me and convince myself that, if everyone saw things my way, services would be better and the children would benefit. I went to work every day on a mission to convince people that because of my lived experience I knew what needed to happen. I even reached the point of believing I needed to leave this kind of work, then I realised what was happening. Just as I'd overcome some personal issues previously, I still had away to go. Other people were working hard enough. I wasn't right that they were deliberately letting children down. I needed to change how I viewed the system and recognise the hard work of colleagues around me.

As soon as I changed my perspective I started to realise not only the limitation of services but also of myself. I'd got carried away because I'd progressed in life so quickly and I wasn't keeping my feet on the ground. I was just one practitioner within a large organization. I'd grown-up anti-authority which was hard to shake off, but these people were my colleagues and friends. Many of the young people were given opportunity after opportunity but, like me, they'd experienced trauma to the point that they were struggling to function and maintain education or employment. Services try and help young people but it is slow progress and they are not always successful. It's not because they don't try or care, which is what I'd been thinking until then. It wouldn't be better if all services were run by ex-offenders or those who'd been in care which was the mind-set I'd wrongly created for myself. I will always advocate that people like me should be given a chance because we can be great with

251

the kids. The truth is, however, that we too need to be supported to be able to overcome the barriers that this kind of transition brings.

❧

I've gone from being a prisoner in 2005 to not only a qualified youth worker but a specialist in just a few years. It hasn't come easy and I have had to overcome barrier after barrier. These have sometimes been practical barriers such as my past. There have been physical barriers such as being placed in prison. They have mostly been personal and individual ones such as self-esteem and problems of identity. Once I'd overcome the fact that I wasn't intrinsically a smackhead, offender or care kid, and that these were labels that other people placed on me, other obstructions were easier to confront. My childhood and young adult life experiences formed how I viewed myself. I realised that I could be viewed however I wanted and I didn't have to be ashamed of my childhood and young adult decisions as there was an explanation for every one of them.

When working with young people we have to help them come to similar conclusions. However, just as I wasn't ready until a certain point, they were often not ready, or unable to engage in a conversation about trauma and recovery. In England and Wales we criminalise children as young as ten. If we picture these children facing lives such as mine it seems illogical to hold them responsible for their environments and decisions over which they have little control within their own lives. Once I was old enough to understand the journey I spoke about at the start of this book, I made better choices. I was 17 when I was sent to prison and that was the right response to my crime. However, was enough done with me and my family before that or, to take just one example, to prevent me being exploited into selling drugs in Wolverhampton? These are the kind of questions I now look at every day with kids in my work.

Postscript

Children who commit offences. Are they just disobedient youngsters or thugs that need to go to prison to keep them on the straight and narrow? Are they vulnerable kids that have been through Adverse Childhood Experiences (ACEs) and need a compassionate response from society? There is no doubt in my mind that there is a direct correlation between how I was raised as a child and my decisions as a young adult. So too for them.

People often say that people make 'choices' and as a result need to understand there are consequences. It can be an emotionally charged statement but, in my view, it means little in terms of helping us to understand why children do offend. It works for the system because it implies that while young people may make bad choices professionals can assist them in making good ones.

I've learnt a lot since I began working in the youth justice field including how to respect my colleagues and their views and this has helped me to review my own life and thinking. There is a great deal of evidence and many explanations concerning the behaviour of children who have suffered ACEs. Key causes of their progress into the Criminal Justice System are recognised as abuse, neglect, absent fathers, experiences of prison within the family, drug addiction and poverty. I score nine out of ten on this matrix. The only one I didn't face is sexual abuse (so far as I'm aware). Research in the USA in the 1990s recognised that the more adversity a child faces the more likely he or she is to not just have negative outcomes such as prison and addiction but also physical and biological difficulties like disease and mental health issues.

My mother was just 16 when she fell pregnant with me and she was a looked after child with little support and unable to accept the support she did have, for whatever reason. This meant I was predisposed to have negative life outcomes. Albeit I accept there are no guaranteed causal effects for offending and not everyone would offend given the same background and circumstances, I believe most would have had poor outcomes with the start I was given. The fact that I was moved from home to home and unable to get a decent education as a result made this ever more likely. I was taken into care and, when returned home, faced every ACE imaginable. It can't be a coincidence that none of us completed school and surely it can't be simply our own choices as children because we weren't making them in the circumstances.

I certainly did make choices about being involved with drugs by the time I was 16. However, I felt comfortable with the criminals I associated with because life had already taught me that they were people like me. After working in the Youth Justice System for a decade I have concluded that, as a nation, we devote far too much effort responding to crime than to preventing it happening in the first place. The political discourse has made it this way, especially after Tony Blair's 'Tough on Crime, Tough on the Causes of Crime' mantra of the mid-2000s onwards. Instead of tackling the root causes of social marginalisation, the Youth Justice System used a 'preventing offending' approach which implied that work needed to take place with the child. One that would effectively 'fix' the child.

In my humble opinion, if we want to prevent offending in children, we must ensure they do not create an identity that leads them down an offending road. Everyone I looked-up to as a kid took drugs, was involved in or close to crime, didn't buy into education, used violence to resolve problems and didn't engage with the 'bad people' from services who were trying to help them. Positively the opposite. This may not have caused my offending which took place in my adolescent years, however the way I viewed the world and myself was certainly due to these experiences, relationships and rejection of authority.

Even though I work in services that address offending when committed by children now, I believe that the most effective way to address trauma experienced by children is to place the emphasis on preventing it happening in the very first place. The answer can't be to place vulnerable children that have experienced such difficult childhoods in a prison environment too early. It didn't help me, in fact, it had a large negative effect, including because I started to act and think like a prisoner.

There will always be youngsters that are not exposed to ACEs that get involved in offending, however those that form the core of youth offenders or are the most prolific and persistent are undoubtedly from households similar to mine. If a child is out through the night burgling, there is a social need within the family, but we respond with a justice hammer and this is confusing for children.

The age of criminal responsibility which begins at ten means that young children are deemed to be offenders, however this is a social construct that needs challenging. When I was 16, drug-dealers had access to my house and therefore all aspects of my life. There were younger siblings there and, as a result of the police being the agency that we were dealing with me over my behaviour, my siblings were not given the support they needed, never mind me. It was a social issue within the family and yet we as a family were being labelled 'criminal' when we were all struggling to cope, compounding the trauma. We needed therapeutic support to help us understand why we were behaving in that way.

In 2016 when Lord Laming published his independent review highlighting the disproportionate over-representation of children in care within the Criminal Justice System, such children were six times more likely to have been cautioned or convicted of a criminal offence than other children (Prison Reform Trust, *In Care, Out of Trouble*, see 'Key Facts' where custodial and other negative outcomes are also noted). This indicates that we place our most vulnerable children in prisons because they are responding negatively to the trauma they are already experiencing. Placing them in custody will only compound the problem and create an identity of someone who doesn't matter and people don't care about.

Our identities are a driver for our behaviour, certainly how we respond to our peers. Take the car crime offence I was involved in which led to my last sentence. I didn't want to get into the car, however because I'd been to prison and the others wanted me to guide them I felt immense peer pressure. I was supposed to be the 'criminal' in the group, which is how I identified and how they obviously saw me (and my brother).

This is something we need to discuss as a society. My story explains, I hope, how prison for children can often be a traumatic experience and paradoxical to healing trauma. I didn't know whether I was a criminal or a child and I couldn't see how custodial intervention supported me to overcome my heroin addiction and understand why I made bad choices in the first place. Politicians and the public alike need to rethink the way we intervene with children that offend and recognise that, if a child is offending persistently before the age of 16, there are quite definitely things happening in that child's life that need addressing, not necessarily that the child needs punishing.

In fact, we should be brave, recognise the circumstances children are living in and, instead of telling the public we will change or fix them, we should let society know we will fight the fight the kids are having alongside them. We should change the narrative and discourse to ensure the public are better informed about the difficulties we all face. All professionals would, I think, acknowledge that in many cases offending is just a chapter in young people's lives and that troublesome children too may be a manager one day (or even write a book).

Please forgive me if I sound as if I am sounding a call for recruitment and training programmes for former child offenders and care leavers who feel they want to work in services such as care and criminal justice. Many young people I have worked with aspire to such roles when they see what I have achieved. It also helps young people to a greater belief that youth workers believe in them. These are significant factors in addressing and preventing offending as children see people that speak like them, walk like them and behave like them making a living from preventing crime and helping young people. One way to counter negative role models is to present visible examples of people like them engaged in the services that work for them. We already know this is imperative for minority groups so we should apply the same approach to children in care or facing criminal justice involvement. It is, after all, the identity they create. We have a responsibility to change that identity and this is one effective way to do this. If all young people see is remote, highly-educated people in such roles, it reinforces their view that social mobility doesn't exist or is unattainable. I guess some youth workers may disagree with this, but what

I am saying is that I see the benefit of involving more service users with backgrounds like mine. I promise you I'm not suggesting we take over!

So what of my life now. I've met and married the most wonderful woman. She's from Spain where she was raised by a very stable family and although she knows about my life story its a world away from the Andi she knows. Its been great for me though. Fulfilling the last of my aspirations, Tami has provided me with a beautiful daughter, Isabelle, who is growing-up fast. My concern when she was born was about my parenting style. How would I manage given my own childhood? Would I be able to be a loving and nurturing father when I'd never known one of my own? Would I be aggressive or lose control like some of the men during my childhood that stepped into the so-called father role for short periods of time? It seems to be working out fine and brings a completely different challenge of course. Parenting has made me recognise not just how difficult I had it but proud given my life circumstances. Thank you for taking time to come with me on this journey. I like to think I walked through storms to reach the sunshine which is what I had tattooed on my arm a while ago.

Turn around stories

Writing as a route out of crime and towards a better life

Prison writing is a valuable two-way process. Education aside many prisoners have changed their lives using writing as a bridge to a new life and career. Our first book in this genre was Bob Turney's acclaimed *I'm Still Standing* back in 2002. Recommended personally by Lord Longford, Bob the one-time prolific burglar turned author actually went on to become a probation officer! Ex-offenders who followed his lead include Alan Weaver (who became a social worker, *So You Think You Know Me?*), Ben Ashcroft (young offender to youth worker, *Fifty-one Moves*) who tells of his constant changes whilst in care and Justin Rollins (ex-graffiti artist and now motivational speaker, *The Lost Boyz* and *Street Crhymes*) whose books have been adopted as set texts on degree courses in Birmingham and elsewhere.

Another ex-prisoner turned author whose book has been widely used in education is Frankie Owens whose *Little Book of Prison* also made the final of the People's Book Prize. There is also a book, *Recovery Stories*, about those who have survived addiction.

Actor Stephen Fry's turn around story was included in a collection called *Going Straight* along with that of the train robber Bruce Reynolds whose life changed after being released from his 25 year sentence. Andi Brierley (the author of this book) who went from prisoner and heroin addict to specialist within a youth justice unit is the latest in this considerable line. Each of these books centres on identifying the changes, choices and threads that led from being an offender to law-abiding citizen.

Further details, information and reviews are available at WatersidePress.co.uk